Four Plays About Histories

Robert J. Litz

Four Plays About Histories

Metron Publications

Cover: Poster for *Mobile Hymn*,
Santa Monica Playhouse / The Other Space,
Santa Monica, California, USA (1997)
Lay-out: Synergie A.M, Sofia, Bulgaria
www.synergie-bg.com

ISBN: 978-1603770910
Library of Congress Catalog Number: 2015917128
Copyright © Robert J. Litz, 1983, 2012
All rights reserved
Metron Publications, P.O. Box 1205
PRINCETON, NJ 08542-1205
http://metron-publications.com/

Robert J. Litz

(1950-2012)

ROBERT JOSEPH LITZ *was born October 3, 1950 in Cleveland, OH, and grew up in Cleveland's Mount Pleasant neighbourhood. He graduated from St. Ignatius High School in 1968. As an undergraduate at Boston University, he was editor of the literary magazine. He earned a MTS in American Studies from Harvard University in 1975. Bob Litz entered the theatre world as a press agent for the New England Repertory Theatre in Worcester, MA. Eventually he had roles in several productions. In the early 1980s, he shifted to writing plays, gaining acclaim in 1983 for his play,* Great Divide, *which was subsequently produced off-Broadway at the New York Theatre Workshop in 1984. Bob Litz wrote seventeen produced plays for Off-, Off-off Broadway, the regional theatres, and for the Elephant Theatre Company where he was Playwright in Residence beginning in 2005. Much of his work focused on social and political themes. He wrote several television shows for* A&E, History *and* Discovery *including the* A&E Biographies George Washington, Benjamin Franklin, Andrew Jackson *and Emmy-nominated* John Travolta. *For A&M Films, he wrote the original screenplay for* Twister. *Other produced films included* House of Cards, Medium Straight *and* Rappin'. *He produced the indie film* Ten Tricks. *Theatre highlights included:* One World *(NAACP Best Play & Best Ensemble nominee);* Douglas *(Portland Critics, Best Play);* Playing the Room *(Juno Award nominee for Best Film on a Musical Subject);* Mobile Hymn *(Dramalogue Award, Best Play) and* Cycles *(Best of 2012 Hollywood Fringe Festival).* Cycles *won rave reviews and had just completed a successful run at The Asylum Theatre and Lab on October 7, 2012, when Bob Litz died suddenly, three days later, on October 10. He was simultaneously working with Michael Nylan on a children's book set in Han China, plays about the U.S. Supreme Court and had a feature documentary,* Madaraka & Jaffar Climb Kiliminjaro *(Becketfilms) in post-production. He won the 2012 Burger Prize for writing on the theatre. He was a member of the Actors Studio (Playwrights/ Directors Unit), the WGAW, and LA Stage Alliance.*

FOREWORD

Robert Litz was both a spectacularly successful human being and a spectacularly good writer. He was a person who loved his work and knew it, whatever frustrations it entailed. I often called him a psycho-optimist, but everyone around him felt better after talking with him – and not primarily because of his incandescent smile, but because he managed, in every single conversation, to make it so clear what the true stakes are in life, and what's worth fighting for.

This publication puts together four of his plays, two contemporary and two historical plays, that were dearest to his heart. The plays were optioned multiple times at the major Hollywood studios (e.g., Paramount), but the options always lapsed, and always for bizarre reasons, including this: at the time when Bob was pushing for Helen Mirren or Annette Benning, the studio executives were sure that these actors weren't famous enough and that they needed to get Julia Roberts to play Cassatt instead.

Like most artists, Bob was usually stone-broke, because producing plays, writing scripts for documentary films, producing experimental work, and writing movies "on spec" does not usually conduce to making money. (Also, whenever he came into big money, as when offered a five-picture deal, he had no trouble giving most of that money away to people he admired, as well as to virtual strangers whom he knew to be poorer than himself.)

As Eudora Welty noted, "No art ever came out of not risking your neck. And risk – experiment – is a considerable part of the joy of doing, which is the lone, simple reason all [writers] are willing to work as hard as they do." Bob had an exceptional talent for writing, as well as a passion for friendship. As a neighbor of mine says, "Bob could do anything, from fixing a piece of plumbing to building a lamp to writing a piece of theater that was so good that it left you breathless." He was a romantic fool in the best possible sense of that word. The only tribute we can pay Bob is to read his work, and this book should further that project in his honor.

Michael Nylan

CONTENTS

MOBILE HYMN

A PLAY IN TWO ACTS

LIST OF CHARACTERS

(in order of appearance)

JULIE (*also* RANGER)

DAD

MOM

TOWTRUCKER

MOLL

BUSDRIVER

SWEETMEAT

PROFESSOR

BETTY

BILL

OPERATOR ONE

OPERATOR TWO

OPERATOR THREE

HITCHHIKER (*also* MOLL)

COP

WAITRESS

VAGRANT

ACT ONE

[Pre-set with JULIE as the RANGER presenting the Parks' slide-show. At first she simply advances the slides as called-for by beeps in the pre-recorded narration. Then, at a slide which resonates for her, the tape mutes and she begins...]

JULIE/RANGER: I used to watch nature shows on TV. ... The mating habits of condors, the propagation of trees. One show was about the biggest species on Earth. Elephants and whales, sequoia and banyans, huge giant squids.

But the single biggest living thing on Earth, bigger than the biggest dinosaur, is... a tree. A stand of aspen in Colorado. It covers an entire foothill of the Rockies. It looks like a whole forest but it's all one plant, connected underneath. One humongous cross-rooted organism.

I really needed to see that tree. To walk through it, lay down in the middle of all that aspen and listen to the wind rattle. ... Just me, the mountain, and the aspen quaking on the wind.

[LIGHTS come up on the TOWTRUCKER working on a motorcycle part. DAD, at his side, surveys a ROAD MAP of the Western States. MOM is discovered distracting herself with some activity – folding laundry, playing music, reading, etc. – waiting for JULIE to come home.]

DAD: Lotta country right here. The roads make a simple pattern, y'know... like mountains and rivers. And there's a sweep to it, from Colorado to California; from down here at Nogales right up to Saskatoon. ... Had the itch ever since I was a kid. Roads, highways, truckstops at 6 AM, driving all night. Fought it my whole life. The day I made the last payment on the house, I thought it'd go away. ... Then the furnace blew. My Chevy

threw a rod and Julie needed a new computer.
[with pride] My kids are out here someplace. Both of 'em. Moll and Julie.

[JULIE enters, drunk, weaving, overcompensating.]

MOM: Julie?
JULIE *[under her breath]*: Oh God.
DAD: Marge too. That's my wife. You from these parts?
MOM: Are you all right?
TOWTRUCKER: Nope.
DAD: Ah… You got it too.
TOWTRUCKER: Got what?
DAD: The "itch."
MOM: I hope Frank behaved himself.
JULIE: As well as could be expected from somebody who got a C-minus in Health.
MOM: Isn't senior Health "human sexuality"?
JULIE: Not in Frank's case.
MOM: Physical love between two people is not something to be taken lightly.
JULIE: I was about to become the oldest living virgin in Upstate New York.
MOM: Liberation's one thing but…
JULIE: Can we talk tomorrow? I gotta lie down.

[JULIE suddenly lies down. "Spins."]

MOM: The first time can be very upsetting.
JULIE: From the beer, Mom. I'll be all right.
DAD: Bet you've seen a lotta guys like me.
TOWTRUCKER *[still working]*: I've seen my share.
JULIE: So what's with Dad all of a sudden? Male menopause?
    Or has he finally just flipped from the fumes at the mill?

[DAD, feeling ignored, begins to fold up his map, starts to go.]

DAD: I oughta get going.
TOWTRUCKER: Just give me a few more minutes.
DAD *[appeased]*: Your bike?

TOWTRUCKER: Naw. Some kid's. … Aw, forget it. Let me see.

[TOWTRUCKER *wipes his hands, tosses his rag, then looks at* DAD'*s map.*]

DAD: I was thinking of heading down through Zion and then on to the Grand Canyon.

MOM [*gently stroking* JULIE'*s hair*]: Your hair's so fine and soft. Like it was when you were a little girl.

[JULIE *groans, tries to evade*]

MOM [*CONT'D*]: Have you been using that new conditioner I got?

JULIE: It doesn't work.

MOM: It has to, it's got egg in it.

JULIE: I put a whole raw egg on yesterday.

MOM: That was for your father's breakfast.

JULIE: He eats toast.

MOM: Because you put all the eggs on your head.

JULIE: Why'd I have to get your hair? Why couldn't I have gotten Dad's. Look! It just breaks off!

MOM: Your father's had to clear the bathroom traps twice in the past month. Maybe you should rinse in the basement.

TOWTRUCKER: Why don't you just follow the route you've got marked out?

DAD: I took that way ten years ago. I'd like to see something new. I'm not in any rush.

TOWTRUCKER: Just goin' around?

DAD: Yeah. Just me this time.

TOWTRUCKER: Only way to go.

MOM: We've all got to be careful not to do anything upsetting to him for a while.

TOWTRUCKER: If I were you, I'd go the same way. Ten years is a long time. You forget a lot. Where'd you say you were from?

DAD: Back East. … Took me a long time to finally make the move and go. Kinda scary, just jumping off like that, not knowing where I'd land.

TOWTRUCKER [*resuming work*]: Still, once you do it, you can't believe you made such a big deal out of it. Hell, by the time I hit high gear, they coulda tore the roads up behind me.

DAD: You ever been back?

TOWTRUCKER: Nope.

DAD: You don't want to? I mean, sometimes, just now and then?

TOWTRUCKER: I had this weird feeling when I crossed the Mississippi that somebody burned the bridge behind me and the road just… evaporated. And way back on the other side someplace there's this guy with a face kinda like mine but who's a total stranger – like somebody somebody like you told me about, like a story that sounded familiar when you heard it but you don't know why. … If I ran into him now, we'd never even recognize each other.

[DAD *folds up his map.*
In another area, JULIE *reads.* MOM *approaches with comb and scissors.*
TOWTRUCKER *keeps working, his concentration tight on the machine.*
DAD *watches him closely, circling around behind him, looking over his shoulder. The Boy, turning his cap, becomes noticeably awkward and nervous. Strips a bolt, drops the tool. Glances up. He's now* MOLL.]

MOLL: You're standing in my light.

DAD: Now what're you doing?

MOLL: What's it look like?

DAD: Like you're making a mess.

MOLL: Plug's just a little tight.

DAD: You're turning it the wrong way.

[MOLL, *feeling foolish, reverses the rachet.*
DAD, *irritated by incompetence, tries hard to stay patient.*]

DAD: How's the job-hunting?

MOLL: Jobs are off-season.

DAD [*not amused*]: Where'd you look today?

MOLL: Nowhere.

DAD: Yesterday.

MOLL: I was working on my bike.

DAD: Did you go see my friend over at the sporting goods store?

MOLL: Not yet.

DAD: Did you at least call him?

MOLL: Didn't get a chance to.

DAD: You had all day. And yesterday.

MOLL: Look, Dad, if I don't get this thing running, I've got no way to get to work even if I got a job. I can't even get around to look without wheels.

DAD: You've got feet.

MOLL [*dismissing him*]: Yeah.

[*Silence.* MOLL *contines to work, ignoring him.*]

DAD: Look at me when I'm talking to you.

MOLL: You weren't saying anything.

[MOM *combs and snips. They can hear the scene between* DAD *and* MOLL.]

JULIE: Just the split ends, huh.

MOM: Take that sweater off – you'll get little hairs all over it and itch forever. … It's Moll's anyway.

DAD: You're almost twenty years old. What the hell's wrong with you? I was out and on my own when I was seventeen.

MOLL [*under his breath*]: Yeah, and look where it got you.

DAD: Your problem is that I've been too easy on you.

MOLL: Dad, believe me, if there's one thing you haven't been, it's "easy." I'll call the guy at the sporting goods store tomorrow. First thing. I promise.

DAD: Call him now.

MOLL: I'm in the middle of something. Besides, it's too late.

DAD [*grabbing the tool*]: I said NOW!

MOLL: Did it ever occur to you that I might not want to spend my life selling jockstraps and tennis balls for some buzzhead?

DAD: Then don't. Find something else. And don't come home 'til you do!

MOLL: Ease up, Dad. Between the stress and Mom's high-fat cooking we can't let these situations get out of hand. … I'll get a job. Don't worry.

DAD: I'm tired of hearing your excuses. Get moving.

MOLL: You know what kind of jobs are out there waiting for me? Stockboy at the 7-Eleven. Busboy at IHOP and pumping gas at the one full-serve station left in Upstate New York! I'm competing with high school kids and old geezers for less than minimum wage. They look at me like I'm some kind of freak. I feel like an idiot. Aw what's the use talking to you?!

*[*MOLL *splits.* DAD *watches him go. Fiddles with the tool, then...]*

DAD: Moll?

*[*DAD *stares at the bike.* MOM *accidentally cuts too much.]*

JULIE *[leaping up]*: Look what you did!!
MOM: I'm sorry, I –
JULIE: My hair's a mess! Everything's a mess!

*[*JULIE *tears off the sweater and hurls it at her mother.* JULIE *stomps off, passing her father.]*

DAD: Julie? *[then to* MOM*]* What's wrong now?
MOM: She's... upset.
DAD: Her hair again?
MOM: No.
DAD: The only thing that hair goop does is plug up the drains. If she keeps this up, she'll be bald before me.
MOM: It's Moll.
DAD: When'd he come back?
MOM: He didn't. ... Julie thinks he's gone for good. She heard you last night.
DAD: And she blames me. So what would you do with him?
MOM: I'd stop badgering him.
DAD: Right. I'm the bad guy. Again.
MOM: He's a good kid. He just needs time.
DAD: Just how much time does he get?
MOM: As much as he needs.
DAD: He's not going to have us around his whole life. He's got to get out there on his own and –
MOM: You're pushing him out of the house.
DAD: For chrissakes, even birds do that much for their kids!
   [pause] I tried to talk to him. I try and try and try... Damn freaky kid. Black nightgowns.
MOM: The boy was ten years old.
DAD: I should have known about that kid.
MOM: He gave it to me as a birthday present. He wanted to give me

something nice. He didn't know.

DAD: I don't even give you that kind of stuff, Marge.

MOM: I know.

DAD: I'm too embarrassed to ask the salesgirl for chrissakes. Ten years old, Jesus.

MOM: I thought it was cute.

DAD: Cute? … Like the motorcycle?

MOM [*grinning*]: Oh, John…

DAD: You think this is funny?

MOM: Not funny. Silly.

DAD: It's time, Marge. [*long pause*] As long as I can remember we've had somebody else to think about. I was his age when he was born and you weren't much older than Julie.

MOM: Maybe we should have waited.

DAD: I've pumped my paychecks into this crakerjack box for twenty years and what've we got to show for it?! … I'm going for a drive.

MOM: Again?

DAD [*exiting*]: We oughta sell this place.

> [*BLUE POLICE LIGHTS begin to flash. Light tight on* MOLL, *giving his version of events to a "Detective."* DAD *reappears at the edge of the spill, his back to* MOLL.]

MOLL: I was just running. I run all the time. I like to run. I was trying to work something out. Something personal.
So I was there, at the shop, so what? I've gone to lots of places looking for jobs. They didn't want me. I've got nothing against sporting goods – some of my best friends are softballs. … Sorry. Look, I might have said something to the guy but I didn't go back and bust his windows.

> [MOLL *squats, as if in a cell.* MOM *enters "the jail."*]

MOLL: Mom?

MOM: Oh, Moll, they said you –

MOLL: I didn't do anything.

MOM: You were frustrated and angry and –

MOLL: Mom, I didn't do anything!

MOM: It's always better if you tell the truth.

MOLL: Go home, Mom.

MOM: I came here to get you but... *[off his look]* I don't have the money for your bail. I tried to use my Shop-Rite card but they won't take it. They need something like the car or house as collateral. So as soon as your father gets home –

MOLL: Don't tell Dad.

MOM: I have to. I'll be back in a few hours, that's all. Everything's going to be all right. I promise.

[MOM exits. MOLL slumps. He stares at the shadowy man at the edge of the light spill. Then...]

MOLL: Dad? ... Dad?

[His second "Dad?" is in the voice of a very young child. DAD wheels around, charged with great energy and a sense of adventure and fun.]

DAD: Okay, Navigator, let's go!!

[DAD bustles the young MOLL onto the floor in front of him as if driving with his son on his lap. They play a familiar game called "Navigator." MOLL relishes the attention and affection.]

DAD: We're just about out of Pennsylvania, way up there at the tippytop of the Pennsylvania smokestack heading West, coming right down along what lake?

MOLL: Uhhhh... Ontario!

[JULIE groans, embarrassed for him.]

DAD: No. We're just west of Erie, PA. Now what lake is it over there on our right?

MOLL: Erie?

DAD: Right! Good boy!

[DAD hugs him. MOLL beams. MOM watches them with pleasure.

JULIE *works hard to play by the rules and not blurt out the answers.]*

MOLL: Lake Erie, right, Dad?

DAD: That's right, son. Now –

MOLL: It's right over there, right next to Pennsylvania.

DAD: You've got it.

MOLL: And Lake Ontario's way back there, ain't it?

MOM & JULIE *[interjecting]*: Isn't it?

DAD: That's right, and –

MOLL: And Lake Erie's –

DAD: Forget about the Lake for a minute. Up ahead, what state are we coming to?

MOLL *[excitedly]*: Ashtabula!

DAD: That's the town, but what state is it in?

MOLL: Oklahoma.

DAD: It starts with an "O" but what state is Toledo in?

*[*JULIE *mouthes "O-hi-o" for him but that only confuses* MOLL *more.]*

MOLL: Omaha?

DAD: No.

MOLL: Oregon.

DAD: No.

MOLL: Uhhh…

DAD: Think hard.

MOLL: Oklahoma.

DAD: You said that already. It's right under Lake Erie.

MOLL: Right over there.

DAD: Right.

MOLL: Ontario.

DAD: No.

MOLL: Oh.

DAD: "O." Now think real real hard.

MOLL: I don't know, Dad.

DAD & JULIE: The state where Grandma used to live.

*[*MOM *mouthes "O-hi-o."]*

MOLL *[finally]*: Ohio!! *[Cheers]*
DAD: Ohio!!
DAD & MOLL: Then on to Indiana, Illinois, Iowa... Nebraska, Wyoming...

[DAD continues to "drive." MOLL rises, ages. So does JULIE.]

JULIE: Dad should have been a bus driver. He always had a yen for travel. It was his way of coping. When things got bad at home, he'd go for a drive.
MOM: Bad days, long drives.
JULIE: If things got super-edgy, he'd plan long trips.
DAD: To Montana, Idaho...
MOLL: The last I saw of Mom and Dad they were leaving. They'd already sold the house, the car, and bought a Jeep Sedan to pull the mobile home.
DAD: To Washington...
MOLL: I was there the day they left. I was going home. I was going to talk to Dad. I was going to tell him I got a job. But they were leaving. They didn't see me. ... I watched them pack the mobile home from some bushes across the street. Then they drove off.
DAD: To Oregon...
MOLL: I stayed there a long time, just looking at the house. New people moved in that afternoon.
DAD: CALIFORNIA!
MOLL: Now they're gone. All of them. Even my sister.

[JULIE wanders lost with her bag.]

JULIE *[to audience]*: Excuse me, is this the Amelia Earhart Memorial Dormitory?
MOLL: Julie went off to school.
JULIE: It doesn't look like the picture in the catalog.
MOLL: Forestry major.
JULIE: Where are all the trees?
MOLL: She did great.
JULIE: And the ivy?
MOLL: A's and B's in everything.
JULIE: The cute guy in the polo shirt and track shorts?
MOLL: Chemistry even.

JULIE: The statue of the guy with the pigeon on his head, with white streaks all over him?

MOLL: When Julie started playing tennis, Dad'd play with her all the time. He never spent much time with me. But he'd take me camping, once or twice a summer, just him and me.

JULIE: I checked the map. This has to be either the library or my dorm.

[SOUNDS of a Bus Station. DAD becomes a BUS DRIVER announcing:]

DRIVER: Outbound local, now boarding at Gate Six! Repeat: Now boarding at Gate Six!

[As MOLL heads for the bus, he brushes past JULIE.]

JULIE *[to the passing young man]*: Excuse me, do you know which way North is?

[SWEETMEAT, a woman whose youthful enthusiasm belies her actual age, enters with her traveling bags.]

SWEETMEAT: Those trees!!!

JULIE *[off SWEETMEAT]*: Where?

[JULIE starts off in the direction of SWEETMEAT entrance. MOLL takes a seat on what will be a "bus."]

DRIVER: Please have your boarding passes ready.

SWEETMEAT: So many colors. God! It's amazing!

[SWEETMEAT gives the DRIVER her ticket and enters the "bus." In the following sequence, MOLL and SWEETMEAT are on a "different" bus from the DRIVER and JULIE.]

JULIE *[to the DRIVER]*: Here's my dorm pass, my pre-registration, my comptroller's voucher, and my... I don't know what this is.

SWEETMEAT *[taking the seat next to MOLL]*: Hi.

DRIVER *[to JULIE]*: Go ahead.

[JULIE takes the seat right behind the DRIVER.]

SWEETMEAT: You got a name?

MOLL: Uh… Mark.

SWEETMEAT: You on vacation? … To see the leaves?

MOLL: Me? No. I'm going…

SWEETMEAT: Where?

MOLL: I just left home see, and uh…

DRIVER: First time away from home?

SWEETMEAT: Runaway?

JULIE: Besides girlscout camp. But that doesn't count.

SWEETMEAT: You look too old to be a runaway. But if you're not going anyplace in particular then I guess it doesn't much matter how old you are, right?

JULIE: How'd you know?

DRIVER: I see a lot of people.

SWEETMEAT: I used to run away a lot, up the coast and back. This time I'm going someplace particular – this place in the country. Lots of big red-orange and yellow trees. Sugar maples with the sap still running. Cook it down and toss that hot syrup on the snow, listen to it sizzle into candy.

MOLL: Sounds great.

SWEETMEAT *[teasing]*: Wanna come?

MOLL: You got family? … There? This place you're going?

SWEETMEAT: I'll start with a garden and see what grows.

MOLL: Kids and everything?

SWEETMEAT: Decorative gourds mostly. God, I hope this is the right bus.

JULIE: You have buses that go to Vermont from here?

DRIVER: We go everywhere. Why do you ask?

SWEETMEAT: I feel like I've been traveling forever. I'm so afraid I'll fall asleep and get off in the wrong place or lose my ticket or my money or my… bags.

[SWEETMEAT looks for her bag. Can't find it. panic. MOLL searches.]

JULIE: My brother's there.

DRIVER: He in school too?

JULIE: Naw. Living with some woman he met.

DRIVER [*moving* JULIE's *bag*]: This your bag?

JULIE: I've got a stub for it someplace.

SWEETMEAT [*when* MOLL *hands over her bag*]: Thanks.

DRIVER: No problem.

[*SOUNDS of BUS on open road*]

SWEETMEAT: I came all the way across the country.

MOLL: By bus?

SWEETMEAT: Mostly. ... I feel so free! I associate the fumes with freedom. I open all the windows, air in my eyes, ears popping, stomach sloshing around...

JULIE [*noticing photo on dash*]: Who's that?

DRIVER: My kids. The summer we all went crosscountry together.

JULIE: Station wagon?

DRIVER: Camper. ... I've got pictures. You wanna see?

[DRIVER *whips out a long accordion of photos for* JULIE.]

SWEETMEAT: This morning was the first time I got afraid of getting lost. Back in California I was heading East. Who could miss, right? Plenty of room for mistakes. So you miss Indiana, there's always Ohio. But now that I'm closing in I've got to be more careful. I'm so tired I'll probably end up in Caribou, Maine.

MOLL: Hardly a place to raise gourds.

SWEETMEAT: You ever cross the country?

MOLL: Once. Dad loaded the whole family into the station wagon. He asked for our tickets then spent the next three weeks accusing us of being stowaways. Real sense of humor.

DRIVER: Great country. I used to drive the I-80 route. Now I'm stuck here on this local run.

SWEETMEAT: You ever been lost?

MOLL: Me? No.

SWEETMEAT: Never? Not even a little lost?

MOLL: Well, maybe once, when I was little.

SWEETMEAT: So where were you?

MOLL: I was lost, how do I know?

JULIE: Who's this?

DRIVER: That's my son.

MOLL: My Dad and I were camping. He was fly-fishing for trout and I was supposed to stay back from the stream and play.

SWEETMEAT: Play what?

MOLL: Play with myself... alone, you know. I don't know. Dad was really into his fishing.

JULIE [off another picture]: Hey, I remember that place, the big tree you can drive through. Moll wandered off.

MOLL: So I wandered off.

DRIVER: Moll?

MOLL: I could hear him calling.

JULIE: My brother.

MOLL: I sat down on a log and waited til he found me.

SWEETMEAT: That's what you're supposed to do.

[SWEETMEAT on MOLL's shoulder.]

JULIE: Weird name hunh? He really hates it. People think he was named after the new shopping center.

DRIVER: Nice talking to you.

JULIE [to audience with glance at MOLL]: It's a wonder my brother didn't grow up totally confused. I mean, he was confused about just about everything. So maybe he was. Or still is. Or isn't.

[SOUNDS of a college lecture hall filling up. "Wizard of Oz" feel.]

PROFESSOR: Today's lecture is on the effects of mobility on the American nuclear family.

JULIE: Isn't this Forestry 101?

PROFESSOR: This is Sociology. I'm sorry. This is "Adventures in Sociology: An exciting exploration of the facts, figures, trends, and chiefly the trendy issues of our times."

JULIE: Can I drop Forestry and take this?

PROFESSOR: Are you –

JULIE: I'm new.

PROFESSOR: Are you a major?

JULIE: I'm a freshman.

PROFESSOR: Yes. I see. Then I don't suppose you've read any of my articles, my studies.

JULIE: No.

PROFESSOR: Have you heard the one about the extended family?

JULIE: No.

PROFESSOR: It fell and broke into a dozen pieces.

JULIE: Hunh?

PROFESSOR: A little academic joke. Well they loved it at the faculty party. … Enough of this levity. The nuclear family and mobility. The first law of motion is that bodies, any bodies –

JULIE: Anybody at all?

PROFESSOR: Yes, any bodies in motion tend to stay in motion unless disturbed by other forces or mobile bodies, and bodies at rest tend to stay at rest unless disturbed by the busy bodies or hardbodies next door. … Get it?

JULIE: What?

PROFESSOR: The joke.

JULIE: Is it time for questions yet?

PROFESSOR: No.

JULIE: When?

PROFESSOR: Later. Afterwards. Now what is it?

JULIE: That sounds like physics.

PROFESSOR: If you don't mind. *[slight pause]* I'd like to share with you a particular case…

[A slide of four people]

PROFESSOR *[CONT'D]*: A family, composed of a father *[slide]*, 2.6 years older than a mother *[slide]*, who has given birth to 2.3 children, i.e., with a miscarriage after 3 months, hence the statistically exact *[rapid series of slides of non-traditional families]* American nuclear family filling every known socio-economic, racial, religious, and ethnic norm.

JULIE *[waving her hand madly]*: Pssst.

PROFESSOR: Not now. … Yes?

JULIE: Can I see them again? The slides?

PROFESSOR: Freshmen. … The father *[slide]* restless, and by his own description "on edge," put out the for-sale-by-owner sign and within three weeks had sold the abode and contents, bought a trailer *[slide]* and became nomadic, i.e., mobile.

The mother *[slide]* resisted hotly, but eventually followed.

The eldest *[slides]*, a boy, drifted. And so set in motion, continued in motion until disturbed from his ways by a woman *[slides]* approximately twelve years older than himself with whom he remained inert until set in motion by his sister *[slides]* who left home and parents for school *[slides]*, an institution that offered –

JULIE: There he is! The cute guy in the polo shirt and track shorts!

PROFESSOR: Yes. *[slide]* An institution which offered the comforts of home, the lax authority with which she was accustomed and the superficiality with which she was most familiar, and young men in polo shirts and track shorts.

[JULIE *raises her hand yet again.*]

PROFESSOR: Yes?

JULIE: What happened to the people in the pictures?

PROFESSOR: They'd uh meet others who'd remind them of someone in their own family and form ad hoc families. Nothing lasted. They moved on. Every holiday they tried desperately to find one another.

JULIE: Did they?

PROFESSOR: No.

[PROFESSOR *and* JULIE *linger.*
Sound environment: a country lane at dusk. SWEETMEAT *enters without luggage.* MOLL *follows carrying ALL of her bags.*]

MOLL: Just how far is this place?

SWEETMEAT: The guys at the gas station said it was just up around this bend. Maybe another mile or so. No more than that.

MOLL *[discouraged]*: Oh.

SWEETMEAT: You sure you can carry all that?

MOLL: Sure. No problem.

SWEETMEAT: I may be older but I'm not decrepit.

[MOLL *struggles to readjust his grip. Starts to lose control.*]

MOLL: They're clumsy, that's all.
SWEETMEAT: And heavy.
MOLL: Not for me.

[SWEETMEAT *moves on.* MOLL *manfully follows.*]

SWEETMEAT: It's really very… big of you, but don't you think you'd better let me take at least one of them?
MOLL [*with an edge*]: I said I'm fine. Okay? … Relax.

[MOLL *moves on, wrestling the bags.*]

SWEETMEAT: Relax?

[SWEETMEAT, *annoyed that he's annoyed, gets a wicked idea. She grabs an armful of leaves, sneaks up behind him. Just as he glances back, she flings them. All the bags go flying. He surveys the chaos, then begins to grin. Wickedly.*]

SWEETMEAT: Oh no… don't you dare…

[MOLL *tackles her. They tumble in the leaves, wrestling, throwing leaves at one another – kids in a preadolescent sexual tussle. Once they finally quiet down…*]

MOLL: Sweetmeat's kind of an unusual name.
SWEETMEAT [*while brushing herself off*]: Not where I come from. Considering some of the names my cousins got stuck with, I got off easy.
MOLL [*coming on to her*]: So what's it mean?
SWEETMEAT: It means … you sleep in the extra room.

[SWEETMEAT *runs off, leaving* MOLL *with the leaves and all the bags.*]

MOLL: Hey! Wait up!

[As MOLL *exits with the bags, we discover* DAD *at a payphone. Rain.]*

DAD: Is there a payphone? In the dorm? Amelia Earhart. ... Thank you.

*[*DAD *jots the number on his road map, then begins pumping change into the phone. He waits. Finally ...]*

DAD *[CONT'D]*: Julie! ... I'm sorry. Is Julie – ... Well there must be a Julie somewhere on your floor. Wait! Please, I – ... This is her father. Sorry.

[He hangs up. He's about to try the number again when MOM *approaches.]*

MOM: Who were you calling?

[He doesn't answer.]

MOM: Julie?

[He nods his head, yes.]

DAD: She's not there.
MOM: Did you try her cell?
DAD: She must have changed companies. So I tried the payphone in her dorm. A girl answered. Said she didn't know any Julie.
MOM: Are you sure you got the number right?

[She checks the phone number he's written on the map, then discreetly compares it with the number on a slip of paper she pulls from her pocket.]

DAD: Maybe we should get a post office box somewhere. For a billing address. So we can reactivate the family plan.
MOM *[as she dials the number...]*: Where? We haven't stayed anyplace more than a day.

*[*MOM *gets a "no service" message.* DAD *checks out the number. It's different from the ones he has.]*

DAD: What is that?

[*MOM says nothing.* DAD *gets suspicious. She avoids.*]

DAD [*CONT'D*]: Have you talked to her?
[*no response*] Marge?
MOM: I must have left fifty messages before we took off. I told you we should have stopped at the school but you were in such a big hurry. We just had to head West.

[*MOM crumbles the slip of paper and tosses it. After a long* MOMent…]

DAD: I tried to write a letter but I couldn't find the words. On paper the words looked clumsy. I sounded like a six year old. Julie writes so well. … Maybe we ought to go back.
MOM [*snatching the map*]: No.
DAD: But –
MOM: John, stop it. Listen to me. … Julie will be fine. We'll get in touch with her.

[*He stares off down the road. He's on the verge of an apology.*]

DAD: I'm…
MOM: I went along with this of my own free will. This isn't just for you anymore. [*pause*] Let's go to… North Dakota.
DAD: We're not going anywhere near the Dakotas.
MOM: Then let's take another route.
DAD: Marge…
MOM [*enthusiastic*]: I want to go to North Dakota.
DAD: Why?
MOM: Why not?
DAD: What's in North Dakota that's all of a sudden so important that you have to see?
MOM [*after a slight pause*]: Sioux Falls.
DAD: Sioux Falls happens to be in South Dakota.
MOM: North, South, who cares. Let's go. Right now.

DAD: It's a thousand miles away!

MOM: We'll drive all night. We'll watch the sun rise over Sioux Falls, North Dakota!

DAD: South Dakota!

MOM [grabbing his hand, tugging]: Come on!

DAD [holding back]: I know why you're doing this.

MOM: Maybe you do, maybe you don't.

DAD [holding her]: Thank you.

MOM: You know, when we were getting ready to leave, it was terrible. The kids were gone. The house was up for sale. I thought I was losing you. Everything I knew. I was so scared, I was numb. But there was something in you, an excitement. You were 20 again. And pretty soon, so was I. It was like being with the man I married all over again.

[She kisses him. Tentatively. Then again. This time, the kiss turns into a "first passion" kiss – which surprises them both. Her hands start caressing him, moving slowly down his body.]

MOM [softly]: Come on.

DAD [with a grin]: North Dakota?

MOM: Further south.

[They exit, holding hands.
JULIE enters the "house" with her bags. It's Thanksgiving Day.]

JULIE: HELLO, Mom! I'M HOME!!

[Long pause as JULIE checks out the space, puzzled at the differences. BETTY enters, open-armed, ready to welcome her unexpected daughter home. JULIE turns. Mutual shock.]

BETTY: Can I help you?

JULIE: Who are you?

BETTY: Who are you?

JULIE: I live here.

BETTY: I beg your pardon.

JULIE: Where's the toaster? And the rug? What's going on here? Where's my Mom?

BETTY: Honey, I think you'd better leave my house now.

JULIE: Your house?! Who are you? Where's my Mom and Dad? My girlscout potholders? They used to be right there, on that wall.

[BETTY *suddenly embraces her.*]

BETTY: You must be Julie!!!

JULIE [*smothered*]: Yeah.

BETTY: I should have known. … So you're Julie. You're so much older than your picture. So much more mature. I saw the picture when Bill and I looked at the house. Your mother and father are such sweet people. All they talked about was you. You and your brother. Moll, isn't it?

JULIE: Yeah.

BETTY: They took the picture with them.

JULIE: Where?

BETTY: They moved out three weeks ago. Bill and I haven't even finished unpacking. Last place we lived we moved before we unpacked from the place before that. Bill moves around a lot with his job.

JULIE: Where did they go?

BETTY: Travelling. You know… They didn't tell you?

JULIE: Nobody told me anything.

BETTY: How strange. Nothing?

JULIE: It's Thanksgiving. I wanted to surprise them. I came home.

BETTY: Isn't there somebody – friends, relatives – you could go to?

JULIE: I want to see my Mom and Dad.

BETTY: Poor baby. [*pause*]

Well… You could stay here with us for a day or so. Lord knows there's plenty of food. Been cooking the last three days, up since six this morning, cooking.

JULIE: I wanted to go home. This is home.

BETTY [*after a pause*]: There's something I want to get for you. You just wait right here. Bill! Bill!!

BILL [*OFF*]: Yeah. What is it? Need a hand with the bird?

[BILL *enters. A goodnatured mid-country man. Too well-fed for too long and moves like it. When he spots Julie from behind, he assumes it is his daughter.*]

BILL [excited]: Oh...

BILL [CONT'D] :

[when JULIE turns to face him] Oh.

[A look to BETTY, then back to...] You must be...

[reading BETTY's lips] Julie! Sure. Hi. I'm Bill. You've met Betty. Never forget a face. The key to good sales.

BETTY: Great sales.

BILL: I'm in RVs. Mobile homes, tent trailers, you name it. Biggest boom industry since the covered wagon. Fixed your folks up with a beauty. That's how we met. So, what brings you back to this neck of the woods? Grew up here, right?

JULIE: Yes.

BETTY: Bill, you chat with Julie. I've got to run upstairs and get that thing.

BILL: What thing?

BETTY: You know. The "thing."

[BETTY exits.]

BILL: The thing, the thing... oh, sure. The thing.

[BILL has no idea what he's talking about but he covers well. He sits next to JULIE, crowding her. He's a very physical man. Nothing mean.]

BILL [CONT'D]: Must be great getting home for the holidays. Catch the high school game, put on a few pounds, stretch the old gut for Christmas. Staying with friends or you have relatives in the area?

JULIE: I was coming home.

BILL: Terrific. Good for you. My kids never come home anymore. It's just me and Betty now. You're in school? My girl's in school. Don't see her much, all I see are the bills. She's busy though. Special trips and projects. Studies all the time. Takes after her old man, busy all the time, a million and one projects. We hear about her from all kinds of people. Never talked much about herself. At home she was always quiet, never said a word at the dinner table, which is when we saw her. Great kid.

[BETTY enters with JULIE's ragdoll]

BETTY: Remember this?

BILL: Bet that used to be your room.

BETTY: I try to keep it fixed up for the kids. The doll was in the closet. Guess they didn't see her.

BILL: Wasn't much room in the trailer. They're roomy, but still – doesn't take much to fill one of those Streamliners.

BETTY: I had this feeling. Mother's intuition I guess. So I kept her.

BILL: Mother and her intuitions.

BETTY: I know how much these things mean.

BILL: Julie, she's called hospitals, fire departments, even the FBI on an intuition.

BETTY: My own girl… well… anyway, I'm glad I kept it.

[PHONE rings]

BILL: There's the phone again. Maybe it's one of the kids. Julie, you'll stay for dinner. After all those cafeteria meals nothing like a little home cooking, right?

BETTY: Father, the phone.

BILL: Going, Mother.

[BILL exits.]

BETTY: That man, give you the shirt off his back. I'm serious. I've seen him do it. His blue pin-striped one. … You stay put. I'll plop your bag in the other room. Your old room okay?

[BETTY exits with one of JULIE's two suitcases. Beat.
JULIE opens her suitcase, packing to go away to college. Considers taking the doll with her. When DAD enters behind her, she sets it aside. Silence. Finally…]

DAD: You're sure you don't want me to drive you?

JULIE: I've got a ticket for the bus.

DAD: It's no trouble.

JULIE: I want to do this myself.

DAD: Sure, sure. [slight pause] Don't you think you should take some extra clothes for winter?

JULIE: I've got loads of clothes.

DAD: Well if you think your mother and I are going to send your clothes parcel post every time it gets cold –

JULIE: I'll be home to pick them up.

DAD: When?

JULIE: Whenever.

DAD: So you'll call.

JULIE: I said I will.

[DAD *hands her a cellphone*]

DAD: I added you to the family plan.

JULIE: I have my own… This one doesn't even have pictures!

DAD: Just take it. Just in case.

JULIE: Whatever.

DAD: I'll give you a ride to the bus station.

JULIE: Frank's picking me up.

DAD: Oh. *[pause]* Julie?

JULIE: What?

DAD: I'm going to miss you.

JULIE: About time you and Mom had some time alone together. Never know, Moll may even show up.

DAD: You've heard from him?

JULIE: No.

DAD: Oh.

[DAD *withdraws.* JULIE *remains, clutching the doll tightly, then starts to put on "Moll's sweater."* BILL *sneaks up behind her with a snapshot camera which has a flash attachment. Just as* JULIE *turns –]*

BILL: SMILE!

[BILL *takes the snapshot pointblank. The flash dazzles her.*]

BILL *[CONT'D]*: A couple holiday snapshots for the scrapbook. Betty! Betty!

BETTY *[OFF]*: In the kitchen.

[With no BETTY *for the photo, he takes another one of* JULIE.*]*

BILL: How about some tennis?

JULIE: It's November.

BILL: So? It's nice out. Cool. A few quick games. Builds up the appetite. Whaddaya say?

JULIE: Well…

BILL *[bustling her off]*: Come on.

*[*JULIE *exits with him, laughing.*
The SOUNDS of an electronic phone system. MOM *at a payphone making a call.* JULIE *goes to a phone. The voice of* OPERATOR ONE *is* DAD*'s;* TWO, MOLL*'s;* THREE, JULIE*'s. All four actors are on stage, voices stylized.]*

MOM: Hello?

OPERATOR ONE: Can I help you?

MOM: Operator?

OPERATOR THREE: This is the Operator.

MOM *[slight overlap]*: Operator…

OPERATOR TWO: Can I help you?

MOM: I dialed direct but your automated system came in and –

OPERATOR ONE: Whom were you calling?

OPERATOR THREE: This is the Operator, can I help you?

MOM: Hello?

OPERATOR ONE *[slight irritation]*: Can I help you?

OPERATOR TWO: This is the Operator, can I help you?

MOM: I think there's somebody else on this line.

OPERATOR TWO: The number you have reached is not a working number.

OPERATOR ONE:	OPERATOR THREE:
Whom were you calling?	Who is it you were calling?

MOLL: Hello?

MOM: My daughter.

MOLL: Julie?!

OPERATOR ONE: The number you have reached is not a working number.

MOLL: Hello, Operator?

OPERATOR ONE & THREE: Can I help you?

MOM: I dialed the number direct.

JULIE: Hello, Moll?

OPERATOR ONE: Shall I place the call for you?

OPERATOR TWO: Can I help you?

OPERATOR THREE: Person to person?

MOM [overlap from "to"]: Person to person.

OPERATOR ONE [overlap from "to"]: Person to person.

JULIE: Where are you?

OPERATOR ONE: The name?

OPERATOR TWO: Can I help you?

MOM: I'm her mother.

OPERATOR ONE: Not you. The party whom we're trying to reach.

MOM: My daughter.

MOM & MOLL: Julie.

MOM: She's at school.

OPERATOR THREE: This is the Operator, can I help you?

OPERATOR ONE: Person to person, Julie from Mom… "lovely."

MOM: Operator?

JULIE: Mom?

MOLL: What?

OPERATOR ONE: It's ringing.

JULIE: Where are you?

MOM: Julie?

MOLL: Vermont.

JULIE: Where in Vermont?

OPERATOR ONE: That number's been disconnected.

MOM: When?

JULIE: I can't hear you!

MOLL:	MOM:
VERMONT!	Julie?

OPERATOR THREE: This is the Operator, can I help you?

MOM: Hello?

OPERATOR ONE: Can I help you?

OPERATOR TWO: That number's been disconnected.

OPERATOR ONE & THREE: Can I help you?

MOM [after a pause]: It's my girl. It's Thanksgiving. I want to talk to her.

> [The sound environment fades to a single loud dial tone that ends abruptly. Or a recorded message: "If you wish to make a call please hang up and dial again."
> MOLL enters reading a passage from "Our Town." He's in SWEETMEAT's Vermont house. Outside, JULIE and SWEETMEAT whoosh and whoop. SWEETMEAT enters, breathless.]

SWEETMEAT: You should see your sister out there whooshing through the leaves.

MOLL: Julie thinks she's an antelope or something.

SWEETMEAT: She do that at home when you were kids?

MOLL: We only had two trees.

SWEETMEAT: Not enough leaves, hunh. ... Hey, let's go out and play.

MOLL: Naw.

SWEETMEAT: Come on. It'll be fun.

MOLL: Nobody's stopping you. If you want to go play home on the range with my sister, go ahead. They're your leaves.

SWEETMEAT: They're just leaves.

MOLL: They fell off your trees. That makes them your leaves.

SWEETMEAT: Okay. They're my leaves. Jeez. I thought you would have liked having family around for Thanksgiving.

MOLL: I'm surprised she hasn't started bouncing on my bed yet.

SWEETMEAT: I'm glad she feels at home.

MOLL: Great.

SWEETMEAT: Well I like her. She's real independent. ... Who's she more like, your Mom or Dad?

MOLL: I don't know.

SWEETMEAT: Who're you more like?

MOLL: I'm not like anybody. Mom maybe. I don't know. [he begins to exit] What difference does it make?

SWEETMEAT: Where are you going?

MOLL: My room.

SWEETMEAT: Why can't you just relax and enjoy the visit? She's only going to be here for a couple days.

MOLL: I'm just going to my room.

SWEETMEAT: It helps to know what you're looking for or running from.

MOLL: I'm not running from anything.

[JULIE *enters, leaves in her hair and sweater. She's glowing.*]

JULIE: Hi.

SWEETMEAT: How're the leaves?

MOLL: Jeez.

JULIE: Great.

SWEETMEAT: You shoulda been here a few weeks ago when they were still up and red. Walk along that path looking straight up, all the colors layers deep passing through each other, like floating in a kaleidoscope.

JULIE: I would have come up sooner but "Mark" wouldn't give me your address.

MOLL: I didn't want you telling Mom and Dad.

JULIE: Afraid they were going to come up here and drag you home?

SWEETMEAT: Here, let me get these twigs and things off your sweater.

JULIE: Thanks.

MOLL: You could have come any time you wanted. All you had to do was call.

JULIE: You said don't call unless it was an emergency.

MOLL: Quitting school isn't? How come you didn't tell anybody?

JULIE: I was going to. When I got home. You could have at least told me they moved. I felt like such a jerk, going back and them being gone. [*slight pause*] It's kinda weird thinking of them alone out there in the middle of nowhere where there's nothing around but coyotes and winnebagos.

SWEETMEAT: Right now they're probably in some trailer park in Arizona watching the sun set over the Rockies or down in Florida listening to the frogs sing to each other in the canals.

JULIE: Yeah. Bet they're having a great time. Dad loves to travel.

MOLL: What about Mom?

JULIE: She went along didn't she?

MOLL: Because Dad sold the house out from under her.

JULIE: It was Mom's house too.

SWEETMEAT: She's got a new house and she's pulling it along behind her. I think it's real convenient having home hooked to the rear axle. Always know right where to find it. Makes it hard as hell to run away though.

MOLL: What's that supposed to mean?

JULIE: A couple years from now we'll probably laugh about it. I mean what's it say about a family that like totally disintegrates?

SWEETMEAT: I've always found those little toasters on wheels cute in a kind of junk-food way. I keep expecting poptarts to sproing out of the roof when I see them on the highway. You should hear my Momma when it comes to trailers. As far as she's concerned, only lowlife, cows, and white trash live in aluminum huts. *[off their looks]* Guess she never met your folks.

JULIE: Where is she?

MOLL: At home where she belongs.

SWEETMEAT: In Oceanside.

MOLL: Not everybody's parents become nomads when they reach middle age.

SWEETMEAT: In a nursing home.

JULIE: Oh.

SWEETMEAT *[no apology]*: A real nice one.

MOLL: At least you know where she is.

SWEETMEAT: And you know where your Momma is. On vacation. Like millions of other people.

MOLL: They'd have to have a place to come back to for it to be a vacation.

SWEETMEAT: Yeah, well…

JULIE: They're probably fine.

[When JULIE starts to take off her sweater, MOLL finally notices it.]

MOLL: What's this?

JULIE: A sweater.

MOLL: I can see that. It's mine.

JULIE: I liked it.

MOLL: So do I.

SWEETMEAT: That is without a doubt one of the finest sweaters ever contrived by man and sheep.

JULIE: You want it back?

MOLL [*grabbing for it*]: I left it home.

JULIE [keeping it away]: There is no home to leave it in.

MOLL: Mom gave me that sweater.

SWEETMEAT: Your family do this every time it gets cold? There some kind of clothing shortage where you come from?

JULIE: I like lambswool. It's soft. Lots of times I wear it with nothing underneath.

MOLL: My sweater?!

JULIE: Not at home though. Mom'd get mad if she saw I wasn't wearing a bra. Liberation's one thing, but floppy tits, that's something else, that's what Mom'd say.

SWEETMEAT: Gawd, do you remember your first bra?

MOLL [*to* JULIE]: That training bra with all the pads and kleenex in it? You must have stuffed half a box in there. Instant puberty! You were what? Twelve?

JULIE: Thirteen.

MOLL: Dad made the big announcement at dinner, right over the pot roast and potatoes: "Say, is that a bra you're wearing?"

[*Something in the privacy of their shared memory moves* SWEETMEAT *to "excuse" herself and withdraw.*]

JULIE: You laughed. All of you.

MOLL: And you locked yourself in your room and cried.

[JULIE *leans on* MOLL's *shoulder, he puts his arm around her, rocking gently, the sweater on their laps.*
In another area of the stage, DAD *is watching TV, alone, late night.*
MOM *enters.*]

DAD: Where the hell have you been?

MOM: Downtown.

DAD: It's almost one o'clock.

MOM: Is it that late already?

DAD: I come home, Julie's out, I don't know where. You're downtown, or so you say. Julie breezes in without even a hello and locks herself in her room. Doesn't anybody stay home and watch TV like in the old days?

Sit around and watch Animal Kingdom? Walt Disney? Tennis?

[JULIE *moves to another area of the stage – not part of the ensuing scene. She addresses the audience.*]

JULIE: One summer Dad thought tennis would bring us all together.
MOM: Moll… Moll is…
DAD: I don't want to talk about him.
JULIE: Moll wasn't interested and Mom wasn't coordinated.
    That left me.
DAD: Not tonight.
MOM: Moll is in jail.
JULIE: It's the only thing I ever did with Dad. If he needed a partner, I was there.
DAD: It's that goddam nightgown, that's where it started.
MOM: Get over it.
DAD: At least I took him camping.
JULIE: Then there was camping. Like a religion with Dad.
DAD: Taught him how to build a fire, chop wood, play touch football, everything.
JULIE: Twice in the summer and once in the fall. Moll got to go with Dad on his fishing trips. Dad thought it made Moll feel important to dig worms and beetles for bait. But the family trips were different.
MOM: He vandalized a store.
JULIE: Moll and I laugh about those trips, but they were really kind of neat. Till I got older. Like about 13.
DAD: Of all the goddam stupid things he's ever done…
JULIE: Dad would have Moll build a fire and then he'd tell us stories. God, was he awful. Ghost stories. Moll and I would pretend to be scared. Mom knew, but she played along. She'd toast marshmallows the whole time. If Dad got to be too much, like with wind sounds and creaky stairs, and Moll and I couldn't stand it anymore without cracking up, Moll'd drop his marshmallow and pick it back up with all kinds of pine needles and dirt and ashes stuck to it. We could fall out laughing and pretend it was the marshmallow.
MOM: I need the money for his bail.
JULIE: We'd sing "America the Beautiful." All of us. Dad'd make us.

MOM: Our son is in jail.

DAD: Maybe that's were he belongs.

MOM: If you hadn't thrown him out –

DAD: I do not want to hear that again! I did not throw him out. I told him to go get a job. That is not throwing him out. Somebody had to do it, and it wouldn't be you.

[MOM hands him his checkbook]

MOM: Here.

DAD: Where'd you get that?

MOM: From the drawer.

DAD *[grabbing it]*: Stay out of that drawer!

MOM: Sign it. It's already filled out.

DAD: For chrissakes, Marge, they're not going to take a personal check for bail.

MOM: They won't?

DAD: No, Marge, they won't.

MOM: Then we'll have to find the money someplace else. Maybe the savings bonds, or the deed to the house.

DAD: I am not going to do anything, don't you understand?

MOM: For our son?

DAD: No son of mine would trash somebody's store.

MOM: You won't do it?

DAD: Why should I?

MOM: You're his father!!

[MOLL enters]

MOM: Moll! *[hugging him]* Did you escape? Are you –

DAD: You owe me an explanation.

MOLL: Later, okay? Mom!

[MOLL tries to extricate himself]

DAD: You were arrested today.

MOLL: I didn't do anything. It was all a big mistake.

MOM: I'm just glad you're home and safe.

MOLL: Mom, will you take it easy. I'm all right. They let me go. I hope you didn't go to a lot of trouble over the bail.

[*Beat.* MOLL *catches the looks between his parents, especially noting his mother's silence.*]

MOLL: You wouldn't do it?!

DAD: That's right, I wouldn't.

MOLL: You would have let me stay in jail?!

DAD: You got yourself put there, not me. And now I want to know what the hell you were doing that you got arrested.

MOLL [*beginning to exit*]: It's not worth talking about.

DAD [*beginning to exit opposite*]: Oh yes it is. And I'm going to find out what the hell is going on.

MOM: Where are you going?

DAD: I'll get the police to tell me.

MOLL: Dad, you're just making a fool of yourself again.

DAD: Shut up. You think you're such a hotshot, a goddam outlaw, well now you'll learn. I tried to teach you something. Now you'll learn the hard way.

MOLL: They let me go. They found the kids who busted up your buddy's shop about an hour after Mom left. They caught 'em trashing the high school. And thanks for believing in me so much. I can't tell you how reassuring it is to know that I've got parents like you behind me.

[MOLL *starts for his room.*]

MOM: I always tried to help.

MOLL: I can take care of myself.

DAD: You? You can't even get a job.

MOLL: I could go out and become the world's oldest living caddy. Is that what you want? Or pump gas?

DAD: Or be a gangster.

MOM: John, please …

MOLL: Listen to me! Will you just listen to me! I didn't do anything. The worst thing I've ever done is get a D in math. I'm not Julie!

MOM: I'm just glad you're home and safe. I was so worried about you down there in that jail, all those men.

DAD: See what you're doing! Go ahead, coddle him, wipe his chin, make excuses. You can't make life easy. Nothing's easy.

MOLL: Not in this house.

DAD: And I don't want any of your smart-assed remarks.

MOLL: I'm going to bed.

DAD: You haven't asked my permission.

MOLL & MOM: For what?

DAD: To stay.

MOM: He's home. He doesn't need your permission.

DAD: Yes he does.

MOM: It was your fault he was out there on the streets and –

DAD: Mine?!

MOM: And your fault he got arrested.

MOLL: Forget it, Mom, I'll sleep in the garage.

DAD: Oh no you won't.

MOLL: I'll be damned if I'm going to beg to sleep in my own bed.

DAD: It's not your bed. It's mine. I paid for it.

MOM: Stop it!

MOLL: Keep your fucking bed then.

[Silence. The challenge sits in the air, charging it, until...]

DAD: Get out. Get your things. Get your things and get out of here.

MOM: No!

DAD: And get that junk heap out of my garage.

MOLL: Don't worry about it.

MOM: Moll, please –

DAD: Shut up. This is my house. I'm the father here. And if he wants to make a shithill out of his life he can go do it someplace else.

MOLL: I will. I will.

[MOLL exits.]

JULIE: We'd sing "America the Beautiful," all of us.

DAD [muttering]: My house. Son of a bitch...

[DAD exits.]

MOM: Fine. If that's the way you feel…
JULIE: Dad'd make us.
MOM: Sell it.

[MOM exits]

JULIE: I don't know, something about us all singing together, watching the campfire… If anybody else'd been around it would have been real embarrassing, I mean hyperblushtime. But there was just us, together, and the quiet after…

[Slow fade on JULIE]

END OF ACT ONE

ACT TWO

[National Park slide show plays. The rhythm is broken by personal "memory" slides. Then, lingering on a slide of huge redwoods...]

JULIE/RANGER: I remember stupid things... like marshmallows, or the day we got a flat on the road to Niagara Falls. I can't even remember what the Falls sounded like but I remember that tire blowing out. All I remember from the Falls is my Mom grabbing my hand and yanking me back from the rail like I was gonna jump or something.

I remember Dad sitting at the kitchen table with his RV catalogs, clicking at his calculator, and Mom pretending not to notice. I remember the smell of laundry on the backyard line, of turkey roasting downstairs, the factory smell in Dad's coat when he got home from work and used to lift me up and spin me around. But...

No matter how hard I try, I can't quite remember their faces. They're like old snapshots that're starting to crumble, the ink on the back with all the names and dates and places smudged and fading out. A couple more years and they'll be dust – garbage, the kind of thing you leave behind when you're gonna travel light.

[BILL enters, breathing deeply, indulging himself. BETTY lugs in a large cooler and a Coleman stove.]

BILL: Smell that air.

BETTY: I don't know why we had to bring so much stuff.

BILL: Come on, take a good chestful. Ahhh.

BETTY: Two thousand miles to play house on a twenty by twenty patch of pine needles and gravel.

BILL: God it's good to be out on the open road. All this fresh air. Makes me hungry. What've we got in there?

BETTY: Marshmallows.

BILL: To eat.

BETTY: What else do you do with marshmallows, play old people ping-pong? You ate everything else.

BILL: We brought a whole chestful of food.

BETTY: You ate it.

BILL: It's this air. Makes me hungry. Let's take a hike.

BETTY: Why don't you hike down to the commissary and buy something for dinner?

BILL *[sexual innuendo]*: There's a nature path over there.

BETTY: Nature's everywhere.

BILL: But it must be better over there because that's where they put the path.

BETTY: I wish we'd taken an RV instead of this tent-trailer. But you wanted to be closer to nature, which we now find is only over there, along the path.

BILL: Look at all these RVs and Streamliners and tent-trailers! God, what a great business I'm in, getting so many people out on the road, out here where there's miles and miles of unpaved nature, where they can breathe and eat and burn a few logs, forget about their jobs and their HEMORRHOIDS!

BETTY *[swatting him playfully]*: Oh Bill.

BILL: It's from sitting too much. Desk jobs. The whole damn country.

BETTY: Looks like an aluminum foil suburb.

BILL: I see those vehicles and by God I see history repeating itself. I want to hitch up the oxen and head out. I feel, down deep, down in my gut, that this is as American as the Oregon Trail. "O Give me a home where the buffalo –"

BETTY: I'll be glad when we get home.

BILL: You're just tired from the drive.

BETTY: I'm tired of picking blackflies and pine needles out of my coffee.

BILL: Hey… *[hugs her]* Thanks for doing this for me. I know how much you wanted to see Paris.

BETTY: I knew how much you wanted this trip. Besides, this is all you would have talked about the whole time.

BILL: Whaddaya mean?

BETTY: You would have compared everything. We'd be standing on the Pont St. Michel looking at the Seine and you'd keep saying how puny it is compared to the Missouri.

BILL: Well it is.

BETTY: How do you know, you've never been there.

BILL: Neither have you. All those moldy old cities.

BETTY: They're not so moldy.

BILL: They're old.

BETTY: No older than here.

BILL: Here's been here since the beginning, just like nature. At least it's clean.

BETTY: Everywhere I look there are beer cans and plastic wrap.

BILL: The air smells like air and you don't have to drink water from bottles. Here you can drink right out of the stream if you want to.

BETTY: I wouldn't.

BILL: You don't have to, there are water taps everywhere.

BETTY: And trailer hook-ups.

BILL: People here travel like Americans. Even the Japanese. People there act different.

BETTY: They are.

BILL: They steal your travelers checks.

BETTY: That's why you get travelers checks, to get them stolen.

[beat]

BILL/DAD: Did you lock the car?

BETTY/MOM: This is a National Park! Do you think people would come all the way out here just to steal our AAA maps.

BILL/DAD *[scanning audience]*: Who are these people? We don't know them, they don't know us. For all we know they may be dangerous fugitives from justice, outlaw bikers, desperadoes on the Santa Fe Trail, six guns and Saturday Night Specials!

[MOLL is discovered over his sister's half-packed backpack.]

DAD *[noting the boy]*: Like that guy hanging around over there.

MOM: That boy?

DAD: Boy?!

MOM: He smiled and said hello.

DAD: Watching to see whose campsites are unprotected.

[JULIE *approaches* MOLL.]

MOM: How would you like people to say that about our son?

DAD: Let'em say whatever they want as long as they put safety glass in their store windows.

MOLL: You're packed already?

JULIE:I want to get an early start. I hope I get a good assignment. Like Yellowstone or Zion. If I do, why don't you come out and visit?

DAD: Christ, I was only joking.

MOLL: How will I get way out there?

JULIE: Take a train. Or a bus. Hitch. You could fix your motorcycle.

DAD: Can't I make a joke? Marge?

[MOLL *finds* JULIE's *road map.*]

MOLL: This is Dad's AAA map, the one with all the blue magic marker routes.

JULIE: You want it? I can get another one.

MOLL: This is his national park map.

JULIE: Bet he's dragging Mom back to all the parks. You know, if you followed this route in reverse, you'd probably run smack into them.

MOLL: It's a little late for that.

JULIE [*teasing*]: There are lots of people out there. Just pick two and call them Mom and Dad if it'll make you feel better. Lots of lonely people'd love to have a slightly used son. Here.

[JULIE *offers* MOLL *the map.*]

MOLL: No. You'll need it.

JULIE: As long as we keep it in the family.

MOLL [*taking the map*]: Yeah.

JULIE: Yeah. Our one family heirloom. Why don't you come with me?

MOLL: It'll be easier if you're by yourself. I don't want you to be late and get a lousy assignment on account of me.

DAD: This trip's not working out. We keep moving but nothing changes except the scenery. We're the same people in a hundred different places. We go to Montana, we go to the Badlands, we're still just us. … This isn't what I left home for.

MOLL: So... You got everything?

JULIE: Everything I need.

MOM: I don't know what you're looking for or what it is you want, but whatever it is doesn't include me. ... I'm not going with you. *[slight pause]* I'm not going back, but I'm not going any further either.

*[MOM can't/won't look at him.
As MOLL helps JULIE on with her pack...]*

MOLL: Send me a postcard as soon as you get settled.

JULIE: Could be a while.

MOLL: Well as soon as you can.

JULIE: What if you're not here?

MOM: I'll be here. You know how to reach me.

JULIE: I'll send it anyway. Be sure you leave a forwarding address. Well...

[Slight pause. Brother and sister embrace. Hold.]

MOM: Just go, dammit!

[DAD exits.]

JULIE: Adios.

[JULIE exits. MOM exits. MOLL follows JULIE to her exit.]

MOLL: Bye.

[MOLL continues to stare off after her. Long pause. Weeks later, MOLL looks out the "window." SWEETMEAT enters behind him. Finally...]

SWEETMEAT: You've certainly been getting a lot of use out of that window since I washed it.

MOLL: West's out that way, isn't it?

SWEETMEAT *[after a slight pause]*: You ever wonder where they went?

MOLL: Who?

SWEETMEAT: Your family. That's who you're thinking about. *[pause]* Yep, the dirt road runs due West 'til it hits the county road. The county road will take you down to Route Seven, Seven'll take you to I-80 West, and before you know it, Route 66.

MOLL: I know that.

SWEETMEAT: I know you do.

> [*A kiss. Then* SWEETMEAT *exits.*
> *As* MOLL *begins to address the audience, his demeanor and tone changes, becoming the young man known as the* HITCHHIKER.]

MOLL/HITCHHIKER: I left the East a big man – rugged, independent, I even bought a pack of Marlboros. I was going to eat up the distance, make that country mine! ... Yeah. Right. You ever been to Nebraska? You know how "big" Nebraska is? I mean on the map it's only this [*thumb and index finger spread to 2"*] big. It took me seven days to go that far. And I felt lucky.

Then Colorado. Instant mountains, right? Wrong. It's two hundred miles before you even see them. You have to earn those mountains. All that rain and dust and peanut butter and five days without a shower, sun so hot it cuts your lips and cold so bad in the morning you can't feel your feet...

But when those Rocky Mountains come rising up out of the earth, it's like no feeling anywhere, anytime. I mean they're so big and you're so small, and they seem to say: "Hey, you! You think you can make it? I dare you." ... And you do it. Or you go back to wherever it was you felt bigger and safer and say, yeah, I've seen the West, it's pretty.

Pretty, hell! It's awesome.

> [*He sits, sticking out his thumb.*
> JULIE/RANGER, *toting pack joins him on roadside, hitching.*]

HITCHHIKER: Hi. ... Which way ya headed?

RANGER: Take a wild guess.

HITCHHIKER: Since we're headed the same way, you wanna hitch together? It'd be a whole lot easier for me to be seen with someone like you, and some girls feel safer if they're with a guy like me.

RANGER: It's faster if I'm by myself.

[She studies the road. He pulls out a pack of Marlboros.]

HITCHHIKER: Suitcherself. Cigarette?
RANGER: I don't smoke.
HITCHHIKER *[putting pack away]*: Me neither.

[She gives him a look. He sits, makes himself comfortable. He whips out a jar of peanut butter.]

HITCHHIKER: Hungry?
RANGER: I feel like I've been living on peanut butter. The past few days I've been having food dreams – fast foods –
HITCHHIKER: Slow foods, junk food, health food…
RANGER: Nightmares of sinking in a vat of creamy peanut butter.

[The RANGER finally sits down.]

HITCHHIKER: That's it, pull up a chair. … Whatcha do?
RANGER: I'm a Park Ranger.
HITCHHIKER: Yeah?
RANGER: Well, a fern-feeler. I'll be doing the nature walks.
HITCHHIKER *[impressed]*: Still, a Federal officer. And a naturalist to boot. … You ain't scared, hitchin'?
RANGER: Of what?
HITCHHIKER: Creeps.
RANGER: Are you?
HITCHHIKER: Hell yeah.
RANGER: That why you have that helmet?
HITCHHIKER: I dumped my bike back in Ohio. I was leaning into this curve, no problem, then my front wheel smacks this corn clod, my back tire slides right out from under me, and before I know it, I'm lying in a ditch. And my bike, which I'd just spent half a year fixing up for this trip, is in a million pieces. … I had this dream of crossing the Great Divide on my bike, way up there in the thin air, looking out across the world from the mountaintops. *[pause]*
I'll get another bike sooner or later, but I ain't about to go back. I keep waiting for a sexy redhead in a sports car to pull up and offer me a free

ride to paradise.

RANGER *[droll]*: Really?

HITCHHIKER: Why just yesterday I got a ride with a real interesting… *[slight pause]* Chicken farmer. And the day before… with a guy who sold lightbulbs. … That chicken farmer took me home with him, and him and his wife put me up for the night and made me a whole fried chicken. A whole chicken! … I'm still holding out for a little taste of paradise in a 380Z, but it's okay the way it is. Can't get everything you want and you can't be everything people expect you to be.

[A car stops.]

HITCHHIKER: Looks like you caught one.

RANGER: Well… Guess I'd better get going.

[She lingers extra moment then takes off.]

HITCHHIKER: Catch ya later, Ranger Danger!

[The HITCHHIKER waves farewell, settles back in as night begins to fall, then suddenly…
Blue flashing lights. A spotlight. With a groan, he spread-eagles on the ground. A COP strolls up, looms over him. Long beat.]

COP: What're you doing?

HITCHHIKER: I know the routine. No hitchhiking.

[The COP checks out his backpack, finds a book: Kerouac's "On the Road." Flipping pages, the COP finds a passage underlined.]

COP *[dripping with puzzlement]*: "What is that feeling when you're driving away from people and they recede til you see their specks dispersing? …"

[Closing the book, the COP turns outrageously "beat" quoting the rest from memory…]

COP *[CONT'D]*: "It's the too huge world vaulting us and it's goodbye. But we lean forward to the next crazy venture beneath the skies."

[The HITCHHIKER's *stunned.]*

COP *[CONT'D]*: If you like that, try this.

[The COP *pulls a dog-eared slim paperback of Whitman from his pocket and gives it to him.]*

HITCHHIKER: First Kerouac, now Whitman?
COP: Keep it. I've got another one. ... Weather's closing in. *[exiting]* Grab your bag. I'll give you a lift.

[The HITCHHIKER *gathers his things and follows.*
DAD, *in his "car," has stopped for the* RANGER. *She hops in with him.]*

RANGER: Where'ya headed?
DAD: West. The Parks. ... Been out there long?
RANGER: Yeah. I'm careful who I ride with.
DAD: You weren't careful with me.
RANGER: You looked nice. I'm a good judge of character.

[They drive on. Occasional fleeting glances. Smiles.
In another area, a truckstop WAITRESS *prepares a pot of coffee.]*

DAD: When I saw you up ahead there I had this strange notion – you'll think I'm weird.
RANGER *[getting suspicious]*: How far'd you say you were going?
DAD: Not like that. I saw you up ahead there and for a minute there ...
RANGER: What?
DAD: Gets so lonely sometimes your mind starts playing tricks. You drive these roads too long and you see things: elk, deer, people, people you used to know, people who've probably changed beyond all recognition, faces from a long time ago, dream faces. ... I thought you were my daughter.
RANGER *[after a pause]*: Are you okay? Mister? *[slight pause]* If you're getting sleepy we could stop for coffee.

[*The* TOWTRUCKER *approaches the* WAITRESS; *their familiarity is almost familial.*]

DAD: I turn on the radio but it doesn't help. You need people, people's voices. Family.

TOWTRUCKER: Howdy, Angel.

RANGER: There's a place we could stop.

WAITRESS [*pouring him a cup of coffee*]: The old man know you're lounging in here again?

TOWTRUCKER: Just coffee. Straight up. No frills.

WAITRESS: I got half a mind to put in one a them cappuccino makers. 'Bout time you grease monkeys and log-haulers got some hot whupped milk in your lives.

TOWTRUCKER [*after sipping his coffee*]: Chi-rist! This stuff tastes like brake fluid!

WAITRESS: You been suckin on wheels again?

TOWTRUCKER: Suck on this.

[DAD *and the* RANGER *enter*]

WAITRESS: Watch your dialect, cowboy, we got a couple a real live human beings in our midst. What can I get you folks?

TOWTRUCKER: Besides directions to a different diner.

WAITRESS: We give him free coffee just to hang around and talk, sort of a poor excuse for a side show. Rest of the time he pumps gas, fixes flats, and restocks the Slim Jims.

TOWTRUCKER: I drive a truck for the local station. Early's 24 hour. AAA affiliated.

DAD: Two coffees.

WAITRESS: Comin' up.

TOWTRUCKER [*to* WAITRESS *but intended for all*]: I saw the damnedest thing just before.

WAITRESS: You look in the mirror?

TOWTRUCKER: There was this Airstream trailer hooked up to a light pickup pulled off onto the shoulder. Guy jumps out, door wide open, unhitches the trailer, pops back in his truck and takes off. So I pull over – thought maybe one of the trailer tires was flat or something. So I'm pokin' around and I'll be damned if an old lady don't come jumping out of the trailer wanting to know what the hell I'd done with her husband. He just took off down the road and she just stood there, staring down that highway like he'd disappeared down a hole. ... I was feelin' real sorry for her, so I brung her into town. She's out there in the cab.

WAITRESS: Well why didn't you bring her in, dummy?

TOWTRUCKER: I asked. She didn't want to. ... Now I don't know what to do with her.

WAITRESS: Only one thing to do, take her home.

TOWTRUCKER: Back to her trailer?

WAITRESS: Home. With you.

TOWTRUCKER: What do I want with an old lady?

WAITRESS: Why'd you pick her up then?

TOWTRUCKER: Maybe I'll haul her trailer over to the trailer park. She can stay there. She's kind of sweet. Keeps saying how she's gonna make me chocolate chip cookies. What do I want with chocolate chip cookies?

[The WAITRESS pats him lovingly.]

TOWTRUCKER: Howdy.

RANGER: Hi.

WAITRESS: You want to leave the clientele alone.

TOWTRUCKER [ignoring the waitress, to DAD]: Where you folks headed?

DAD: West.

TOWTRUCKER: Your daughter?

RANGER: He's just giving me a ride. We don't really know each other. His kids are out here somewhere. A son and daughter, right?

[DAD nods, yes]

TOWTRUCKER: Where're they holed up?

DAD: I ... don't really know. My boy left home a while back and headed West – just like his old man, I guess. And my little girl is, well she's not so little anymore, but she's...

DAD [CONT'D]: [forcing a smile.] You know how kids are, once they're out on their own, they can't afford to look back, gotta keep moving, blaze their own trails, make their own...

RANGER: Mistakes?

TOWTRUCKER: I liked it best when I was tearing down some desert flat and all I could think about was keeping my wheels on the road.

RANGER: Sound like a lot of noise to me.

TOWTRUCKER: Yeah well some people's music's other people's noise.

RANGER: I like the quiet of trees.

TOWTRUCKER: Things get too quiet you just end up listening to yourself think.

RANGER: What's so bad about that?

TOWTRUCKER [*nudging* DAD]: Depends what you're thinkin' about.

RANGER: Can we go?

DAD: We're just trying to have a conversation here, all right!

RANGER [*exiting*]: If the country weren't so littered with strip malls, I'd walk.

TOWTRUCKER [*once she's gone*]: If that's the way she is with people, no wonder she wants to hang with trees.

DAD: I used to be a lot like that.

TOWTRUCKER: You'll get over it. It's just edginess. Eastern edginess.

WAITRESS: You have no idea where they are? None at all?

[DAD *shakes his head, no. Pause.*]

DAD: He got arrested. My own kid. Christ. I didn't know what the hell else to do with him. I mean, between the motorcycle and … So I threw him out. Took off, not a word. Nothing.

[DAD *gets lost in a furrow*]

TOWTRUCKER [*aside, to* WAITRESS]: Hey, darlin, here's a quarter. Buy the old guy another coffee. He needs somethin and it ain't on your menu.
[*exiting, to* DAD] You have a good trip now, hear?

WAITRESS: Good kids.

DAD: Yeah.

WAITRESS: More coffee?

DAD: If I'd touch him, even by accident, he'd shrink away and flinch. … I think he was closer to Marge. He'd give her presents – he'd give me presents too, but not personal things. Tennis balls, aftershave, a tie.

[The WAITRESS *slips away]*

DAD *[CONT'D]*: I always had this idea of what a father and son should be. I never had it with my old man but I thought I could have it with my own son. We'd go camping, every summer, just him and me, up to the mountains. Do a little fishing, sit around the campfire, do things, quiet, you know. ...
At night we'd sit by the fire and – jeez, the number of times we did this, I can't believe – we'd play Cat's Cradle. The game with the string? We'd sit and play for hours with the fire burning. Almost head to head, pulling the string off our fingers. But our hands would never touch.
Cat's Cradle... that's as close as we ever got.

*[*MOM *is discovered climbing, high in the mountains. She gropes as she inches forward, then freezes. She tries backing off. Can't. Frozen.
The* RANGER *approaches, with safety ropes and in harness.]*

RANGER: Just stay calm.

MOM: I am calm.

RANGER: Come this way. Take your time, just one step at a time. Don't be afraid. I'm right here. One step.

MOM: No.

RANGER: Look, you can't stay up here your whole life.

MOM: I can if I want to.

RANGER: True. Frozen to death. Covered with ice and snow, maybe an occasional mountain goat, or maybe a rock climber'll pass by and toss you a chunk of dried fruit. It'll get real boring, so why don't you come with me?

MOM: No. I started. I'm going to finish.

RANGER: You're two thousand feet from the summit. You're not even wearing the right shoes!

MOM: I don't care.

RANGER: Nobody climbs Terminal Peak without boots.

MOM: This isn't Mount Lord?

RANGER *[her irritation finally showing]*: Jesus...

MOM: I wanted to climb Mount Lord.

RANGER: There are trail markers every twenty feet!

MOM: I didn't see them.

RANGER: All you had to do was look!

MOM: I did look. I just didn't see them.

RANGER: I know, you were so taken with the scenery. Let's go. I don't have all day.

MOM: You just go do whatever it is you're supposed to do.

RANGER: Unfortunately, it's my job to keep people like you from killing themselves.

MOM [a bit huffy]: I'm sorry if I put you out.

RANGER: Look, M'am, I don't know why they sent me up here after you – probably some kinda sick test – but if I don't bring you back down safe and sound…

[MOM begins climbing higher.]

RANGER [CONT'D]: Where the hell do you think you're going?

MOM: Up.

RANGER: You think this is a bad spot, wait 'til you hit the ledges.

MOM: I'm looking forward to it.

RANGER: You didn't even know which mountain you were on. You'll never find your way back.

MOM: I'll figure it out.

RANGER: Which way is North?

MOM [after a slight pause]: There.

RANGER [after a long pause]: Wrong.

MOM: There?

RANGER: You don't know where the hell you are, do you?

MOM: I –

RANGER: You have no right to be up here! None at all!

MOM: If I want to climb a mountain, I will. Any one I want, and you can't stop me.

RANGER: You… people… with your marshmallows and stoves and TV sets, you come out here and think you're all a bunch of pioneers.

MOM: The reason I didn't pay any attention to your damn trail markers is because they're ugly! I didn't come up here to look at splotches of paint on every fifth rock. I want to go someplace where you "clubbies" aren't telling me where to go or what I should be seeing.

RANGER: Why don't you all just pack up your Price Club frying pans and go back to your shopping malls and leave these places to the people who deserve them?!

MOM: Yell all you want. It was real quiet up here before you came along. If you want something to do, go empty the trashcans.

[MOM *moves on up the mountain.*
The RANGER *watches until she's gone. The* RANGER *finds herself "stuck."*
DAD *is discovered at a Payphone. Sound of ringing. Finally...*]

MOM: Hello?

DAD: Hi.

MOM: John? Is that you?

DAD: How are you, Marge?

MOM: Better.

DAD: Good.

MOM: You?

DAD: All right... I guess. You hear from the kids?

MOM: No. Have you?

DAD: No.

MOM [*after a pause*]: John, are you –

DAD: I'm in Death Valley. The desert. I was at the Grand Canyon last week.

MOM: You have a nice Christmas?

DAD: Not bad. I went to a truckstop. How about you?

MOM: Mine was... fine.

DAD: I had dinner with this family. A mother and her two kids.

MOM: That's good. ... John, I've got to go.

[MOM *exits.* DAD *continues as if she were still on the line...*]

DAD: The Canyon's changed.

[*He walks away from the phone without hanging up the receiver*]

DAD [CONT'D]: The River's cut another inch or so into the rock since... the last time we were there... The wind's blasted its face and stripped away another layer of skin. The lines around its eyes and mouth are deeper. ... I keep looking for myself, but the mirror's too deep.

[*Then BANG! A flat tire.* DAD *goes to work on the flat, changing it.* MOLL *as child enters behind him.*]

MOLL: Whatcha doin', Dad?
DAD: Fixing the tire.
MOLL: How come? Did it break?
DAD: It's flat.

[MOLL *moves in for a closer look.*]

DAD: You're in the way, son.
MOLL: How come you got a stick in there?
DAD: No tire iron.
MOLL: How come?
DAD: I left it at home.
MOLL: Why?
DAD: Just go over there and play with your sister.
MOLL: Can I help?
DAD: Not now. Marge!!
MOLL [*big discovery*]: Look, Dad! ANTS!! [*on the tire*]
DAD: Maybe you should go help your mother.
MOLL: Wow, look at 'em all. There must be a hundred zillion million of 'em. They're all over your leg.
DAD: Damn...

[DAD *swats his trousers furiously.* MOLL *finds this hilarious.*]

MOLL: You have ants on you, Dad.

[DAD*'s losing it. Hallucinations*]

MOLL: Are we going to that same place with the river we went to last time when it was just you and me?
DAD: Yes.
MOLL: You said I could fish just like you and we could cook up the fish on

the fire and I could light it, didn't you say I could?

[no response from DAD*]*

MOLL: How long's it gonna be til we get there?
DAD: We're not going to get anywhere if you don't stop bothering me. ...
Dammit! I said get away from here! Get out! Get your things and get
out of here!!

*[*DAD *wails at the air. SOUNDS of highway traffic swirl around him.
HEADLIGHTS, BRAKES. Stranded in a vast empty space, losing his
mind.]*

DAD: Keep the house! Keep the trailer! Keep everything!

*[*DAD *hurls his tire iron at a passing car – dopplered horn.]*

DAD: I know where I am. I know where I'm going. I don't need ...

*[*DAD *wrestles with his roadmap.]*

DAD: Aftershave... tennis balls... twenty years... a tie, a watch, a... All I
ever wanted was... was...

*[His muttering turns gruffer, deeper. As he sinks lower he pulls on an
old coat. The* RANGER *appears, as if at the end of her Park slide show.
Three slides of National Park show, lingering on the last, then ...]*

RANGER: The best thing my folks ever did was vanish. And getting out of
Dodge when I did was the best thing that ever happened to me. When I
went back and found it all gone – mom, dad, the house, my brother, all
the crap I saved from when I was a kid – I said, good riddance. I mean
I look around and all I see is the garbage kids go through with their
families.
I'm lucky. I'm totally free, no ties holding me back. I mean, after crabs
ditch their shells, they don't go back. They grow new ones. Same with
butterflies and snakes.

So I'm supposed to get all kinds of warm and fuzzy over some old shell that's no more to me than some raincoat I had when I was half my size and half my age? … Get real.

[Then, she spots the VAGRANT.*]*

RANGER: Dad?

VAGRANT: Hunh?

RANGER *[starting to go]*: Sorry.

VAGRANT: Hey, you got a buck? Five bucks? A dime? Anything?

RANGER: Uh yeah, sure. *[slight pause]* What's it for?

VAGRANT: I'm investing heavily in the dot-com market. Search engines mostly.

RANGER: This isn't for wine?

VAGRANT: You've seen too many movies. A prisoner of cliches. I am no bum. I am a freelance scavenger. A professional.

RANGER: Then you don't need the money.

VAGRANT: Sure I do. Who doesn't. I'm padding my portfolio to pay my daughter's college tuition. I mean the price of an education these days, tsk, tsk, tsk.

RANGER *[giving him a dime]*: Here.

VAGRANT: Wow. A whole dime. *[he throws the dime away]*
I'll call my broker collect. Could you make that a quarter?

RANGER: No.

VAGRANT: No, SIR.

RANGER: I gave you a dime.

VAGRANT: I don't need a dime. I need a quarter. Thousands. Life is not cheap. Man does not thrive on dimes.

RANGER: What kind of life is this anyway, sleeping on the ground?

VAGRANT: Look at all these people camping. Where do they sleep? Hunh? On the ground. They've got an inkling, but they don't know. That's why they're here. To find out. To find out what I already know. I'm closer to basics. A little food, a little warmth, a few friends, a couple safe investments.

RANGER: What about family? Wife? Kids?

VAGRANT: I had kids once. But I threw them out. You want a couple?

RANGER: No.

VAGRANT: One? Two for a buck? How about this one?

[The HITCHHIKER *enters, possibly pushing or riding – a motorcycle.]*

HITCHHIKER: Hey, Ranger Danger, howya doin'?

RANGER: Peanut Butter! Where'd you get that motorcycle?!

HITCHHIKER: Bought it off some guy at a truckstop.

VAGRANT: Hey! *[off his look]* Yeah, you. You looking for a mother?

HITCHHIKER: Hunh?

VAGRANT: A mother.

HITCHHIKER *[puzzled]*: You've seen my mother?

VAGRANT: I've seen everything. Show him where his mother is.

RANGER: How do I know where his mother is?

VAGRANT: It's your job – find lost people, put 'em back together. Little boy lost his Mommy and Daddy. Lookin' for your old man, right?

HITCHHIKER *[playing along]*: I wouldn't be surprised if I ran into him someplace.

VAGRANT: So what's he look like?

RANGER *[drawing* HITCHHIKER *away]*: Let's go.

HITCHHIKER: About your size. Maybe a little taller. He's hard to describe.

VAGRANT: Tell her, don't tell me. It's her job, not mine.

RANGER *[begrudgingly]*: Okay, what's his name?

VAGRANT: What's in a name – hell, on data bytes we're just binary bleeps and numbers. Guys call me Dow Jones.
[to HITCHHIKER*]* Don't just stand there, talk to her. Tell her something interesting. Make her blush. No, huh?
[to RANGER*]* Give him a dime, he'll talk.
[to HITCHHIKER*]* She gave me a dime and I talked.

RANGER: He threw it away.

VAGRANT: I am not a jukebox! I do not sing for dimes! For a buck I'll sing a campfire song. Half a buck I'll tell a story. For five bucks I'll give you a tip on the market. For ten I'll be your father. For fifteen I'll be a father to both of you. C'mon, don't be a bear.
[slight pause, then nailing the HITCHHIKER*]* What's he look like?! You got a picture?

HITCHHIKER: No.

RANGER: C'mon, he'll talk like this all day.

[She exits, fully expecting him to follow, but the HITCHHIKER *is held by the* VAGRANT'S *gaze. Mesmerized.]*

VAGRANT: Always carry a picture, or something a person wears. Helps you remember. I've got nothing in this world but what I carry: a few pictures… people, places, things… and this…

[The VAGRANT *draws a black nightie from the pocket of his seedy coat. The* HITCHHIKER *is transfixed. Then, he bolts.*
In another area of the stage, MOM *gathers deadfall kindling. She hears the distant yips of coyotes. She listens, electrified. She yips back. At first tentatively, then with force.*
The RANGER *comes across* MOM. *Before she sees who it is…]*

RANGER: No open fires, M'am.
MOM: You again.

[Awkward pause, then…]

RANGER: Did you have a nice hike?
MOM: Did you?
RANGER: Yes. … I'm just glad you made it okay. Still …

[Pause. Laughter. The RANGER *takes over arranging the "campfire."]*

RANGER: It's way too dry for a fire.
MOM: Too bad. Wood fires always makes me feel at home, like a fireplace does. … Do you like working here?
RANGER: What's not to? Every day I wake up with the Canyon outside my window and all day long it's right there beside me. On my days off, I go to this canyon I know. Listen to the wrens.
MOM: Were you ever a girlscout?
RANGER: The hat huh?
MOM: Not just the hat. … I went with my daughter once to girlscout camp, a helper to the leader. Julie and I used to stay up way past everybody and watch the coals. I'd put my blanket around her. It's not the same without a fire.

[Smiles. When the RANGER *starts to go...]*

MOM: Stop by later, I'll toast you a marshmallow. *[before the* RANGER *can object]* Over the stove.

[The RANGER *exits.* DAD *discards his hat, faces* MOM. *Pause. Then...]*

DAD: Hello, Marge.
MOM: You came back.
DAD: I got you a little something.

*[*DAD *presents her with the black nightie. Silence. Finally...]*

DAD: Let me get a picture.
MOM: A picture?
DAD: Why not?
    [after arranging her pose] A little to your right. Okay, now squat down maybe four, five inches. I want to get you and the mountain in the picture. ... Smile.
MOM: This hurts my legs.
DAD: One more second and...
MOM: Just take the picture.
DAD *[finally taking the picture]*: There.
MOM: Lucky you don't come back every day.
DAD: One more on the roll.
MOM *[taking the camera from him]*: Oh no... Your turn.
DAD: Careful, don't smudge the lens.
MOM: All these things set?
DAD: Did you just change the f-stop?
MOM: The what?
DAD: The f-stop. That thing, there.
MOM: I thought that was the focus.
DAD *[trying hard to be pleasant]*: Here. This is the focus and that's the f-stop. This is how you hold it and this is how you focus. Got it?
MOM: Better to remember things than to take pictures anyway.
DAD: They help you remember. Details.

MOM: Why should I remember this?

DAD: If you don't want to do it, you don't have to. You're the one who wanted to take my picture.

MOM: So pose already.

DAD: Where were you standing?

MOM: A little to your right. Good. Now squat! ... Lower. Lower. ... A little lower. There. That's good. Now hold it. Keep smiling. ... How're your legs?

DAD: Just take the picture.

MOM: Hold still. ... Smile. Good. ... *[taking picture]* There.

DAD: I think you jiggled the camera.

MOM: Well you moved.

DAD: Maybe we both moved in the same direction.

[Silence. MOM waits for him to say what he's got to say. Finally...]

DAD: Did you miss me?

[MOM says nothing; she leaves him hanging. This is a much stronger woman than the one he left behind.]

DAD: When I left I could have gone anywhere, and all I could think about was that I had no place to come back to.

MOM *[after waiting a long time]*: That's it?

[DAD fiddles with his camera.]

MOM: Do I seem different? *[pause]* I am.

DAD: I missed you. *[pause]* I'd go into bars and truckstops and buy people coffee or a beer. I wanted to share my adventures with somebody. They weren't interested. All they wanted was somebody to tell their stories to.

MOM: While you were away, I climbed that.

DAD: That mountain?

MOM: It wasn't easy. I took it step by step.

DAD: Why'd you do it?

MOM: I wanted to see what I could see from the top with my own eyes.

DAD: So what'd you see?

MOM [laughing]: Nothing. It got cloudy. Climbed a whole mountain and all I could see were clouds. Oh a few peaks sticking up. But now I know why people do it. It did something to me to be alone like that, nobody else to turn to. I kept hoping I'd be able to look down and see the trailer. A house. Something familiar. But that's not why you climb a mountain. I'm glad there were clouds. Made me look up and out.

DAD [after a pause]: Let's go in.

MOM: It's a beautiful day.

DAD: So?

MOM: So I want to stay outside. Take a walk or something. There's a trail that goes down to a stream, and there's a waterfall. It's beautiful this time of day, the way the sun mixes in the mist, the sound, the rush.

DAD: I'll wait here, if that's okay.

MOM: I'll see you in a couple hours. ... If you want to start dinner, the stove's right there.

DAD: You'll be back ...

MOM: In an hour or so.

[MOM exits. DAD gets out his slide projector to look at slides of his recent trip. RANGER and HITCHHIKER cross.]

HITCHHIKER: Did you know that old guy?

RANGER: The Parks get all kinds. Some people who come, never leave. It changes them. For good. He'll be fine. ... Where's your campsite?

HITCHHIKER: Don't have one.

RANGER: I might be able to find you a place for the night.

HITCHHIKER: With you?

RANGER: In with the trailers. C'mon, I'll take you over.

HITCHHIKER [sidling up to her]: You do this all the time?

RANGER: Mostly the nature walks and slide show. [off a bird call] Hear that? ... That's a canyon wren, marking her territory.

HITCHHIKER: You know who they all are by the sound of their voices?

RANGER: That's a Gamble Oak. Over there's an aspen. ... Amazing thing about birds and trees is that each family finds the place that's best for it and that's where it stays. You don't find these back East.

[MOM, *beaming, returns from her walk to find* DAD *watching slides. The* RANGER *and* HITCHHIKER *observe. When* DAD *realizes* MOM *is there...*]

DAD: Slides.

RANGER [*stepping up*]: Hi. ... I've got a young man here who needs a place to sleep. Campground's full. We try to put them in with trailer people. Just space enough for a sleeping bag outside.

[DAD *looks to* MOM – *this is her home, her decision. She nods yes.*]

DAD: Sure. Say my son were to come along. I'd want him to be with good people.

RANGER: Terrific. He'll only be here one night. [*exiting*] Thanks.

MOM: Wait. I promised you a marshmallow.

RANGER: Some other time maybe.

MOM: Stay a while. Please.

[HITCHHIKER *enters.* DAD *rises. They stare at one another. Long pause.*]

DAD: Hi.

HITCHHIKER [*after a pause*]: Hi.

MOM: So, you're traveling.

HITCHHIKER: Yeah.

DAD: Just you and the open road.

HITCHHIKER: Yeah. The Parks.

DAD: Same with us.

[*A long look between* MOM *and* DAD.]

HITCHHIKER: Your slides?

[*The slides offer welcome distraction.* HITCHHIKER *sits.*]

RANGER: That one looks familiar.

DAD: California. Yosemite.

MOM: We didn't go there.

DAD: When we took the trip with the kids.

MOM: Didn't you only have that little snapshot camera when we took that trip? These pictures are...

DAD: I took them last month. ... I went to all the Parks.

[As the slides progress...]

MOM: These are the same places we went on the family trip.

DAD: They're worth going back to.

MOM: Did you expect to find...

DAD: Pictures.

[pause]

HITCHHIKER: Where are your children?

MOM: We don't see them much.

HITCHHIKER: I mean in the pictures. Usually you take pictures like these for the people in them. These look like postcards.

DAD: I was by myself.

[Pause. DAD moves last slide off]

MOM: Who wants a marshmallow? We can toast some.

RANGER: No fires.

MOM: We have a stove. *[to HITCHHIKER]* Would you?

[HITCHHIKER pumps up the stove and lights it. MOM gets marshmallows and puts them on ends of sticks.]

MOM *[to RANGER]*: How do you like yours? Rare? Well done?

RANGER: Burnt.

MOM: Oh good.

DAD: That's the only way she makes them.

MOM: Oh stop it. *[to RANGER]* You'll have to wait, first one's for him *[HITCHHIKER]*.

DAD: I'll pass tonight.

MOM: He says that every night. If you want more I can make more. We've got plenty. Here.

[MOM *gives the* HITCHHIKER *a flaming marshmallow which he blows out.*]

DAD: Would have a been a great night for a campfire. Story-telling. Singing.

[*The* HITCHHIKER *tries to pluck the hot marshmallow off the stick. He burns his fingers, dropping it.*]

HITCHHIKER: Oww.

[MOM, *the* RANGER, *and* HITCHHIKER *laugh.* MOM *ignites another one for the* RANGER. *Lots of oohs and ahhs.*]

MOM: There you go.
RANGER: That was fast.
MOM: Burning them's easy, toasting's hard.
RANGER: You're not going to have one?
MOM: Me? No. I just like making them. I used to make them all the time for the kids when we went camping. They loved 'em.
DAD: We did a lot of camping when they were younger.
MOM: When we were all younger.
HITCHHIKER: I used to go with my father.
RANGER: I was a girlscout.
HITCHHIKER [MOLL]: We'd sit by the fire and play Cat's Cradle.
MOM [BETTY]: Hear that, Father? He loves it. Still a kid at heart.
DAD [BILL]: We have a string anywhere, Mother?
HITCHHIKER: I've got a piece.
MOM [SWEETMEAT]: Give him a piece of string and a cardboard box and he's happy as a clam.
DAD: Tied and raring to go.
HITCHHIKER: You first. Respect for elders.
DAD: There's an old proverb: He who ties knot, starts not.
HITCHHIKER: Whatever you say.
DAD: Actually, it's not a proverb. I just don't like to start.
HITCHHIKER: That's okay, I don't respect my elders.

[DAD *and* HITCHHIKER *begin to play.*

The HITCHHIKER *idly begins to hum "Amazing Grace."*
DAD *unconsciously joins in, humming in unison.]*

MOM *[to* RANGER, *softly]*: Look at them.

*[*HITCHHIKER *begins to softly sing the lines "was blind but now I see. When we've been here ten thousand years/ Bright shining as the sun" then hums the rest of the verse.*
DAD *hums "America the Beautiful."]*

RANGER: Brrr. It's getting cold out.
MOM: Would have been a nice night for a fire.
RANGER: I should go get a sweater.
MOM: Here. ... We can share this blanket.

*[*MOM *wraps the blanket around her. They huddle together, watching the blue flame of the stove fire.*
DAD *sings very softly the lines: "For purple mountains' majesty, above the fruited plain ...," continues to hum while he and the* HITCHHIKER *play Cat's Cradle.*
MOM *and the* RANGER *hum in unison, then softly begin to sing the campfire song: "Fire's burning, fire's burning, draw nearer, draw nearer. In the gloaming, in the gloaming, come sing and be merry."*
They repeat the verse. The men join in, singing one verse with them softly as lights slowly fade.
This is not a grand chorus but the sound of four people on a quiet night somewhere in the vastness of America, sharing their passing hour on Earth.]

THE END

GREAT
DIVIDE

A PLAY IN TWO ACTS

TIME

The main action of the play takes place during two different eras, one in the present, the other beginning in the 1930's.

PLACE

The main action is set in the town of Wisdom, Montana, about thirty miles east of the Idaho line and the Great Divide, chiefly in and around a service station and a neighboring trucks top diner. The other chief locations are a dairy farm in Caledonia County, just south of St. Johnsbury, Vermont, and a house in a small city somewhere in Upstate New York. Other locations include a place high in the Bitterroot Mountains, and outside a college dorm. [Because of the play's fluid movement in time, space, and character, these locations should be suggested only minimally, allowing for the greatest freedom of imagination for the audience and a smooth continuity between scenes.]

CHARACTERS

[Four actors play a total of twelve characters chiefly distinguished by their specific life concerns, speech patterns, and by simple signal shifts in costumes – a hat, glasses, apron, etc.]

EARLY, an older man who runs the service station in Wisdom. The same actor also plays: JAMES, an older man, a Vermont dairy farmer; JOHN, a millworker from Upstate New York; and a MOUNTAINMAN of undetermined age, an ancient.

MARLE, a young man who comes to Wisdom and stays. The same actor also plays: YOUNG EARL, a Vermont farm boy and JAMES' only son; and MOLL, a postadolescent, JOHN's son.

MADGE, a middleaged woman who runs the trucks top in Wisdom. The same actress also plays: EDNA, *a Vermont farmwoman and* JAMES' *partner;* MARGE, *a housewife,* MOLL *and* JULIE'*s mother.*

RUTH, a young woman, YOUNG EARL'*s wife. The same actress also plays* JULIE, *an independent young woman,* MOLL'*s younger sister.*

GREAT DIVIDE was originally conceived as a companion piece to my other full-length play MOBILE HYMN though both plays are intended to stand alone as separate works. If produced in conjunction, the same casts can be used for both plays.

GREAT DIVIDE was first presented as a staged reading on November 18, 1982 at the Westside Mainstage in New York by the Actors' Producing Company. Directed by Richard Humphrey withHumphrey with

*Herman O. Arbeit.............................*EARLY *et al.*
Carole Lockwood............................ MADGE *et al.*
Frances Robertson.......................... RUTH *et al.*
*Jonathan Fuller...............................*MARLE *et al.*

A revised version of GREAT DIVIDE was presented as a staged reading at the Eugene O'Neill Theater Center, 1983 National Playwrights Conference on August 4-6, 1983, in Waterford, Connecticut. Michael Feingold, Dramaturg. Directed by Dennis Scott with

*James Ray.......................................*EARLY *et al.*
Caroline Coates............................... MADGE *et al.*
*Julie Boyd.......................................*RUTH *et al.*
Kevin Geer...................................... MARLE *et al.*

ACT ONE

[Wisdom, Montana, just outside EARLY*'s service station. The present. AS LIGHTS COME UP we discover* EARLY, *a toughened older man watching something coming up the road toward him. Eventually,* MARLE, *a young man enters, pushing his motorcycle camping equipment lashed to the backrack and bar.]*

EARLY: If you're plannin on pushin that thing to Idaho, you better getcherself a runnin start. It's all uphill from here to the pass.
  *[*MARLE *stops, out of breath, in no mood to be teased.]*
  What seems to be the problem, son?
MARLE: It ain't runnin.
EARLY: Neither're you.
MARLE: It died about two miles down the road.
EARLY: You come in here to get it buried or fixed?
MARLE: Fixed.
EARLY: You got money?
MARLE: I'd do it myself if I had the tools.
EARLY: We got a flat rate for labor – nineteen an hour. Twenty-nine if you watch, and thirty-nine fifty if you worked on it first yourself.
MARLE: I didn't have the airmix adjusted right for the altitude. That, and the firing advance. Now everything's fouled.
EARLY: That'd just make 'er run bad, not kill it. Seems to me you got more serious problems you ain't admittin.
MARLE: I don't have much money left.
EARLY: Like I was sayin, you got some serious problems.
MARLE: Look, you think maybe we could make some kind of deal?
EARLY: Sure. I fix your motorsickle and you pay me parts and labor.
MARLE: How about if I work it off? I'm not the greatest mechanic in the world but I ain't bad.

[EARLY strolls around the bike, looking it over.]

EARLY: Ain't too good neither. *[slight pause]* Ain't much of a recommendation to come pushin your means of transport up to your prospective employer's front door. *[another slight pause]* You ever pump gas?

MARLE *[not enthused at the prospect]*: Yeah.

EARLY: How long?

MARLE: Years.

EARLY: You drive?

MARLE: If I didn't drive what would I be doing with a motorcycle?

EARLY: You weren't driving when you got here now were you?

MARLE: I can drive.

EARLY: Good?

MARLE: I can't do stunts.

EARLY: Can you keep the wheels on the road and the doors on their hinges?

MARLE: Depends on the wheels and doors.

EARLY: Hmnnn.

MARLE: Well?

EARLY: Might just have somethin for you. You ever drive a towtruck?

MARLE: A few times. Little service runs: flat tires, gas, jumping – the usual.

EARLY: Ever tow?

MARLE: No.

EARLY: You interested?

MARLE: In what?

EARLY: See that truck over there? Reason that one's parked where it is is because I ain't got a driver. Don't make much sense to have a towtruck and no driver.

MARLE: Well...

EARLY: Now you could try pushin this thing up over the mountains, but I wouldn't advise it.

MARLE: I've got no place to stay.

EARLY *[slapping the camping gear]*: This's your bedroll ain't it?

MARLE: Yeah.

EARLY: You got a tent to go with it?

MARLE: You sayin I should camp?

EARLY: I suppose you could put the bedroll in the tent and sleep outside.

MARLE *[mimic]*: But you wouldn't advise it.

EARLY *[after a pause]*: There's space out back and a hot shower inside. The restrooms are as clean as you'll keep 'em. You can either cook on your own or there's Madge's Diner over there if you're up for some indigestion… We got a deal?

MARLE: How long's this "arrangement" gonna last?

EARLY: All depends.

MARLE: On what?

EARLY: Your work and my patience.

MARLE: I'll work til you're paid off and that's it. After that I'm gone.

EARLY: Suitcherself. *[slight pause]* Leave 'er over there and I'll have a look later.

[MARLE *begins to wheel the motorcycle into the station.*]

EARLY: Name's Early.

MARLE: First or last?

EARLY: That's it. Just the one. Day I showed up here in Wisdom my pickup'd blown some rings. Tried to bandaid it and got myself soaked in fortyweight. Name stuck.

MARLE: 'Cuz you were covered with oil?

EARLY: It was five o'clock in the morning.

[THEY *exit with the motorcycle.*
EDNA, YOUNG EARL's *mother, enters wearing a kitchen apron over her simple 1930's farm dress. She's been hard at work as usual. She's been canning. She wipes her hands on her apron as she calls for her son.*]

EDNA: Earl! Earl!

[YOUNG EARL *played by the same actor playing* MARLE, *enters.*]

EARL: Ayeh?

EDNA: I need a hand to take them cans down cellar.

[JAMES, EDNA's *husband and* EARL's *father, enters. He's been working on the truck.*]

EARL: I'm helpin Dad with the engine on the truck.

JAMES: That c'n wait. You go give your mother a hand.

EARL: I'll do it later.

EDNA: I got mason jars all over the kitchen. If you want dinner this evenin, you better get in there.

JAMES: Better do what she says, son.

[EARL *exits.*]

EDNA [*after watching him go*]: I don't know what's gonna come a that boy, James.

JAMES: He's just findin his way. Hain't much of a future lookin at him up here.

EDNA: There's the whole farm and...

JAMES: Winters so long, it's enough to make the boy cabin crazy.

EDNA: It's been good enough for us.

JAMES [*wiping his hands with a rag*]: Boy's in love, that's all. Mind's all over the place.

EDNA: Love?

JAMES: Nelson girl. I seen 'em the other day when I was to town. An he's been slippin off in the night.

[*In another area of the stage* EARL *and* RUTH *a young woman, enter. They are having an unheard, serious conversation.*]

EDNA: I know.

JAMES: Figured you did,

EDNA [*after a pause*]: Oh James...

JAMES: He ain't the first an' he sure hain't gonna be the last. What's the matter?

EDNA [*after a pause*]: What if...

JAMES [*after a pause*]: Hain't nothin to worry about. Ruth Nelson's a right proper girl.

EDNA: Hain't her I'm worried about.

EARL: Is it mine?

RUTH: There ain't nobody else. What kind a girl you make me out to be?

EDNA: They're so young.

JAMES: Boy's eighteen. You think sometime how we were when we was eighteen.

EDNA: I am.

JAMES: Hmnnn.

[After a moment, JAMES *withdraws to another area of the stage.]*

RUTH: What're we gonna do?

EARL: You told your Aunt?

RUTH: I can't. You know how she is. Soon's she knows she'll set me out. *[pause]* We're gonna have to get married. Real soon. *[pause]* Earl?

EARL: I gotta get back to home. I said I'd bring the cows in tonight.

*[*EARL *begins to exit.]*

RUTH: We gotta talk, Earl.

*[*EARL *moves away from* RUTH.
MOLL *approaches* JOHN, *his father, who is musing on a road map in a room of a small suburban house in Upstate New York, the present.]*

MOLL: Dad?

[As soon as JOHN *sees* MOLL *he begins putting away the map. He doesn't like to be disturbed.]*

MOLL: You planning another trip?

JOHN: No.

MOLL *[trying to look at the map]*: God, do you remember that flukey trip we took ten years ago? Julie and me in the back seat, staring out the back window? We must have driven a couple thousand miles.

JOHN *[pulling the map away, finishes folding]*: Six thousand two hundred.

MOLL: Yeah.

*[*MOLL, *brushed off, begins to exit.]*

JOHN: You hear about that job at the gas station?

MOLL: They hired somebody else.

JOHN: There's more than one gas station in town.

MOLL: I was really hoping for something with a little more status, I mean pumping gas again's –

JOHN: Have you looked?

MOLL: Yeah.

JOHN: Hard?

MOLL: There's nothing out there.

JOHN: How do you know if you haven't looked?

MOLL: I was talking to this guy I know. He was thinking of heading West, get a job on an oil rig or something. Alaska maybe.

[JOHN *just stares critically and witheringly at* MOLL. JOHN *begins to exit.*]

MOLL: We were just talking, that's all.

JOHN: That's all you ever do, talk about getting a job. You've been out of school two years. ... I just want you to make something of your life. Take some pride in yourself. You can't tell me you like hanging around the house.

MOLL: I'm stuck here.

JOHN: And whose fault is that?

MOLL: I don't have any way to get around.

JOHN: You've got feet.

MOLL: I was thinking of buying a motorcycle.

JOHN: With what?

MOLL: A used one. They're not too expensive. That way I could go out and look for work. If you could lend me a couple hundred dollars...

JOHN: Get a job first, then we'll talk.

MOLL: I can't get a job til I have a way to get to it.

JOHN: Come down to the mill with me tomorrow. There's got to be something you could do there.

MOLL: Yeah. Get laid off.

JOHN: At least go down and fill out an application.

MOLL: As long as I can remember you haven't had a good thing to say about the place, and now you want me to work there?

JOHN: I worked there my whole life so that maybe you wouldn't have to. Now you can' even get a job pumping gas.

MOLL: All the stations are selfserve now.

JOHN: You've got an excuse for everything.

MOLL: Just lend me two hundred and fifty dollars. I'll pay you back.

JOHN: No.

MOLL: You're going to take out a loan for two thousand so Julie can go to college and you can't even give me two hundred fifty?

JOHN: Your sister earned it.

MOLL: It's not my fault she was born smart.

JOHN: She also worked hard.

MOLL: So did I.

JOHN: It didn't show.

[MARGE *enters.*]

MOLL: I went back didn't I?

JOHN: Because I made you.

MOLL: You didn't take the equivalency exam, I did. Give me credit for something, will you?

MARGE: What's going on here?

MOLL: Nothing.

JOHN: We were just having a talk.

MOLL: Otherwise known as I listen while Dad tells me what to do.

MARGE: John, do you really have to?

JOHN: This is between him and me.

MARGE: I can't stand having the two of you at each other all the time,

MOLL: I love it. It brings a little variety into my otherwise dull life.

JOHN: If he brought a little less variety and a little more money, we'd all be happier,

MARGE: He's doing the best he can.

JOHN: Which isn't much.

MOLL: Dad thinks I have a bright future as a mill worker.

JOHN: If it was good enough for me, it's sure as hell good enough for you. It put clothes on your back your whole life.

MOLL: You did it for you, not me. And if you're waiting for a "thank you," you can just forget it.

[JOHN *checks his anger, then begins to exit.*]

JOHN: I'm going for a drive.

[JOHN exits. Pause.]

MOLL: Stupid son of a bitch.

MARGE: Don't you ever talk about your father that way. Do you hear me? *[slight pause]* You know how he is sometimes.

MOLL: With me it's all the time.

MARGE: What were you two talking about?

MOLL: The usual.

MARGE: Work?

MOLL: Actually my lack of it.

MARGE: He only wants the best for you.

MOLL: He's got a hell of a way of showing it.

MARGE: It's the only way he knows. ... He's worried about you.

MOLL: Then why can't he lend me two hundred fifty dollars?

MARGE: For what?

MOLL: A motorcycle. I saw an ad for a used roadbike. I could get around, look for work. I said I'd pay him back. I'm not asking for a gift, just a loan. If Julie asked for a loan, he'd whip out his checkbook so fast...

MARGE: Motorcycles are dangerous.

MOLL: I sure can't afford a car.

MARGE: Two hundred fifty dollars?

MOLL: The guy's asking three hundred, but the ad's been in the paper for almost a month. I'm sure I could get it for two fifty. But I might as well forget it.

MARGE: I have a little money.

MOLL: No, Mom, that's all right.

MARGE: It's mine to do what I want with.

MOLL: I don't want you and Dad mixing it up over this. I'll find the money somewhere.

MARGE: Your father doesn't know. I keep the bankbook hidden in the attic.

MOLL *[this strikes him funny]*: You're kidding? You hide it in the attic?

MARGE: My mother told me a woman should always keep a little money tucked away that her husband doesn't know about.

MOLL: Where in the attic?

MARGE: In Grandma's cedar chest.

MOLL: That's a riot.

MARGE: She gave me eight hundred dollars as a wedding present and it's been gaining interest ever since.

MOLL: Keep it, Mom. It's yours.

MARGE: I know it's mine. That's the point, I could lend it to you.

MOLL: No.

MARGE: You need it.

MOLL: So do you.

MARGE: I want you to have it. It would make me feel good.

MOLL [after a slight pause]: I'd pay you right back.

MARGE : I know you will.

MOLL: I promise.

MARGE: It's been hard for you. I know. You deserve a chance.

MOLL: Thanks, Mom. Really.

MARGE: You go call up that person and tell him you've got the money. And I'll get a little extra out for a good helmet. The helmet will be a present, from me.

MOLL: Thanks.

[They do not hug but they do touch hands.]

MARGE: Now you just go make that phone call. I'll get my bankbook.

[MOLL exits. MARGE lingers. RUTH enters.]

RUTH: You seen Earl?

EDNA: Him 'n James was workin on the truck.

RUTH: Again?

EDNA: Cain't seem to keep it runnin right.

[MARLE approaches EARLY, watches him work for a moment.]

RUTH: He spends more time with that truck than he does with me.

EDNA: Pay it no mind. Every Spring's the same – too much to do an' everything breaks down.

RUTH: Before we was married, we used to always find time to sit or walk or do somethin together. Seems now he's always off by himself.

EARLY: I hate to tell you this, son…

MARLE: Just put it to me straight.

EARLY: She's a lost cause. You say you tried fixin her yourself?

MARLE: Well...

RUTH: I've been tryin.

EARLY: Tryin ain't good enough. Sometimes tryin only gets you deeper inta trouble.

RUTH: I just can't seem to make things right.

EARLY: There's a few good parts but you been pushin her pretty hard.

EDNA: Now, now, hain't nothin to worry about.

EARLY: Just how far'd you reckon you'd get?

EDNA: Where's baby Jesse?

MARLE: No place particular.

RUTH: Out back.

EARLY: Lookit this.

[MARLE *leans in to take a closer look at some part.* EDNA *looks toward them, they're almost head to head.*]

EDNA: Lookit him, sleepin away in James' arms, an him just smilin. Oh land... James certainly does love that boy, same's it was his own. [*she laughs*] He's sure taken to being a Pa again.

[EARLY *rises.*]

EARLY: You ever think about going back to where you come from?

MARLE: Can't.

EARLY: Seems a man's gotta think he knows what's best for himself even if he don't.

MARLE: You ever been to California?

EARLY: Nope.

MARLE: Why not?

EARLY: Same reason I never been to China, Never got there. Can't get to everyplace.

MARLE: You born here ?

EARLY: Shoulda been.

MARLE: Where then?

EARLY [*avoiding the question*]: Let's go over to the Diner and get us some coffee before I show you how to run that truck. Don't want you doin to it what you done to that motorsickle.

MARLE [*pressing the question*]: So?

EARLY: What?

MARLE: Were you born on the side of a road or somethin?

EARLY: Just because you know where a man's been don't mean you know him.

MARLE: I ain't pryin, I'm just curious.

EARLY: If you can't read a man's past in his face, then what he says's just so much talk. Maybe I was born like a hailstone and just kept gettin harder til I landed here. And maybe you was born on that motorsickle.

MARLE: And maybe it don't make a damn bit a difference.

EARLY [*looks him in the eye, then says*]: Maybe you got possibilities, boy.

[*EARLY exits.
After a beat, EARL approaches EDNA and RUTH.*]

EDNA: Why don't you two just sit out here a bit. Air's nice tonight.

RUTH [*beginning to exit*]: I gotta set dinner.

EDNA: You just stay put. I can manage.

[*EDNA exits after a glance at EARL. Pause.*]

RUTH: Jesse said a word today.

EARL: What'd he say?

RUTH: "Snow."

EARL [*finding a bleak humor in this*]: Figures.

RUTH: 'Course it coulda been he was sayin "No." Hard to tell.

EARL: Maybe he was just makin sounds.

RUTH: Oh he was talkin sure. [*pause*] Earl?

EARL [*his mind elsewhere*]: Hmnn?

RUTH: How come you never spend time with Jesse?

EARL: I do.

RUTH: Not much.

EARL: I got the farm to run ain't I? And when I ain't, he's sleepin.

RUTH [*after a pause*]: What's wrong, Earl?

EARL: Nothin. … Tired, that's all.

RUTH: I ain't seen you smile in a long time.

EARL: Ain't nothin much's struck me funny.

[Pause. Something crosses EARL's mind and he begins to grin.]

RUTH: What?
EARL: Nothin.
RUTH *[wanting to share in the experience]*: Come on, what?
EARL: That little dapple brown calf...
RUTH *[eager]* :Yeah?
EARL: Slipped on a cowpie.
RUTH *[disappointed]*: That's it?
EARL: Well, yeah. Like I said, hain't much to get excited by round here.

[Pause. RUTH tries to snuggle up to him. EARL is distant, removed.]

RUTH: Your mother said it'd be okay if I went into town with you tomorrow.
EARL: I'm just goin in to pick up some seed.
RUTH: We could go by the drug store. Have us a soda like we used to. Your mother said she'd stay with Jesse.
EARL: I'm just goin in and comin right back out.
RUTH: Can't I at least come for the drive?
EARL: It's the same road you've been goin up and down your whole life. *[slight pause]* I need to get off by myself a couple hours.
RUTH: You're always by yourself.
EARL: Workin.
RUTH: Still...
EARL: I like drivin by myself. I can't think when I'm on the fence line or milkin. *[EARL starts off.]* Come on. Dinner's probably ready.

[EDNA enters. SHE watches EARL exit.]

RUTH: Earl?
EDNA *[after a pause]*: Come on in, Ruth, Dinner's set.

[RUTH curls in on herself, EDNA senses the problem and tries to comfort her.]

EDNA: Special time a year up here, what with the snow gone 'n mudtime past. Me 'n James been livin here our whole life. Can't see us no place else. Same's you. But Earl… boy's got a restlessness I can't figure.

RUTH: Scares me.

EDNA: Give him time, daughter, you just gotta give him time.

[LIGHTS UP on EARLY in another area of the stage. He's working on an engine. MARLE enters with two cups of take out coffee.]

MARLE: I got us some coffee.

EARLY: Take a quarter outa the register.

MARLE: It's on me.

EARLY: Big spender huh? Next thing I know you'll be wanting to strut on down to Jackson Hole, party it up with the gals.

MARLE: Here's just fine with me.

EARLY: Hmmph.

[RUTH withdraws slightly from EDNA.]

RUTH: I know he ain't comin back. I can feel it.

EDNA: Don't you worry.

EARLY: Hand me that box wrench. So what was it?

MARLE: Threw a rod. Overheated on the grade. Guy probably never checked his compression. Valve just tightened up over time til the pressure got too high then "kthunk" – that's all she wrote. I left 'er outside on the tow.

EARLY: I'll get under it tomorrow. What'd you do with the people? Leave 'em on the Pass?

MARLE: Left 'em at the Diner.

EARLY: Worse.

[MARLE helps EARLY on the engine. EARLY continues – the offhanded storytelling of a man who's working with his hands.]

EARLY: The morning I pulled into this dumbbutt town – quietest place I ever been – I could hear the wind blowin, not over anything, but all by itself, right over my ears. I could see them mountains up ahead and figured if I could just get up 'n over 'em I could coast all the way to

California. Wasn't too up on my geography just then – a few tough spots between here and there. Took goin up to the top to see that. Gimme that other wrench.

EDNA: Not long after James 'n me got married he took off to France. Said it was the war an' his patriotic duty, but I shouldn't wonder but James just needed time. Earl twarn't but two. I feared he wouldn't come back, same as you. But he did. Hain't been gone since.

RUTH: Mebbe so.

EDNA: Far places call a man sometimes and if they don't go least once, them places keep pullin at 'em their whole life.

MARLE: I had this picture of myself when I left, riding high in the saddle of my Kawasaki – just lookin to "let the good times roll. "

EDNA: Hain't sayin it's a good thing, but reinin in a horse all the time ain't never gonna make a mule. Horse's gotta run now and again or they lose the spirit God give 'em.

MARLE: I was comin down through Illinois, just shy of the River, when I saw that bridge up ahead. I let loose this holler – I was crossin over. And then this big old son of a bitchin june bug took a dive down my throat. I spent fifteen minutes gagging my guts out underneath a billboard.

[EARLY *laughs, kind of a snort, followed by a small cough.*]

EDNA: Had me an Aunt took sick ten year ago down Boston. I took care of her for nigh on a month.

EARLY [*asking Marle to go on*]: So?

EDNA: Shouldn't wonder but I needed some runnin time a my own just then.

MARLE: That twelve foot Marlboro man just sat there, cool as you please, suckin on his smoke, starin out across the River countin clouds. I chucked a beer bottle at his head.

EDNA: Earl'll be comin back sure.

MARLE: But up there on that bridge, I was floatin. I could see the Mississippi through the road grid. I wasn't ever comin back. I was goin places that cardboard cowboy never even dreamed.

EDNA: Come on.

[EDNA *and* RUTH *exit.*]

EARLY: An' look where you ended up.

MARLE: When I save up enough I'm gonna buy me a little place of my own.

[EARLY *laughs – a snort.*]

MARLE: I'm serious.

EARLY: I know.

MARLE: There're worse places on Earth to be.

EARLY: Some better too.

MARLE: Name one.

EARLY: Bitterroot.

MARLE: Montana?

EARLY: Depends which way you're lookin. Turn West you got Idaho.

MARLE: Up on the Divide.

EARLY: You never been up there have you?

MARLE: No.

EARLY: Oughta cross over, see the other side before you go talkin about settlin in down here.

MARLE: I like it here.

EARLY: Too many tourists. Not wild enough.

MARLE: Way I see it, tourists've got cars and cars break down, and that means work.

EARLY: Think you got it all figured, ain'tcha?

MARLE: You settled didn't you?

EARLY: Truck blew up. Can't leave if you got no way to haul your ass out.

MARLE: That was a million years ago.

EARLY: Forty. [*slight pause*] I kept thinkin I'd save up enough to get back up there. Get me a place. Hunt, fish, count deer. Just kept layin in here, figurin I'd someday sell out. But who the hell'd want to buy this stuff now? Everybody wants to buy new, 'cept fools like you. Right man could get this junk for a song. [*pause*] You know any snappy ones ?

[MARLE *weighs the implied offer for a moment then asks:*]

MARLE: You got no family?

EARLY: Everybody's got family. Somewhere. [*slight pause*] My old man sent me into town one morning with his pick-up for some seed and I kept on goin. Left 'em all. Wasn't sure where the hell I was goin but I knew damn well I wasn't gonna stay.

MARLE [to himself]: Never even looked back.

EARLY: Spent the first month starin in the rearview before I started lookin for somethin up ahead. Coulda had my old man's farm in Vermont: cows, corn, all the snow I could eat.

MARLE: Vermont? You never told me –

EARLY: Didn't have to. You been there. You know.

MARLE: How'd you know?

EARLY: That machine you pushed in here has a license plate on it, don't it?

[MADGE appears in another area of the stage working in her Diner.]

MARLE [after a pause]: I borrowed the money for it from my mother. Never even paid her back.

EARLY: I got a theory about lendin. If you want to get it back, you shouldn't lend it out in the first place. Lendin's like a gift, kind of a way of spreading yourself around some – givin things. Things don't just disappear 'cause they're in somebody else's hands. They got a life a their own. Some of 'em last longer than the body who give 'em. Like these here tools.

[Pause. They sip their coffee.]

EARLY: Go on in and finish up on that station wagon. Brake lines're shot. Cylinders're out and the brake fluid's in the back. I'm gonna step over to the Diner 'n give Madge a hard time.

[MARLE becomes the pivot of both scenes. MADGE speaks to MARLE. EARLY speaks to MARLE. EARLY and MADGE influence one another. EARLY is in the station, MADGE in the Diner, MARLE is in both, shifting from moment to moment.]

MADGE: You'd think that old man'd come up with somethin a little more original.

MARLE: Same could be said of your menu.

EARLY: You notice what they got for lunch today?

MARLE: Chili.

MADGE: Same as every Tuesday.

MARLE: Looks like the same stuff they had last week.

EARLY: Same stuff they had for six months. Think I'll have the eggs.

MARLE: Stomach actin up again?

MADGE: If he'd go to the doctor like I told him, he might find out what's wrong with him. But it's easier to blame the food.

EARLY: After twenty years of eatin at that Diner what I got is a gizzard not a stomach.

MADGE: Then go to the vet.

[EARLY *begins to exit.*]

MARLE: Smell of the fluid make you sick again?

MADGE: If it ain't one thing, it's another.

EARLY: Brake fluid's like aftershave to me...

MADGE: I can believe it.

EARLY:... but the air up there in the Bitterroot's like perfume, sweet enough to make ya sing.

[EARLY *exits.*]

MADGE [*after a pause*]: What happened to your tent? I looked out this morning and saw it was gone. Figured you went with it.

MARLE: Just into Early's cabin. What with all the rain, he figured I oughta come inside. For the time being anyway. Hell, I woulda got more sleep in the truck what with him coughin all night.

MADGE: He was ?

MARLE: Probably just a cold from all this damp.

MADGE: When was the last time you seen a cold last a year? Just before you come he was claimin it was the influenza and before that the grippe. Pretty soon he'll be runnin out of common ailments.

MARLE: He's just gettin old. Probably ain't nothin serious.

[JOHN *is discovered in another area of the stage studying a catalog for mobile homes and recreational vehicles.*]

MADGE: To hear him talk it ain't nothin at all. If you see any change for the worse, you come tell me, hear?

MARLE: Sure.

[JULIE enters near JOHN. MARLE exits.]

JOHN: Which of these do you like best?

JULIE: Which of what?

JOHN *[displaying the catalog to her]*: These are my first choices.

JULIE: Are you buying a mobile home?

JOHN: Maybe.

JULIE: Why?

JOHN: Travel around, see some of the country without having to cram everything into two weeks. I could take an early retirement. You'll be at school and Moll will be… somewhere. Between the money from the house and my pension –

JULIE: You're going to sell the house?

JOHN: Why not?

JULIE *[she thinks this is oddly funny]*: And live in a trailer?!

JOHN *[earnestly serious]*: I've worked it all out. It's much cheaper. I read a whole article about it. And if we get tired of one place we can just hitch up the Jeep and drive someplace else.

JULIE *[still amused]*: What's Mom say?

JOHN: Come on, let's take a drive down to the showroom, look 'em over.

JULIE *[slightly patronizing]*: Look, Dad… I've got to get to work. For some reason it's very important that yesterday's ketchup bottles and salt shakers are refilled for lunch.

Don't ask me why. It's just one of the many deep spiritual satisfactions of my summer job. After August 31ˢᵗ I never want to see another cheeseburger plate as long as I live.

[JOHN is looking down at the catalog. HE feels a bit foolish, slightly embarrassed. JULIE notices, then points to one of the pages.]

JULIE: I'd check that one. It's got nice lines.

[JULIE exits. Pause. JOHN slowly puts away the catalog. MADGE watches him, EARLY approaches her.]

MADGE: You're early.

EARLY: Think maybe one of these days you'll come up with a new joke?

MADGE: Coffee?

EARLY: Yep, your coffee's a joke all right.

MADGE: You want a cup of coffee or not?

EARLY: Had the coffee. Actually, the coffee had me. Just a couple eggs scrambled and some toast.

MADGE: Stomach actin up again?

EARLY: Jesus Christ, since when's the state of my stomach the only news worth talkin about in this sillyass town?

MADGE [calling order to cook]: Two eggs scrambled easy and a side of toast.

EARLY: White.

MADGE: We're out of rye, white's all we got. Sent those folks with the car trouble over to the motel. Where's the boy?

EARLY: Gettin grime under his nails. He's been lookin a little too clean lately. If he wants to be a mechanic it's about time he started lookin and smellin like one.

MADGE: If he starts smellin like you I'll have to seat you two down at one of them end tables.

EARLY: Never heard you complain about my scent before.

MADGE: Spoils the customers' appetites.

EARLY: Ever think it's the food?

MADGE: Never hear any complaints except from you.

EARLY: Me 'n the boy're the only ones dumb enough to keep comin back.

MADGE: The rest of 'em are just passin through.

EARLY: Just like the food.

MADGE: You're lookin pretty peaked. You all right?

EARLY: Ain't nothin the matter with me that a few eggs and some fresh air can't cure.

MADGE: You're such a damn stubborn sonuvabitch sometimes. I've been telling you to go see that doctor since last summer.

EARLY: Got no use for doctors. Or lawyers. Or nosey waitresses.

[EARLY bends over, supporting his forehead with his hand. MARLE enters.]

MADGE: Well look who's here.

MARLE: Howdy, Madge.

MADGE: Let me see them hands, boy.

[MARLE *sticks out his hands. He's not sure why she's asked him to do it and she's not about to let him in on the joke. She chuckles.*]

MARLE: What?
MADGE: You're gettin there.

[EARLY *is still supporting his head in his hands.*]

MARLE [*shrugging off* MADGE*'s joke*]: Hey, Early, where the hell'd you say you put them brake lines. I've been lookin all over for 'em.
[EARLY *coughs.*] Early?
EARLY: What?
MARLE: You okay?
EARLY: I'm fine dammit, I gotta get me some air.

[EARLY *exits. Pause.* MARLE *and* MADGE *are quietly concerned.*]

MADGE [*finally, softly to the cook*]: Hold them eggs.
MARLE: I better go see if he's okay.
MADGE: Leave him be, [*softly to cook*] Oh, and the toast. Hold the toast...
That man can be so muleheaded sometimes I could kick him.
MARLE: I better get back to work. He'll be all riled up if I leave the station unattended.
MADGE: You been keepin an eye on him like I told you?
MARLE: Yeah. It's gettin worse.
MADGE: Damn old coot. I can see I'm gonna have to drag him down to the clinic myself.
MARLE: Doubt you'll be able to.
MADGE: Sooner me than you. You just go along with everything he says. He snaps his fingers and you jump.
MARLE: I just do my job.
MADGE: Now that you moved into the cabin, he don't even try to cook his own meals. I bet he hasn't washed a dish since you moved in.
MARLE: I gotta live there too... Hell, with his stomach, your cookin'd kill him.
MADGE: I've been cookin for him for twenty years. When you finally up

and leave, we'll be back to what was. You're spoilin him. I'm the one who'll have to put up with it when you're gone.

MARLE: Who says I'm goin anywhere?

MADGE: How long you think it's gonna be before you get sick of fixin fan belts and panfry lamb chops for that old man? You ain't cut out for this life. You ain't been here but two months. You grew up livin a different life. Wisdom ain't no suburb.

MARLE: Nobody asked me where I wanted to grow up. It just happened.

MADGE: If your motorcycle didn't break down you woulda been in San Diego by now.

MARLE: It ain't no different from Early. Or you.

MADGE: I got left. What do you know about bein left? Nothin.

MARLE: You coulda left any time. Any time at all. Maybe you're sittin around waiting for your old man to come truckin into town and wisk you off again, but I ain't. I got nobody comin for me and I got nobody out there waitin, so you damn well better get used to me.

MADGE *[curt]* Fine.

[MADGE *begins to exit.*]

MARLE: Besides... I come to develop a taste for your lousy chili.

MADGE *[stopping]*: You can say anything you want to, but I ain't hearin no more denigration of my chili.

MARLE: I said I liked it dammit.

MADGE: 'Scuse me if I ain't thrilled.

[MADGE *exits,* MARLE *lingers or moves to another area of the stage.* EARLY *enters.*]

EARLY: There you are. Did you bleed the lines on that brake job?

MARLE: You mean...

EARLY: Did you bleed the brakes when you was through?

MARLE *[realizing his mistake]*: Oh no...

EARLY: He hit his brakes and blew two lines. What the hell's the matter with you? You coulda killed that whole family. He come in fit to tear my head off.

MARLE: I'm sorry.

EARLY: Sorry?! The hell're you talkin about, sorry. I can't trust you with nothing.

MARLE [starts to go]: I'll go talk to him.

EARLY: I got a good mind to fire you.

MARLE: On account of one lousy mistake?!

EARLY: I can see the signs. You ain't nothin but a drifter. Your mind's on everything but what it's supposed to be.

MARLE: I was thinkin about you. I'm worried.

EARLY: Then you can just take your worries someplace else. I ain't payin you to be my nursemaid.

[EARLY exits. MARLE, alone, kicks around the stage. He takes out his frustrations on inanimate objects.]

MARLE [muttering]: Son of a bitch.

[After kicking and moping for another moment, he goes for the motorcycle and wheels it downstage. He jumps on but just as he's about to kick the starter he stops. He looks around. Takes in the space. In another area of the stage, JAMES is discovered sitting on the porch of his farmhouse, watching the wind in the trees, thinking.]

MARLE [finally]: I LIKE IT HERE DAMMIT!

[He dismounts, then shouts off to EARLY as EDNA enters behind JAMES.]

MARLE: I belong!

[MARLE exits. EDNA watches JAMES from behind for a moment before speaking.]

EDNA: James? What you be lookin at so fierce?

JAMES: Wind. Wind 'n trees. Winter be comin on early this year. [pause] Wished he'd leastways brought back the truck.

EDNA: You don't suspect he'll be comin back.

[Silence. EDNA *puts her hand on* JAMES' *shoulder - a comfort for both.* JAMES *however continues to brood upon the distance with unwavering severity.* RUTH *enters another area of the stage but does not join them, nor is she seen by the old couple.]*

JAMES *[finally]*: Boy asleep?

EDNA: Ayeh.

JAMES: Strange he ain't never asked about his daddy.

EDNA: He's just learned to talk. *[pause]* You don't talk much about Earl neither.

JAMES: Hain't much to say about somebody you ain't seen.

EDNA: I suspect if he'd found hisself in trouble we woulda heard by now.

*[*RUTH *approaches them. She sits beside James on a lower step. It is as if the three were clustered on the stoop watching and waiting for an arrival.]*

RUTH: Chill in the air.

JAMES: Ayeh. *[long pause]*

RUTH: I allow he's settin some place right now takin in the same breeze.

JAMES: Mebbe so. Mebbe so.

RUTH *[after a pause]*: You been real good to me an' Jesse.

EDNA: We done what we had to. Tain't been easy on you.

RUTH: Or you.

JAMES: A man's bound to take care of his own. [pause]

RUTH: Hain't right to stay, now that I give up on Earl comin back.

EDNA: Hain't no reason to go neither. *[slight pause]* Work's been gettin too much for me an' James. Mebbe we come to lean on you too much. *[slight pause]*

JAMES: Farm's Jesse's now, by right. *[long pause]*

RUTH: Tomorrow we best be gettin out the blankets.

EDNA: Ayeh.

*[*RUTH *rises.* EDNA *looks at her. They nod "goodnight."* RUTH *exits.* EDNA *waits a moment, pats* JAMES *on the shoulder. He touches her hand.* EDNA *exits.* JAMES *continues to stare off into the distance.]*

JOHN: Where'd you get the money?

MOLL: Borrowed it.

JOHN: From who?

MOLL: A friend.

JOHN: What friend? You don't have any friends.

MOLL [accusing]: One.

JOHN: And how do you intend to pay him back?

MOLL: I'm getting a job.

JOHN: About time.

MOLL: As soon as I get 'er running.

JOHN: What do you mean "get it running"?

MOLL [cutting him off]: She keeps stalling out.

JOHN: You bought a motorcycle that doesn't even run?! What the hell's the matter with you?

MOLL: She was running fine when I bought it.

JOHN: Figures you'd buy a lemon.

MOLL: Give me a break, willya.

JOHN: One stupid thing after another. How are you going to get it fixed?

MOLL: I'll do it myself.

JOHN: You don't know the first thing about machines.

MOLL: I'm learning.

JOHN: And while you're learning, how are you planning to get to work?

MOLL: I don't have the job yet.

JOHN: You just said you did.

MOLL: I said I'm going to get one.

JOHN: Well I'll believe that when I see it.

MOLL: I'm really trying, Dad.

[For a moment, JOHN drops his assumed mantle of severe parental responsibility and is genuinely affected by his son's sincerity.]

JOHN: I know. I just wish you'd asked me to look this thing over with you before you bought it.

MOLL: If you'll remember, you weren't particularly thrilled with the idea when I brought it up.

JOHN: Because you didn't have any way to pay for it. You still don't. Do you know what happens to people who buy things they can't afford?

MOLL *[making a joke]*: They get credit cards.

JOHN *[not amused]*: They go broke.

MOLL: Or end up working their whole lives at things they don't like.

JOHN: How much did you pay for this junkheap?

MOLL: Three hundred dollars.

JOHN: How much was he asking?

MOLL: Three hundred.

JOHN: You didn't make a counteroffer?

MOLL: She wouldn't sell for less.

JOHN: "She"?

MOLL: Yeah.

JOHN: So you just gave in. Well that figures. I'll bet you didn't even shop around.

MOLL: This was the cheapest one in the paper.

JOHN: It looks it.

MOLL: What the hell do you know about motorcycles?

JOHN: A helluva lot more than you do. At least I recognize a piece of junk when I see it.

MOLL: I told you it was running fine when I bought it.

JOHN: But it's not running now, is it?

MOLL: I said I'll fix it. You've got all kinds of tools in the garage.

[JOHN considers how to respond to this implied request to use his tools.]

JOHN *[finally]*: Just take care of them.

MOLL: I will.

JOHN: And clean up when you're through. If I find one wrench mucked up in some corner, that's it.

MOLL: I'll be real careful, I promise.

[Pause. JULIE enters and quietly observes the end of their scene.]

JOHN: If you have any questions…

MOLL: Thanks, Dad.

JOHN *[uncomfortable with this unfamiliar relationship]*: Sure.

[JOHN exits.]

JULIE: If I ever have a kid, I hope it pops fullblown into the world at twenty-six.

MOLL: Hopefully with no sister.

JULIE: What'd you do this time?

MOLL: Nothin. If Dad would just get off my back for fifteen minutes…

JULIE: At least he notices.

MOLL: Yeah, I love it.

JULIE: I could blow the roof off the house and Dad would spend the next two weeks telling you to get a job as a roofer.

MOLL: I gotta get out of here, go someplace. West maybe.

JULIE [laughing]: You?

MOLL: There's nothing keeping me here.

JULIE: Besides a bedridden motorbike.

MOLL: Cycle!

JULIE: Go ahead. Get technical. You could always turn it into a lawnmower. But that's not as sexy.

[MOLL gives her a quizzical look. He didn't get the "sexy" part. JULIE explains.]

JULIE: Males and machines. It's all part of an elaborate surrogate sexuality.

[MOLL still doesn't get it.]

JULIE [condescending]: You're just horny.

MOLL: Among other things. Frustrations come in bunches.

JULIE: "Please, Miss Piston, let me touch your valves. I know you've been with other guys but they didn't respect you. I love you for what you are."

MOLL: The previous owner happened to be a girl.

JULIE: Your bike's a dyke?

MOLL: Cycle! MOTORCYCLE!

[MOLL exits. MARGE enters.]

MARGE: Julie? Where's your brother going?

JULIE [droll]: Montana.

MARGE: Moll never said anything about –

JULIE [beginning to exit]: I think he's going out to the garage.

MARGE: Where are you going?

JULIE: Out.

MARGE: Where ?

JULIE: Out! With Frank.

MARGE: I thought you and Frank had stopped –

JULIE [cutting her off]: We got back together. He's still a jerk, but at least he's a jerk with a Mustang. If I had a choice between the two, I'd take the Mustang.

MARGE: What are you going to do with him?

JULIE: The same thing we always do, the same thing everybody does in this mindless town. Look, Mom, I'm just trying to avoid brain-death until September Third. If you can't trust me now, what're you going to do when I'm off at school? I take precautions. No way I'm going to end up like…

[JULIE checks herself.]

MARGE: Me?

JULIE: I didn't say that.

MARGE: I want to know exactly what you're planning to do this evening.

JULIE: I don't know yet.

MARGE: That's not good enough.

JULIE: I don't know! Probably something inspired – like a movie or a cheeseburger.

MARGE: The drive-in?

JULIE: Probably.

MARGE: Then you can just stay home.

[JULIE starts to leave.]

MARGE: Have you asked your father?

JULIE: You ask him.

MARGE: Why are you wearing a skirt?

[JULIE stops.]

JULIE: I decided to wear a skirt. Is that okay with you ?

MARGE: Why?

JULIE: My jeans are dirty! Christ, if some guy wants to get into my pants and I don't want him to, I could be wearing a tutu and it wouldn't make any difference… What's the matter, you worried I'm not wearing any underwear?

marGE: You've stopped wearing a bra.

[Facing upstage to MARGE, JULIE *lifts her skirt.* MARGE *turns away, embarrassed.]*

JULIE: Go on, take a look. Are you satisfied? Well?

*[*JULIE *lowers her skirt and smooths it out gently, almost demurely. She puts on a shawl.* EDNA *turns to her. She senses the girl's disquiet and hugs her.]*

EDNA: You look right fine, Ruth.

RUTH *[after a pause]*: It don't seem right, goin to town this way. Without Earl.

EDNA: Church picnic's a time for seeing them you ain't seen for a while. Give you a chance to be with folks your own age.

RUTH: They're gonna be askin' after Earl.

EDNA: Ayeh. *[pause]* Tain't you that's to be ashamed. Not that you won't feel it so. But I 'shouldn't wonder but by hidin from others eyes makes it harder to see yourself. You go on now. Have a good time. And when folks ask, you just look 'em in the eye and say whatever you've a mind to. Go on now, daughter.

*[*RUTH *exits.* EDNA *exits. In another area of the stage, we see* MADGE *and* EARLY *walking along outside.]*

EARLY: Did you see what that blame fool went and done? Bought another motorsickle.

MADGE: It's his money. He earned it.

EARLY: He's gonna kill himself on that thing one a these days.

*[*MADGE *laughs.]*

EARLY: The hell's so funny, woman?

MADGE: You're actin more like his Pa every day.

EARLY: The hell I am.

MADGE: You even yell at him like you were. It's touchin.

EARLY: You're the one who's tetched. Now where the hell is he? I told him to get the front lot cleared out by suppertime.

MADGE: Ain't no hurry.

EARLY: Says you.

[MARLE approaches.]

MARLE: Howdy.

MADGE: Marle.

EARLY: I thought you said you was gonna buy yerself a pick up truck.

MARLE: Couldn't pick one up.

EARLY: You ain't supposed to, dummy.

[EARLY whacks MARLE with his cap.]

MARLE: I better be gettin on the front lot like you said.

EARLY: Oh, hell... leave 'er be. Pretty soon she'll be two feet in snow. We'll get 'er come spring.

[MADGE laughs.]

EARLY: She got somethin stuck on her funny bone today.

MADGE: You're really somethin, old man.

EARLY: Old hell! You don't see me wearing no support hose like somebody I know.

MARLE: If I ain't gonna do the lot, then maybe I'll fix us somethin decent for supper.

EARLY: Boy's actually a worse cook than he is a mechanic. If you can believe it.

MADGE: You two could come on over to my place.

EARLY: Some choice.

[MARLE whacks EARLY with his cap.]

EARLY *[playful challenge]*: Watch who you be hittin with that cap, boy.

MARLE *[to MADGE]*: You want me to bring anything?

MADGE *[beginning to walk away]*: I reckon you'd better bring him – on a leash. With a six pack under his arm. Come on over any time.

EARLY *[loud enough so MADGE can still hear]*: I oughta just do it too.

MARLE: Do what?

EARLY: Come in on a leash. Lift my leg on her rocker.

MARLE: Don't tell me you got problems with your plumbing now too. Jesus Christ, Early, ain't you embarrassed not even being able to take a decent piss?

EARLY *[for MADGE's benefit]*: If she didn't want me pissin in her house she shouldn't a told me to bring beer.

[MADGE is now off, THEY laugh. The laugh brings on a slight coughing fit in EARLY. It subsides. MARLE makes no comment. They linger in silence, taking in the late afternoon air and feel the chill.]

EARLY: Kinda reminds me of the Montreal Express.

MARLE: What does?

EARLY: This wind. Comin down from Canada, cuttin right through Vermont, bringin winter down the line. My old man used to sit out and wait for it.

MARLE: What part of Vermont'd you live in?

EARLY: Upcountry. St. Johnsbury way.

MARLE *[after a pause]*: You ever think about going back, just for a look see?

EARLY: Nope.

MARLE: But you think about it.

EARLY: Hell, I been here almost forty years. Time to think a lot of things. … I wonder now and again what's become of my boy.

MARLE *[surprised]*: You got a son?

[EARLY really didn't want to get onto this topic.]

EARLY: Yessir, fine cold wind. Got the teeth a mountains in 'er.

MARLE: You never told me you –

EARLY: No I never did and I ain't about to again. Just sorta come up. Unexpected like.

MARLE: Then you've got a wife too?

EARLY: If I got a son it makes sense I got a wife somewheres too don't it? Sometimes you got about as much sense as a flat tire, boy.

MARLE: Is that why you and Madge never got married?

EARLY: Jesus. Of all the galdurned idiotic idees. Me 'n Madge ain't the marryin type. Besides, she had herself a husband once too. Run off just like me'n you. ... This here country's filled with folks who left things behind. We ain't in no hurry to make the same mistakes. *[slight pause]* You still thinkin of settlin in out here?

MARLE: I feel at home.

EARLY: Home, hunh?

MARLE: Yeah.

EARLY: A man gets old in a place like this.

MARLE: Like you.

[EARLY looks him over closely, then perks up shifting the focus.]

EARLY: Better get down to the store and pick up that beer. Come on, gimme a ride on that new motorsickle a yours.

MARLE: You?

EARLY: I ain't that old dammit.

MARLE: I'd let you ride 'er all by yourself, but I left off the trainin wheels.

[MARLE laughs. EARLY tosses him an old rag.]

EARLY: Finish up inside.

[EARLY exits.]

MARLE: Where you goin?... Early?

[EARLY mounts the motorcycle.
MARLE stops, turns, then rushes over to him.]

MARLE *[laughing]*: Hey, whaddaya think you're doing?!

EARLY: What's it look like?

MARLE: Where you going?

113

EARLY: California, join me an outlaw bike gang. Mind the shop, boy, I'll be back in about ten years. If I ain't, it's yours.

[EARLY *kicks the starter. It doesn't start. He tries again. Nothing.* MARLE *shuffles.*]

EARLY: I see you been workin on it again.
[EARLY *dismounts.*]
EARLY: You got a real knack for turnin perfectly good machines into museum pieces, you know that.

[MARLE *squats down to take a look at the engine.*]

MARLE: I'm good with cars. Cycles are supposed to be easier.

[EARLY *watches him for a moment, then starts to grin. He tousles the boy's head, then exits.* MARLE *glances at him. He doesn't put back on his cap. He then refocuses on the engine.*
JULIE *approaches him.*]

JULIE: Give up.
MOLL: I think I've almost got it.
JULIE: You said that a month ago.

[JULIE *plops down nearby.*]

JULIE: I quit my job. Some jerk asked for a "dead" burger. I figured it was some kind of bizarre come on, his idea of cute, so I took the order and brought him back a medium.
He starts yelling that he wanted it "dead." "Dead" apparently meant very well-done. Who knows. He's yelling and screaming: "I asked for it dead! This thing's so rare it's still moving!" So I grabbed his knife and stabbed it. There was some question of whether I quit or got fired. Either way, I'm gone. I just want to go someplace where there are more trees than people.

[MOLL *tosses a tool into a can, picks up a rag to wipe his hands.*]

MOLL: On behalf of the human race, I'm sure the feeling's mutual.

[*HE tosses the rag on the ground and exits.*
JOHN enters. JULIE exits. HE looks around. He picks up the rag,
throws it into the can, sees the tools in the can and gets very angry. He
takes the can and charges across the stage toward MARGE who's in an
apron.]

JOHN: Where the hell is he?
MARGE: He's in the bathroom, cleaning up for dinner.

[*JOHN starts toward the bathroom.*]

MARGE: John, wait. What's the matter?
JOHN: You know where I found these tools? Here. In the trash can.
MARGE: So?
JOHN: He threw my tools in the goddam garbage.
MARGE: Maybe they just fell in there by mistake.
JOHN [*starting off again*]: Oh there was a mistake all right…
MARGE: John!
JOHN: You should see the garage. Oil and rags everywhere. He could have
   burned the house down.
MARGE: Cool down a minute, then talk to him.
JOHN: I'm through talking.
MARGE: At least give him a chance to explain.
JOHN: I told him, if he ever messed up those tools –
MARGE: For God's sakes, they're only tools.
JOHN: I asked one thing, one small thing: take care of the tools and keep
   the garage clean.
MARGE: That's two things.
JOHN: Lazy son of a bitch…
MARGE: You're talking about your own son!
JOHN: That's it, take his side again. Christ. No wonder he won't do anything.
   Every time he turns around, you're there coddling him. Do you think I
   like harping on him all the time?
MARGE: Sometimes I think you do.
JOHN: What the hell's that supposed to mean?

MARGE: You haven't said a kind word to him in years. All you do is bellow.

JOHN: THAT... is not true.

MARGE: He needs encouragement.

JOHN: I let him use the whole garage. I have to park in the goddam driveway. I let him use my tools. I let him live here, free of charge, working on that... that piece of shit he calls a motorcycle. I offer advice. I give suggestions. I've asked every friend I have if they hear of a job anywhere to let me know. He won't even go meet the people. He's always got something more important to do.

MARGE: Giving him ultimatums won't change anything.

JOHN: What would you do with him?... I was out and on my own when I was seventeen. The boy's twenty for chrissakes.

MARGE: He's not you.

JOHN: He and I had a deal.

MARGE: I know. Try to be a little more patient. He'll be fine. Just give him a few more months.

JOHN: Every time I draw the line with those kids, you erase it. No wonder they have no sense of responsibility. They screw up, and you make excuses. Nice is not the answer. It never was.

MARGE: Neither is shouting at them all the time. I wish you'd try to understand what it must be like for him.

JOHN: I have. Too many times. And this is it. He's going to learn this lesson once and for all.

[JOHN *begins to exit.*]

MARGE: What are you going to do?

[MOLL *enters, wiping his hands on an old towel.*]

MOLL: Dad...

JOHN: There you are.

MOLL: I was just looking for you. I've got a question about my distributor.

JOHN: Well I've got a few questions for you. See these tools? You know where I found them?

MOLL: In the garage.

JOHN: In the trashcan, that's where.

116

MOLL: Is that the big adjustable? I was looking all over for it.

JOHN [*punctuating by hitting wrench on can*]: It was here. In here. Right here. In this can.

MOLL [*smiling*]: Oh, and you thought…

JOHN: I don't think anything, I can see for myself.

MOLL: That's my cleaning can. I put the dirty tools in there to soak in gasoline.

JOHN: That can was filled with rags and paper.

MOLL: It was not.

JOHN: What the hell do you call these then?

[JOHN *reaches into the can, grabs a handful of rags and throws them at* MOLL.]

MOLL: I never put rags in there.

JOHN: Maybe they fell in there by mistake, just like the tools. Maybe the rags all over the garage got there by mistake too. I had to clean the whole garage myself.

MOLL: I have a separate pile for rags. I'd never put rags in my cleaning can.

JOHN: Well somebody did.

MARGE [*to* JOHN]: You did. You were the one who was cleaning out the garage. You get so mad you don't even know what you're doing.

JOHN: That's it, make excuses for him.

MOLL [*emphatic*]: I didn't put the rags in the can.

MARGE [*to* JOHN]: I told you to give him a chance to explain. If you want to look like a fool, go ahead. It serves you right.

[MOLL *smirks but tries to hide it from his father.*]

JOHN [*embarassed but covering*]: How the hell did I know this wasn't a trash can. I've been using this thing as a trashcan for ten years.

MOLL [*openly smiling*]: Way to go, Dad.

[MOLL *and* MARGE *laugh.* JOHN's *humiliation burns inside. Their attempt to point out the humor of the misunderstanding only drives him further away, deeper into himself.*]

MOLL [ribbing JOHN]: Thanks for cleaning up for me, I'll go out and finish up later.

[MOLL reaches for the can. JOHN stops him.]

JOHN: Get out. Get your things and get out of here.

MARGE: Stop it. Right now.

JOHN: Shut up.

MOLL: It was just a mistake, Dad. Come on.

JOHN: I told you to get out.

MARGE: You stay right where you are. This is my house too.

JOHN: Then you support him.

MARGE: I do.

MOLL: This is crazy.

JOHN: Crazy?! You want to know what's crazy? That I didn't kick your ass out the door ten years ago. I've had it. With all of you.

MARGE [to Moll]: I want to talk to your father alone.

JOHN: You want him to stay? Fine. Stay as long as you want. Stay til you're fifty. [to MARGE] You go down to that paper mill. See how you like it. I've been standing over those goddam pulp cookers since I was seventeen. I dream about those machines. I can't get the stink out of my nose. I taste it in everything I eat. For two lousy weeks a year I go someplace where the stink of woodpulp isn't making me sick to my stomach. I live for those two weeks.

MOLL: So go! If you hate it so much, why the hell don't you just quit. At least I know I don't know what I want, but you don't even have that. You've got this big dream with nothing inside it.

MARGE [trying to interject]: Moll, please...

MOLL [running on]: You think if you can get rid of me and shove Julie off someplace and pretend Mom doesn't exist, everything will be fine. You made your life, now live in it.

[JULIE has entered cautiously, drawn by the commotion. She hangs back.]

MOLL [to Marge]: I'll send you the money I owe you as soon as I can.

[MOLL begins to exit.]

MARGE: Wait. John, say something.
MOLL: Bye, Mom.

[MOLL *exits.*]

MARGE [*to* JOHN]: How could you?

[JOHN *drops his head, the tools moving in his hand.*]

JULIE: Dad?

[*No response from* JOHN.]

JULIE [*to* MARGE]: Where's Moll going?
MARGE: Ask your father.

[MARGE *exits.*
JOHN *begins to pick up the soiled rags from the floor and put them in the can.* JULIE *watches him, sensing his deep disturbance. She hangs back.* JOHN *finally puts down the can and exits to another part of the stage.* JAMES *picks up a mallet and wedge and goes to a section of hardwood. He sets the wedge. SNOW begins to fall lightly over him.* RUTH *approaches* JAMES.]

JAMES [*finally*]: Fever broke?
RUTH: 'Bout the same. There's six cords in the shed and nice and warm inside.

[MOLL *enters another area of the stage. He mounts the motorcycle. A slight "prayer" that it will finally start.*]

RUTH: Jesse's gonna be fine.
JAMES: Hain't doin this for him.

[*SLIGHT RUMBLE OF THUNDER is heard in the distance. James takes note of it.* MOLL *is up, ready to kick the starter.* JAMES *splits the section.* MOLL *kicks the starter. It starts. His fists go up in triumph. SOUND of motorcycle continues as if it is heard heading off as LIGHTS FADE.*]

END OF ACT ONE

ACT TWO

[*As LIGHTS come up, we discover* JOHN *alone in front of the service station. His folded map is in his hands. He keeps watching for* MARLE. *A light SNOW is still falling.*
MARLE *enters with change from John's fuel purchase.* JOHN *glances at him furtively as if seeing his son's face in the face of this stranger.*]

MARLE: Don't worry, I didn't forgetcha. Here.

[MARLE *hands him the money.* JOHN *pockets it.*]

MARLE: Thanks for not counting it. I like being trusted, same as the next. I'd check your oil next time. You're down about half a quart. Which way you headin?

[JOHN *clumsily opens the map.* MARLE *moves in for a closer look.* JOHN *has trouble taking his eyes off the boy.*]

MARLE: Followin your blue line South?
JOHN: Uh, no… There.

[JOHN *points to a spot on the map.* MARGE *enters. At first she does not see* MARLE's *face. But when she sees the two of them together, she stops.*]

MARLE: Lost Trail Pass huh?

[JOHN *notices* MARGE *and notes the look on her face.*]

JOHN: We'd better get going.
MARLE: Wait.
MARGE: What?

MARLE: Hell, I'd be nervous too If I was plannin on driving up over the mountains.

JOHN: A little snow won't stop us.

MARLE: That's down here. But further up, I don't know. Road's probably pretty bad. State Police oughta close the pass.

JOHN: It'll only get worse if we wait.

MARLE: That's a rough stretch of road in this weather, and with that trailer…

JOHN: I've been pulling it for almost a year now.

MARLE: In your condition?

JOHN: What condition?

MARLE: You seem awful shaky. Somethin troublin you? Somethin I did?

MARGE: Could we… park here for the night?

MARLE: If you asked Early he'd probably let you stay right here, at least til tomorrow. In them cross winds and with a slick road, it ain't the same as summer.

MARGE: Maybe we should wait.

JOHN: We'll be fine.

MARLE: Suitcherself.

JOHN [tugging at MARGE's arm]: Come on, Marge.

[JOHN exits. MARGE lingers. Pause.]

MARLE: Somethin I can do for you, M'am?

[Another uncomfortable pause while MARLE waits for MARGE to do or say something. MARGE finally goes up to him, hesitates, then hugs him. She releases him and runs off.]

MARGE [exiting]: You take care of yourself.

MARLE [puzzled]: Sure thing.

[HE watches them go off. EARLY enters behind him.]

EARLY: You take care a them people?

MARLE: Yeah. They was really strange. Like they seen a ghost or somethin.

EARLY: Hell, lookin at you'd be enough to scare anybody.

[EARLY *laughs*, MARLE *smiles, but he's still a bit shaken by the encounter. THEY are about to exit when they hear the distant rumble of THUNDER. THEY watch the sky.*
In another area of the stage we discover RUTH, *sitting on the porch of the Vermont farmhouse reading a Bible. MORE THUNDER, sound of a far-off storm approaching.* EDNA *enters looking at the sky.*]

EDNA: Where's James ?

RUTH: In the high field. Him 'n Jesse's try in to get the hay in before it rains.

[*ALL FOUR on stage are watching the sky as we hear another rumbling peal of THUNDER.*]

EARLY [*telling a funny story*]: Looka there, over the range. See that lightnin ticklin the mountain tops? Damn strangest thing, first storm a winter. Comes in actin like a summer squall, like it forgot what time a year it was. ... I was up there once when the thunder come in. Hunkered down back a this big old rock. Damn if the wind didn't all of a sudden hook around on me.

EDNA: Hain't safe to be pitchin this kinda weather, up there on the hayrick.

EARLY: Them thunderclouds got a way a turnin in on themselves just before they break. First wind's just a suckin up, like a man takin in a deep breath. Then wham! It all comes blastin out, big and deepbellied, bolts in both hands.

RUTH: Want me to go fetch them in?

EARLY: Damn near blew me right off the mountain. And there I was, standin there like a lightnin rod, lightnin smackin all around. I figured it was just a matter a time before one of 'em popped me. I took it for a fact I was a goner... not that it woulda much mattered to anybody. I thought long and hard just then, 'bout all kinds a things – babies, cows, my Pa.

[*LOUD THUNDER CLAP, FLASH OF LIGHT.*]

EDNA: James!

[EDNA *rushes off, ultimately in the direction of* EARLY. RUTH *watches her go.*]

EARLY [*continuing*]: Made this here kind a peace with myself. Figured when my time come, I'd cross over same as the next. Still… I'd just's soon he come to git me later than sooner.

[*Another RUMBLE OF THUNDER, now receding* EARLY *and* MARLE *laugh, but the laugh brings on a cough for Early. He seems weaker than we've seen him.* MADGE *rushes up to them and tries to help* MARLE *support him.*]

EARLY: Quit fussin after me. Both a ya.

[EARLY *exits. DISTANT THUNDER, receding. Pause.*]

MARLE: Seems to me he's gettin worse.

MADGE: Some ways maybe. His appetite ain't improvin, that's for sure.

MARLE: He's lettin go.

MADGE: Lettin go? Of what?

MARLE: Can't say for sure. His reasons, I guess. Like the way he talks about them mountains.

MADGE: Him and them damn Bitterroots. I wish he'd just up 'n go there and quit talkin about 'em all the time.

MARLE: It's like part of him got broken off and just stayed there the last time he come back. The stronger part.

MADGE: He ain't been up there in years. Least not since you come.

MARLE [*softly*]: I dunno what to think, Madge.

MADGE: Y'know, I used to think San Francisco was where I wanted most to be. Sounded to me like the most beautiful place on Earth. So about five years back, I went there. Took my money, bought me a ticket, and just went there.

Oh it was beautiful enough – all them houses and the fog and whatnot, but I guess I'd just gotten used to this godforsaken spot. Pretty as any old San Francisco, sittin out back 'bout dusk, watchin the sunlight turnin the snow up there a fine color of salmon.

And we got a much better grade of junk. People 'n things've been left all over this country ever since there've been people passin through: old wagons, lame mules, anything 'r anyone too weak, busted up, or worn out to keep up.

I got over my feelins about bein left a long time ago. All I left in San Francisco was my hat. "I left my hat... in San Francisco." *[she laughs]* In a park, down by the water, right down there on a bench lookin up at that Golden Gate. Hmmph.

Early's kinda lucky. He's been to his place, got to know it firsthand. I give up lookin for mine. He knows he can't go back there too much, maybe he can't go back there at all. If he does...

MARLE: What?

MADGE: Maybe he won't come back. Now ain't that a silly notion. You got a place like that?

MARLE *[after a slight pause]*: Yeah.

[*Pause.* MADGE *smiles and pats* MARLE's *hand.*]

MADGE: Who'd a ever dreamed this dumb crossroad'd be a place for anybody.

MARLE *[after a pause]*: Madge?

MADGE: Hmnnn?

MARLE: How come you'n Early never got married?

MADGE *[blushing]*: Well...

MARLE: He ever ask?

MADGE: I did. Once. The next morning it didn't seem like such a good idea. We been close enough though for a long time. ... Kind of a shame actually. After a while somethin shrivels up when you ain't been touched.

[MARLE *begins to withdraw.* MADGE *continues.*]

Ain't much that's soft 'round here. If you ain't careful you get hard as this here country so even the rain runs off and nothin works its way in.

[MADGE *begins to contract inward until she is lying on the ground, very still.* RUTH *looks up from her Bible.* EARL *is now somewhere in front of him. He does not look at her. They are not engaged in a real-time conversation.*]

RUTH: Earl? Where you been so long?

EARL: How's Jesse?

RUTH: Gettin lanky like you were, says your Ma. He's been helpin your Pa with chores. He's a good boy. Where you been, Earl?

EARL: Winter come in yet?

RUTH: First snow fell but didn't stick. Yesterday the puddles was paned over, thin ice like a window. Shines like it always does in the first sun, but it don't stay. Where you been?

EARL [seeking confirmation of a report]: I heard the river overflowed last spring all up 'n down the valley. Bottom land got flooded.

RUTH: Lost two cows. Milkers. Your Pa hauled the washed up trees into windrows. Mud piled up in the low spots but we got it turned under and the corn's growin fine. Had a good crop this year. Earl?

EARL: Good. That's good.

RUTH: Where you been?

EARL: Used to be so green. I rememba the green. Ain't so here. Even in spring when the aspen bud, it's light, like it's been mixed in with too much yellow. Brown country here most times, but the sky… oh Ruth, the sky's so big…

[SOUND of CB RADIO crackling with static. EARL moves off.]

RUTH: Where you been so long? Where you been?

[MARLE puts on his down jacket. He's lost in thought for a good long moment before EARLY enters.]

EARLY: You been monitorin that radio like I told ya?

MARLE: Sorta.

EARLY: I know, you done drifted off again. Daydreamin. Well get on out there. Call come in about an accident up on the pass. Some damn fool with a trailer.

[MARLE is taken aback. YELLOW TOWTRUCK lights begin to flash.]

EARLY: Well don't just stand there, get your gear and get a move on.

[MARLE starts out.]

EARLY: And, son... be careful.

[BLUE POLICE LIGHTS begin to flash as well. A light SNOW begins to fall on the prostrate. MARGE and JOHN who is standing in a tight pool of light. MARGE shifts and groans slightly.]

JOHN *[to the audience]*: I could feel the trailer slip sideways in the turn.

[MARLE rushes to MARGE's aid.]

MARLE: Hey, lady! Hey! You all right?

[MARGE groans. The STATIC RADIO diminishes.]

JOHN: The downgrade wasn't bad and I tried to steer out of the skid but the trailer pulled the back of the Jeep with it.
MARLE: Don't move. Just lie still. The ambulance'll be here in a couple minutes. I just called them in.

[MARLE covers her with a blanket.]

JOHN: I felt the bump of the shoulder then the slowmotion float of the fall and the camp stove coming at Marge from the back seat. I tried to stop it with my left hand and then the door seemed to explode into my back and the rearview mirror came rushing at my face.
MARGE *[very dazed]*: John? John! JOHN!
MARLE: Easy. You gotta lie still.
MARGE: Where's my husband?
MARLE: He's being taken care of.
MARGE: Where is he? JOHN!
MARLE: You could be hurt.
MARGE: What's happened to him?
MARLE: You just had a bad accident. You're gonna be okay.
MARGE: Is he...
MARLE: Lady, please.

[MARGE crawls part way toward JOHN.]

JOHN: I remember looking into the mirror, into my eyes in close-up for what seemed like hours.

MARGE: Oh, God, no.

JOHN: A strange hum started…

MARLE: I'm sorry.

MARGE: John…

JOHN: A thousand screaming electric angels.

MARLE: There's nothing you can do for him anymore.

JOHN: Then the sound faded.

[MARLE withdraws. MARGE stands silently.]

JOHN: Then the light started to close in around me, brighter and brighter, til the sun, til all the light there ever was seemed streaming from a pinhole. I was being drawn into the light, into the heart of it, then it stopped. I stopped.

[MARGE begins a low keening.
EARLY begins to cough. RUTH, in yet another area of the stage begins reading her Bible aloud.]

RUTH: And Naomi said, 'See how your sister-in-law has gone back to her people and to her gods. Follow her.' But Ruth the Moabite said…

[MARLE rushes to EARLY to support him.]

MARLE: Take it easy. Easy.

RUTH *[continuing]*: 'Ask me not to leave you, for where you go I will go…'

EARLY: Don't be hoverin around me. Go on. Git.

RUTH *[continuing]*: '…and where you lodge I will lodge, your people shall be my people and your God my God…

MARLE: I ain't leavin you here like this.

EARLY: Like what?!

MARLE: Coughin your damn guts out.

RUTH *[continuing]*: … where you die, I will die and there will I be buried.' "

EARLY: They're my guts, I'll do whatever I damn well want with 'em.

MARLE: You're sick!

EARLY: You just now figured that out?! A real by-god medical wizard aintcha?

[Pause. RUTH *exits.* MARGE's *keen has decrescendoed to silence.]*

EARLY: What the hell you hangin around here for anyway? Ain't you got better things to do with your life? You got your motorsickle, why don't you just get on 'er and go. Ain't nothin here worth hankerin after.

MARLE: Ain't no place I wanna go.

EARLY: Well that's pretty goddam pathetic if ya ask me.

*[*EARLY *weakens suddenly.]*

Goddamit. Pack yer things. You ain't wanted here no more.

MARLE: I been kicked outa one house and I run off from another. I ain't about to go leavin again. You hear me, I ain't goin.

EARLY: Go on, before I gotta chase you off.

MARLE: You ashamed of me seeing you weak?

*[*EARLY *threatens to drive* MARLE *away.]*

MARLE: I love you...

*[*EARLY *attacks.* MARLE *holds him off.]*

... you goddam sonuvabitch.

[As they struggle, EARLY *weakens.* MARLE *ends up supporting the old man,* EARLY *hangs onto him as* MARLE *helps him to sit.* MADGE *enters.]*

MADGE: What the hell?

MARLE: Come on, help me get him to bed.

MADGE: He have another fit?

EARLY: Take yer hands off me.

MADGE: I'm takin you into the clinic.

EARLY: Ain't nobody takin me nowheres. All I need's a little rest.

MADGE: Take him over to my place.

EARLY: I got a bed.

MADGE: I ain't leavin you in that goddam cabin.

MARLE: You might be more comfortable over at Madge's.

EARLY: I been in that cabin forty years and I ain't about to be put out now.

MADGE: And you been closin me out of every private thing ever since I've known you. You don't let nobody in. You don't let nobody care. I deserve more than bein pushed away and being joked with. This ain't no private thing. What's hurtin you is hurtin me too.

[EARLY *looks at her, then says, very coolly:*]

EARLY: When I feel like goin, I'm gonna get there on my own two feet.
MADGE: Ain't no use talkin to him.

[MADGE *exits.*]

MARLE [*after a pause*]: She was only tryin to help.
　　[*No response from* Early.]
Come on, I'll walk back with you.
EARLY: Go on. Leave me alone.

[MARLE *takes a beat, then exits. HE goes to another area of the stage (outside) where he stands alone, quiet, thinking about the old man.* JULIE *approaches with a backpack.*]

JULIE [*very friendly*]: Hi.
MARLE [*preoccupied*]: Oh. Hi.
JULIE: I was thinking of spending a few days up in the mountains just West of here. Who do I tell?
MARLE: You mean…
JULIE: Notify. You know, of my whereabouts.
MARLE: Why?
JULIE: It's crazy enough to head up into that country alone. You're always supposed to notify somebody where you're going, just in case.
MARLE: Yeah. I see what you mean.
JULIE: So who should I tell?
MARLE: Well… nobody's ever asked me that before. Sometimes they tell me where they're going while I'm fillin their tanks.
JULIE: So I could tell you.
MARLE: I suppose so.

[MARLE *is still very distracted by thoughts of* EARLY.]

JULIE: You all right?

MARLE: Yeah. Sure.

JULIE: So why don't I sketch out where I'm going and leave that with you.

[*JULIE searches for a pen.*]

Do you have a pen?

MARLE: What's that?

JULIE: A pen.

MARLE: Uh, no. There's one inside.

[*MARLE makes no move to go in.*]

JULIE [*suggesting they go*]: This way?

MARLE: Yeah.

[*Still no movement from* MARLE. *When* JULIE *finally heads off in the direction of* EARLY, *he follows.*]

JULIE [*to Early*]: Hi.

[EARLY *just looks at her. She's not quite sure what to make of this reception.* MARLE *enters behind her but hangs back.*]

MARLE: She's lookin for a pen or somethin.

[*JULIE sets her pack down near* EARLY, *trying to act at ease.*]

JULIE: I'm going to sketch out my route but I didn't have anything to write with.

[EARLY *keeps looking at her.*]

Uh, yeah. [*to* MARLE] Talky ain't he?

[MARLE *looks away and doesn't answer.*]

I'll check in with you when I come out. After that I'll be heading North. To Glacier Park Service.

MARLE: She just came in.

JULIE: From Yellowstone. I'm heading up into the Bitterroots for a couple days.

EARLY: Hmmph.

[*HE looks over her pack.* JULIE *draws away and begins looking around the station. She doesn't see* EARLY *pull a blanket from her pack and draw it around himself.*]

JULIE: Nice place you got here. Must keep pretty busy. These places get a real feel to them after a while. So much so you can almost sense the kind of people who work in 'em.
     [*SHE turns and sees* EARLY *with her blanket.*]
     Hey! What do you think you're doing?
MARLE [*to* EARLY]: You got a chill?
JULIE: That's my blanket. [*slight pause, then to* MARLE] Is there something wrong with him?

     [MARLE *draws back again.* EARLY *continues to sit, the blanket pulled around himself, staring at* JULIE.]

JULIE: You don't have blankets of your own?

     [*When* EARLY *doesn't respond,* JULIE *becomes a bit uneasy. After another pause,* MADGE *enters with a cup of tea.*]

MADGE: I brung you some hot tea.
EARLY: Who asked you?
MADGE: It's good for you.
EARLY: Says who?
MADGE: Says me.
JULIE: How about that, he can talk.
EARLY: Girl's goin up into the Bitterroots.
MADGE [*to* EARLY]: Don't you go getting started on them mountains again.
JULIE: You've spent time up there?
EARLY: Reckon it ain't much of a secret.
MADGE: If you want a ride up to the pass, just come on over to the Diner. Most folks are heading that way. You spendin the night?
MARLE: There's a motel just down the road.
JULIE: I'd rather sleep out. I've got a tent.
MADGE [*to* MARLE]: Sound familiar?
MARLE: There's space out back. I used to live there.

JULIE: In a tent?

MADGE: If you want, you can stay with me. I got room.

JULIE: Thanks. *[to* EARLY*]* So what're they like? The Bitterroots?

EARLY: If that's the kind of question you're goin up there to get answered you ain't gonna make it, girlie.

MADGE: She was just tryin to be friendly for God's sakes, no need to jump on her.

JULIE: I've spent time in the mountains before.

EARLY: Where?

JULIE: Green Mountains. White Mountains.

EARLY *[droll]*: Blue Ridge?

JULIE: No.

EARLY: Good. Startin to sound like you had a notion for colors instead of height. These mountains are black and white, rock 'n ice. Hard. Mountains back East ain't nothin but hills – worn down, tired, slump shouldered.

JULIE: I was climbing in Yellowstone.

EARLY: Girl does have a thing about colors.

JULIE: I missed Red Rocks.

EARLY: Smart ass too.

JULIE: I can take care of myself.

EARLY: You better. There ain't nobody up there gonna do it for you.

MARLE: Come on, Early, ease up on her.

EARLY: You ain't been neither, so how the hell you know what I'm talkin about?

MADGE: What's the matter with you tonight? Just because you're sick don't give you the right to be nasty.

EARLY: I ain't sick dammit. I'm sick a everybody tellin me how sick I'm supposed to be. All I got's a bad cold.

MARLE: Right. Look how you're sweatin.

EARLY: It's this goddam tea… Too damn bitter.

MADGE: I'll go get you some honey.

*[*MADGE *exits.]*

EARLY *[to* MARLE*]*: Whatchou lookin at?

MARLE *[turning away]*: Nothin. *[pause]* I'll go get you that pen.

*[*MARLE *exits.* EARLY *and* JULIE *scope each other out.* EARLY *grabs her pack.]*

JULIE: Hey!

EARLY: This all you got?

JULIE *[grabbing it back]*: All I need.

EARLY: You couldn't last two days with what you've got in there.

JULIE: I could make it two months on what I've got up here. *[she taps her head]*

EARLY: You think you get up there in the high rock with nothin but yourself and you proved somethin – only there ain't nobody to prove it to. Ice don't give a damn about anybody and the air'd just's soon suck you up as blow you over.

[Long pause. JULIE *is anxious for* MARLE *to return.]*

EARLY: You got people?

JULIE: Got no need for them.

EARLY: Hmmph. [slight pause] Tellin folks where you're goin's no different from bringing 'em with you. If you didn't have no need for 'em, you shoulda just disappeared. You got too many ties you ain't broken yet. "Got no need for people." Hmmph. You gotta cut deep if you wanna be that free.

JULIE: Think you're pretty rough, don'tcha?
    [No response]
So why don't you come with me?
    [No response]
Well?

EARLY: I heard ya.

JULIE *[very challenging]*: So? Whaddaya say?

EARLY: I couldn't make it across the goddam road.

JULIE: Is it that bad?

*[*EARLY *doesn't answer. Long pause.]*

EARLY *[finally]*: Take the boy.

JULIE: He doesn't seem much interested.

EARLY: You asked him?

JULIE: No.

EARLY: Then how the hell do you know if he is or ain't? *[pause]* I'd appreciate you askin.

JULIE: You think I'm experienced enough to take care of your son?

EARLY: He ain't… as experienced as you.

JULIE: You mean to tell me that in all the time he's lived here he's never been up in those mountains?

EARLY: Not off the road.

JULIE: Okay. I'll ask him.

[MARLE enters with a ballpoint pen.]

MARLE: Here's the pen.

JULIE: How would you like to come with me?

EARLY: Don't waste no time, do ya?

MARLE: Where?

EARLY *[teasing]*: Boy ain't been around too many girls for a while.

JULIE *[coy]*: In that case, maybe I just changed my mind.

MARLE: About what?

EARLY: She was gonna ask you to go up into the mountains with her.

MARLE: I gotta look after the station.

EARLY: I'll look after the goddam station. Go on. You ain't had a day off since you started here.

MARLE: How the hell're you gonna do all the work yourself?

EARLY: Since when'd you become indispensable? *[slight pause]* I'm gonna be all right. I got mother hen Madge lookin after every move I make and a couple dozen I don't.

JULIE: First thing tomorrow morning.

MARLE: Some other time. Thanks.

EARLY: What other time? The girl's headin north when she comes out.

MARLE: I don't want to. All right?

JULIE: Can't say I didn't try.

MARLE: Did he put you up to this?

EARLY: I mighta mentioned it as a possibility.

MARLE: Well the answer's "no."

[MARLE exits.]

EARLY: Now where the hell're you going? Git on back here, boy.
JULIE *[after a slight pause]*: You want me to go get him?
EARLY: Do whatever you want.

*[After a pause, JULIE exits. EARLY remains.
In another area of the stage, MARLE is (outside) brooding.
JULIE approaches him.]*

JULIE: Hi.
MARLE: Hi.
JULIE: Nice night.
MARLE: Yeah.
JULIE *[after a pause]*: What's the matter with your father?
MARLE: You mean… *[pause]* Don't know. He won' t go see a doctor.
JULIE: Some people are like that.
MARLE: I guess so.
JULIE: Why was he so hot on getting you up into the mountains with me?
MARLE: That's where he wants to go. Only he can't.
JULIE: Have you lived out here your whole life?
MARLE: Seems like it.
JULIE: Must be nice.
MARLE: Yeah.
JULIE *[after a slight pause]*: Nice town.
MARLE: Ain't much to Wisdom.
JULIE: Weird name for a town.
MARLE: Somebody with a sense of humor. … Makes people think twice
    before heading over the Divide.
JULIE: Yeah.

[MARLE begins to exit.]

JULIE: Well. Goodnight.
MARLE: Yeah.
JULIE: If we'd gone up there together, would you have tried to make me?
MARLE: You mean…

JULIE: Make me. Gotten it on at ten thousand feet.

MARLE: I dunno. Maybe.

JULIE: From what the old man said I would have thought you'd be horny enough to hump an engine block.

MARLE: You got some mind, you know that.

JULIE: You've got some problem.

MARLE: I got a lot of 'em.

JULIE: Such as?

MARLE: People askin too many questions.

[MARLE *begins to exit.*]

JULIE: Give me a lift up to the pass in the morning?

MARLE: This ain't a taxi service.

JULIE: Let me come with you.

[No response]

RUTH: Shouldn't wonder but you want to be alone again.

EARL: Mebbe so.

RUTH: Earl?

EARL: If I drive them cows in one more night with Pa tellin me what's got to be done an' how to do it an' how his Pa did it, I'm gonna kill them cows… or somebody. An' every time I find some quiet, there you are, tellin me how I got to be or where I got to go. I gotta be off by myself.

RUTH: You ain't here now.

EARL: I wasn't born to this life. None of this.

RUTH: I been makin the best of what is ever since I come here and I hain't never been good enough for you.

[MARGE enters another area of the stage and sits.]

EARL: Tain't you, Ruth.

RUTH: I'm shut of it, Earl. You hear me, shut of it. If you can't be home for me and husband to me, then it's time you be shut of me too.

[EARL turns away.]

Go on to France or wherever it is your drivin takes you and get it out, an' don't come back til you're empty of it.

[RUTH *exits.* MARLE *sees* MARGE *sitting alone. He puts on his cap and approaches her.*
In another area of the stage, EARLY *begins to cough.* MARLE *rushes to him.]*

MARLE: Early?… You gotta see the doctor.
EARLY: No.

[EARLY *sits.]*

MARLE: I'm takin you down to that clinic If I gotta tie you up in a blanket and lash you to the fender.
EARLY: Go on about what you were doin and leave me alone.
MARLE: How long's this been going on?
EARLY: What?
MARLE: This attack.
EARLY: You come in here for something in particular or just for conversation? Go take a shower. You stink. I can smell transmission oil all over you.
MARLE: The shower can wait.
EARLY: Your smell's makin me sick to my stomach.
MARLE: Yeah? So how come you were sick before I even came in?
EARLY: How do you know if I was or wasn't, you wasn't here.
MARLE: I'm gonna go call Madge.
EARLY: Stay away from that phone, you hear me. *[softly]* I got something to say to you.
MARLE: This's no time for you to be talkin.
EARLY: Now listen up…
MARLE: C'mon, Early. Just stay still.
EARLY: This station… this station's all I got. That and a little land and the cabin out back. Trucks and tools…
MARLE: Will you shut your mouth for once.
EARLY: I want you to have it.
MARLE: Goddamit will you stop talkin and stay still.
EARLY: I want you to have it all.

MARLE: We'll talk about it later.

EARLY: The whole shootin match.

MARLE: Let me go get a towel. You're all sweated up.

EARLY: Forget the towel and listen to me. I want you to take over the place.

MARLE: Quit sayin that.

EARLY: Quit interruptin me. Didn't anybody teach you any manners?

MARLE: You sure as hell didn't.

EARLY: I had other things to teach, now get back here… You're gonna be needin to fix up that hydraulic lift in the left bay and I don't want you takin any money from any franchise company men. You stay independent, son. You hear me. You let them big dealers get a toe hold on you they won't let go til they got everything. I got some money saved back in the shack. Under the floorboard against the back wall. Between that and what you got saved oughta cover it.

I gotta lie down now. Give me a hand here.

[MARLE helps EARLY lie down on the floor supporting the old man's head.]

EARLY: When I die…

MARLE: I ain't listenin to no more a this talk.

EARLY: I want you to close the place down for a week.

MARLE: Early!

EARLY: One solid week, ya hear me. Go up to the Bitterroots. Look 'er over real good. Listen to things by yourself. One week. If you decide that's where you want to be or you see someplace else you gotta go, you come back here and sell this place. Sell everything, every last crescent wrench, you hear me, and you go up there and you look 'er over real good and you think, and listen. From up there you got but two choices. If you come down you'll always know what it is up there, you'll know what you've seen and heard and you'll see things different from then on. One week. No more, no less. You got that?

MARLE: Yeah.

EARLY: You stay independent, son. Don't let nobody take you in. You look 'er over real good and then do it, just go ahead and goddam do it. Them Bitterroots… air's so sweet…

[EARLY dies quietly.

138

[MARLE *lays him gently on the ground. He picks up* EARLY's *cap and withdraws slightly.* EDNA *enters and approaches.* RUTH *enters from another direction with a blanket. The three stand over the man as if at a graveside.*]

EDNA: Oh, James... Hay's been left in the field to dry and Jesse keeps askin for you. He just don't understand. It was all so sudden.

It's gonna be a long winter – me 'n Ruth 'n Jesse in the house.

[MARLE *exits.*]

Neighbors been comin by. Folks is gonna miss you, James. I'm gonna... ... go now. I'll be back. Real soon.

[RUTH *and* EDNA *very formally, unfold the blanket and spread it over the body, covering him completely.* EDNA *exits.*

RUTH *lingers a bit long alone.*

MARLE *enters another area of the stage. He's got a backpack and he's wearing* EARLY's *cap.* MADGE *approaches* MARLE.

EDNA *and* RUTH *ceremonially unfold the blanket and spread it over the body, covering him completely.* RUTH *exits.*

The older woman withdraws slightly.

MARLE *approaches* MARGE. *It is shortly after John's funeral.*]

MARLE: M'am... I put your bags in the office. Bus'll be by in about an hour.

MARGE: Thank you.

MARLE: I'm real sorry about your husband.

[MARGE *silently accepts the condolences.*]

MARLE [*after a slight pause*]: Where will you go?

MARGE: I don't know. [*slight pause*] I can't go back. I thought maybe I'd go down to San Francisco for a while.

MARLE: You got family there? In California?

MARGE: No. That's where we were heading... before the accident.

MARLE: Me too.

[SHE *glances at him, slightly puzzled.*]

MARLE: I became a different person when I crossed the Mississippi, and the further I went the more different I got. Now I'm so different, if I ran into who I used to be we'd never even recognize each other… Y'know, if you get a notion to stay, you could probably work something out with the folks here at the Diner. Hell, Wisdom ain't so big it can't take one more stray.

[SHE smiles at him and begins donning MADGE's *work apron.* MARLE *puts on* EARLY's *cap and picks up a small pack.]*

MADGE: You leavin?
MARLE: Got to. For a while. I made a promise.
　　[RUTH exits.]
　　Shoulda took his ashes up to the mountains with me, left 'em there. But I didn't know his spot… Maybe we shouldn' ta buried him whole.
MADGE: Fire wasn't Early's way. I suppose if he'd ever talked about it, he woulda wanted to be put up in a frame like the way the Indians do. *[slight pause]* How long you gonna be?
MARLE: A week.
MADGE *[looking off into the distance]*: Them mountains scare me.
MARLE *[after a pause]*: Is it always this way?
MADGE: Each time's different. But some things are the same. The feeling that they ain't really gone. Things and people go on the same way they always did, then you turn around expecting to see 'im and you find yourself talkin to yourself. It ain't like missing somebody. Missing's when you know they're comin back. This is more like knowing that sooner or later you're gonna go join 'em.
MARLE: You gonna be all right by yourself?
MADGE: I've been left alone before. I'll manage. Probably overcook the eggs.

[SHE laughs lightly, sadly.]

MARLE: He always did like his eggs runny.
MADGE: Yeah.

[THEY touch hands. MARLE *exits.]*

MADGE *[to audience]*: Folks come in and ask how come the station's closed. I tell them the owners've gone away for a while. No reason to tell them more, they wouldn't understand. Oh they would, in the way any person understands, and they'd drop their eyes and say they were sorry. This way they look up and out and ask where they've gone, and the ones that don't ask, they just fill the future in with where they're going and with journeys they ain't taken yet.

[JULIE has approached MADGE, her backpack on her back.]

JULIE: Hi.
MADGE: You have a good trip.
JULIE: Great.
MADGE: You run into anybody up there?
JULIE: Not a soul. Where's the old guy and his son?

[MARLE enters the highest point of the stage pack on his back, out of breath, his cap on. He is high up in the mountains looking out from a high place. He has stopped to rest.]

MADGE: They… went up to the Divide.
JULIE: Really? That's terrific, I didn't think he'd make it. Too bad I didn't run into them. Too much country up there to see anybody unless you were really lookin for them and even then it'd be hard. Well, I just stopped by to let you know I made back all right.

[JULIE begins to exit. MARLE takes off the pack and sits.]

MADGE: Where ya off to?
JULIE: I got a job with the Park Service. It's all lined up.
MADGE: Sounds great.
JULIE: Yeah.
MADGE: Good luck.
JULIE: Bye.

[JULIE exits. After a beat, MADGE exits.]

MARLE *[as if to Early]*: I been up here six days and ain't nothin happened. Jesus, Early…

*[The MAN rises up from under the blanket and climbs up toward
Marle with the blanket.]*

MARLE *[continuing]*: ... I don't know what it is you sent me up here to see.
I seen a couple goats, and a she-bear and her cub. I heard a cat in the night.
    But mostly it's just rock and ice, and the air.
    Air's too thin. Like the sky got sucked away.

*[The MOUNTAINMAN approaches MARLE form behind.
MARLE doesn't see him.]*

MARLE: Damn, it's cold.
MOUNTAINMAN *[harsh and gruff]*: The hell you doin on my mountain?
MARLE: This is yours?
MOUNTAINMAN: More mine'n anybody's.
MARLE: I didn't know. Early said -
MOUNTAINMAN: People says a lot. Can't trust what people says.
    [MOUNTAINMAN tosses the blanket to MARLE.] You was cold.
MARLE: Who are you? Where'd you come from? *[pause]* You got a name?

*[The MOUNTAINMAN doesn't answer. HE squats down, surveying the
valleys below as if watching for something approaching. MARLE finally
squats down next to him trying to see what the old man sees.]*

MOUNTAINMAN: Left it. Left all of it.
MARLE: What do you live on?
MOUNTAINMAN: This mountain.
MARLE: I mean food.
MOUNTAINMAN: Wind. Wind 'n trees. *[slight pause]* You got any food?
MARLE: Uh, yeah. Hang on a minute...

*[MARLE rummages through his pack and takes out a piece of something
resembling jerky and hands it to the old man. He takes it, sniffs it, then
throws it off the promontory.]*

MARLE: Whatcha do that for?

[Silence. The MOUNTAINMAN *stares off into the distance. Finally, he asks]*

MOUNTAINMAN: You think he's dead, dontcha?
[slight pause] Dead as rock? Dead as ice?... Nothin's dead. See them rocks? Changin all the time. Slow changin. And the ice – quick changin, like light. The dyin change, the dead don't. *[pause]*
He ain't here. Go on, look around. Look all you want. You ain't gonna find nothin but what you brought and what you left.

[Pause. MARLE *begins to leave.]*

MOUNTAINMAN: I been waitin... I knowed you was comin. I knowed from way back, before you did even. How many you left behind?
MARLE: How many what?
MOUNTAINMAN: See that rock a way down there. Got busted loose from right here where you're standin. Now there's a hole rightchere where it was. How many holes you left behind gettin here?
MARLE: I better be movin on.
MOUNTAINMAN: You're just gonna leave another hole. Now on, I gotta live with her, all around 'er, right smack side a her, careful I don't fall in.
MARLE: I can't stay up here for ever.
MOUNTAINMAN How long you think I been here?
MARLE: How the hell do I know?
MOUNTAINMAN: Maybe I been here six days. Maybe three. Maybe I been here forever. Maybe not. Maybe I been here since the mountains was born. Maybe I be here when the mountains ain't nothin but holes in the sky. I got all your holes rightchere.

[The MOUNTAINMAN *seems to be gathering in things from the air around him, sweeping them with long graceful movements of his hands and arms, making no sounds. He gathers whatever it is into a heap floating at chest level. He glances at* MARLE, *holds gaze for a moment, then begins to compact them with his hands, rolling the mass into tight dense ball which he "pops" into his mouth and swallows in one quick gulp. He smiles wickedly.]*

MOUNTAINMAN: You can go now if'n you want. You don't have to look back no more. Long's I'm here you're a free man. I gotcher whole past rightchere.

[*The* MOUNTAINMAN *pats his belly.*]

MARLE [*after a pause*]: Did you know Early?
MOUNTAINMAN: Same's you. All the same. One life, all the same. Gimme back my blanket.

[MARLE *gives him the blanket which the* MOUNTAINMAN *snatches and then moves a few steps away.*]

MOUNTAINMAN: Watch.
MARLE: What're you gonna do?
MOUNTAINMAN: Disappear.

[*The* MOUNTAINMAN *pulls the blanket up over his head.* MARLE *stares at the blanket and the lump underneath. It is dead still. He approaches cautiously, then begins to lift the blanket.*
JOHN *pops up with a map. He talks to* MOLL *as if* MOLL *were a very young boy.*]

JOHN: Come here, son, I want you to see where we've been. Come on.

[MOLL *approaches and sits beside his father. He is a boy of seven.*]

JOHN: See that blue line. That's where you and me and Julie and your Mom have been and this is where we're going.
MOLL: We going to that green spot, Dad?
JOHN: That's a park. Called Glacier, You know what a glacier is?
MOLL: Un-unh.
JOHN: It's a river. Only it's made of ice.
MOLL: So it doesn't move.
JOHN: Very very slowly. It's a river that runs from way back in time.
MOLL: Where's it go?
JOHN [*holding up the blanket*]: Under here.

[MOLL *stares at the blanket. It scares him.* JOHN *pulls the blanket over his head, and becomes very still.*
MOLL, *still a child rushes around, looking for his father.*]

MOLL: Dad? Dad? Dad?

[JAMES *rises up, looking out across the land below.*]

JAMES: Looka here, boy. See them cows. Gonna be your'n someday. We been Vermont people nigh on two hunert years, 'n shouldn't wonder but we'll be Vermonters when the cows come home.

[SOUND *of distant rumbling* THUNDER.
JAMES *throws down the blanket and wheels around on* Marle. *It is now* EARLY.]

EARLY: You seen enough or do I gotta bend yer eyes for ya?
MARLE: Early?

[EARLY *snatches the cap from* MARLE'*s head.*]

EARLY: You made up your mind yet? You sellin out and movin on or you goin back to Wisdom?… You're standin on the spot… Fronta you's West, backa you East… One way's for movin on, the other's for stayin.
MARLE: It ain't the same with you gone.
EARLY: Don't go gettin sappy on me. You gotta be rid a me, you hear?
MARLE: Then why'd you leave me the station?
EARLY: You got some strange notion that when I died I turned into a gas station? Here's where I am. Rightchere.

[MARLE *sits. The* THUNDER *keeps rumbling in the distance.*]

EARLY: Oh now that's a fine howdy-do. Get up, dammit. Git up on yer feet.

[EARLY *offers the cap with one hand and the map in the other.* MARLE *still doesn't choose. The* THUNDER *is growing stronger.*]

EARLY: Hear that? Old son of a bitch's comin in to getcha. Better make yer move now. You might shake me but you ain't never gonna get free a him.

[EARLY *persists in the offer of the map and cap. MORE THUNDER. After a pause,* MARLE *takes the map.* EARLY *seems disappointed.*]

EARLY: Well... Guess I can't blame you for having spunk.

[*After another pause,* MARLE *begins to tear the map into smaller and smaller pieces.* EARLY *grins.* MARLE *tosses the scraps into the rising wind and a light snow begins to fall as if brought on by the toss of the "confetti."* EARLY *puts the cap on the boy's head.*]

EARLY: Looks good on you. Better on you than on me.

[MARLE *starts away from him.*]

EARLY: You tell that old woman Madge I'll be lookin out for her. You mind her, boy. She's a good woman... And remember, get that left bay fixed up. Stay away from those franchise men.

SNOW begins to fall more heavily, falling on the audience as well.

EARLY: And take this... you're gonna need it come winter.

[EARLY *tosses the blanket into the air right over* MARLE's *head. LOUD CLAP of THUNDER. BRIGHT FLASH OF LIGHT. BLACKOUT.*]

THE END

CASSATT
&
DEGAS

LIST OF CHARACTERS

(in order of appearance)

DRIVER	ZOE
MARY CASSATT	BERTHE MORISOT
LYDIA CASSATT	EUGENE MANET
FLOOR MANAGER	EDOUARD MANET
CLAUDE MONET	STABLE HAND
ASSISTANT	BERTHA PALMER
MEISSONNIER	SARA HALLOWELL
JURORS	GENDARME
CAMILLE PISSARRO	JULIE MORISOT (*as a* TODDLER)
EDGAR DEGAS	CAMILLE
PAUL DURAND-RUEL	YOUNG MODEL
THERESE	DOCTOR
LOUISE ELDER	HENRY HAVEMAYER
AUGUSTE RENOIR	JULIE MORISOT (*as a* YOUNG WOMAN)
MATHILDE	MODEL
PHILLIPS	NEIGHBOR WOMAN

EXT. NEAR THE PALACE OF INDUSTRY [PARIS, 1874] - DAY

[A "grid-lock" of horse-drawn carriages and wagons, many loaded with huge historical paintings. Stymied Teamsters curse and shout. On equally congested sidewalks, PAINTERS and their HIRED HANDS tote framed canvases up the street. In a city consumed with art, this is the big day for its legions of painters – of 7000 works submitted, only 2500 will be chosen for the French Academy's official Salon.

SUPER: "SUBMISSION DAY"

"FRENCH ACADEMY OF FINE ARTS - PARIS 1874"

A monstrously overloaded WAGON has stopped all traffic. The old MARE in harness will not and cannot move. Spewing curses, her DRIVER *climbs down, undoes his belt and begins to methodically beat the Mare. Some among the passing crowd object, others jeer, but no one risks intervention. The Mare strains in her traces but she's too weak to rear or move. Then…*

Two impeccably dressed women in their 30s – MARY CASSATT *and her more fragile older sister,* LYDIA *– emerge from the crowd.* MARY *is carrying a small, gilt-framed oil painting, a portrait of a woman.]*

CASSATT *[to the* DRIVER*]*: Stop that! Stop it!!

[The DRIVER *doesn't miss a beat.* CASSATT *shoves her painting into* LYDIA's *hands and charges the* DRIVER.*]*

LYDIA: Mary, don't!

[Ignoring LYDIA, CASSATT *grabs the* DRIVER's *arm in mid-blow.]*

CASSATT: I said stop!!!

[The startled DRIVER *wheels on her.* MARY *clutches the belt. As they eye-ball each other, passersby taunt the* DRIVER.*]*

LYDIA: Mary… Let it go.

DRIVER: Out of my way.

[With a violent tug, the DRIVER *yanks the belt from* CASSATT's *hands. When he winds up for another swipe,* CASSATT *steps between him and the horse. With steel in eye and spine…]*

CASSATT: Don't you dare.

[The blocked Teamsters continue screaming. Some bystanders cheer, others hiss. The stymied DRIVER *rails…]*

DRIVER: What am I supposed to do?!

*[*CASSATT *looks to the horse, back to the* DRIVER, *then…]*

CASSATT: How much? For the mare. *[off his look]* I'll give you thirty francs.

[He "poofs" at the notion.]

CASSATT *[CONT'D]*: That's a month's wages for you.

*[*CASSATT *drops the reins and begins a thorough and expert examination of the animal – the woman knows horses.]*

CASSATT *[CONT'D]*: Shin-splints.
DRIVER: Sixty.

[While checking the mare's teeth and gums…]

CASSATT: I'll go forty. Final offer.
DRIVER: Forty-five.
CASSATT: Lydia, pay the man.
LYDIA: But…
CASSATT: Just give him the money.

[LYDIA *digs money from her purse;* CASSATT *unharnesses the Mare. The* DRIVER *counts the cash delighted with his bargain.*]

DRIVER: I would have settled for forty.
CASSATT: And I would have gone fifty. Good day.

[CASSATT *leads away the Mare. On-lookers gossip and point. In B.G., workmen push the overloaded wagon off to the side.*]

EXT. FURTHER DOWN THE STREET - CONTINUOUS

[*Passersby ogle the eccentric image of two seemingly proper ladies –* LYDIA *carrying a painting in her gloved hands,* CASSATT *leading a bedraggled limping Mare.*]

CASSATT: If it makes you feel better, I'll take the money from my art account.
LYDIA: Don't be ridiculous.
CASSATT: Father only agreed to pay living expenses. No paints, no frills. Definitely no horses.
LYDIA: That fifty francs was set aside for your new frames.
CASSATT: I'll build the frames myself. *[off* LYDIA*'s look]* I'll learn.
LYDIA: And where are we supposed to stable this nag? In our parlor?!
CASSATT: We'll find a place. And I'll groom her myself.
LYDIA: When?
CASSATT: When I'm not painting.
LYDIA: You're always painting!
CASSATT: For God's sake, Lydia, what was I supposed to do?!

[*After a few more paces…*]

LYDIA: Held out for thirty francs.

[MARY *catches* LYDIA'*s tight little grin. The Mare whinnies.*]

CASSATT [*grinning*]: You're terrible.

EXT. PALACE OF INDUSTRY - DAY

[*At the entrance to the hall, blue-bloused WORKMEN wrestle with paintings, some balanced precariously on wheeled barrows. PAINTERS shout at their charges. Workmen shout at one another. The Creator of a huge historical/allegorical oil painting, harangues the four Workmen wrestling with his ungainly canvas. The doorway is utterly jammed as...* CASSATT, LYDIA, *and the Mare approach.* MARY *is intrigued by the chaos;* LYDIA *is overwhelmed.* CASSATT *plants the reins in a startled Workman's hands, slipping him a few francs.*]

CASSATT: Look after my horse. We shouldn't be long.

[CASSATT *grabs her painting, then plunges into the throng. With* CASSATT, THE CAMERA *slides through the crush of bodies, blouses, frames, and pictures into...*]

INT. THE EXHIBITION HALL - CONTINUOUS

[*A tumult. The cavernous hall is packed with yet more blue-bloused Workmen, Painters, white-bloused museum-keepers, and haute bourgeois JURORS moving as a pack. As* CASSATT *and* LYDIA *press deeper into the crowd...*]

CASSATT'S VIEW

[*White-bloused Keepers shuttle paintings out for appraisal by the Jury, then remove them in opposite directions depending on their fate – accepted or rejected.*
A howl of protest attends the rejection of a gargantuan historical painting. The Jurors, in whispered conference, revise their decision.]

The Keepers reverse direction, hauling the painting toward the wing holding "the accepted."]

FLOOR MANAGER *[to* CASSATT*, pointing]*: You! Yes, you! Over there!

[A white-bloused Keeper grabs CASSATT*'s painting and heads for another part of the hall. She pursues.* LYDIA *follows.*
CASSATT *is jostled into a red-roped barricade beyond which the Jurors have gathered.*
CASSATT*'s painting, a well-drawn portrait of an older woman ("Portrait of Madame Cortier" also known as "Ida"), has been planted on one of the many easels set up in this wing. The Jury is passing judgment – but on which painting?!*
CASSATT *crosses her fingers. Holds her breath. In a flash, a Keeper removes her painting and rushes off with it.]*

CASSATT: Excuse me! Excuse me!! Where are you taking my painting?!

*[*CASSATT*'s painting is instantly replaced on its easel by another – a shockingly bright landscape. The new painting causes a stir.* CASSATT*, riveted, is drawn back to the ropes.*
The brightly colored landscape ("Impression: Sunrise") is apparently the work of the tall handsome man, CLAUDE MONET *(34), now jostled next to* CASSATT*. An* ASSISTANT *to the* FLOOR MANAGER *shoves a form into* CASSATT*'s hand, barking orders.]*

ASSISTANT: Name. Name of work. Description of work. School. And sign.
MONET: Congratulations. You're in.

[Then, a bit sharply when it seems she doesn't understand…]

MONET: You've been accepted!

[While distractedly filling out the form…]

CASSATT: Apparently so.
ASSISTANT *[snatching back the form]*: Foreigners!

[MEISSONIER, *one of the plumpest of the Jurors, one with a particularly superior air, brays with vicious laughter as he turns his attention to* MONET's *landscape.* MONET *clutches as the other jurors, painters, and keepers join the burlesque.*]

MEISSONIER: Is that the sun?! Or a fried egg!!
JUROR: Who is responsible for this travesty?!
OTHER JUROR *[reading]*: Claude Monet.

[MONET *stiffens defiantly as the Jurors eyes zero in on him.* CASSATT *puts painter and painting together.*]

OTHERS IN CROWD: Take it away! Hide it! Burn it!!
MEISSONIER *[Zeus passing judgment]*: Refused!

[*Applause. Some cheers. A few derisive whistles.*]

CASSATT: Refused?! That's impossible!
MONET *[turning away]*: I think not.

[*Just as the RED-INKED STAMP ("R" for Refused) is poised over the frame of* MONET's *landscape,* CASSATT *steps past the rope.*]

CASSATT: Wait! You're making a mistake!

[*This unheard-of behavior stops everyone dead. Shocked whispers as* CASSATT *intervenes. Among those taking an interest are two gentlemen,* EDGAR DEGAS *(45) and* PAUL DURAND-RUEL *(37), who observe from a distance.*]

MEISSONIER: Who is this woman?

[*We overhear a* JUROR *whisper the word, "American."*]

MEISSONIER *[enough said]*: Ah.
CASSATT: How can you accept mine but not his?

[Mean laughter.]

MEISSONIER *[dripping condescension]*: Obviously, my dear, you do not understand our procedures. In this hall it is every man for himself!

[General laughter. Off MEISSONIER's *signal, the* ASSISTANT *stamps the frame of* MONET's *painting with a big red "R."*
MONET *retrieves his painting, trying to maintain his dignity despite the public humiliation. He leaves under a flurry of catcalls, laughter, and abuse.]*

CASSATT *[to* MEISSONIER & JURORS*]*: You find this amusing?!
MEISSONIER: Unfortunately, no. The experience is unforgettable, like an utterly indigestible meal. The nausea lasts and lasts, alas.

[More sycophantic laughter. The Jury moves on. CASSATT, *not-so-delicately ushered back behind the ropes, spots* MONET *at the doors, battling the incoming tide.* CASSATT *pursues.]*

EXT. PALACE OF INDUSTRY - CONTINUOUS

*[*CASSATT, *struggling, finally breaks from the crowd into the open. She side-steps another quartet of workmen hauling yet another huge historical/allegorical painting into the hall.]*

CASSATT'S VIEW

*[*MONET, *painting under his arm, stomps off. A prematurely white-bearded man,* CAMILLE PISSARRO (44), *also carrying a painting stamped with an "R," falls in alongside, tosses a sympathetic arm over* MONET's *shoulder.* MONET *shrugs it off.*
The Workman plants the Mare's tether in CASSATT's *hands.]*

LYDIA: Why must you always make a scene? First the horse, now this!
CASSATT: I never make scenes.

[As the two women walk off leading the old horse, we see…

DEGAS *and* DURAND-RUEL *behind them, just outside the doorway, curiously observing them.]*

DURAND-RUEL: Perhaps she's an equestion.

*[*DEGAS *charges back inside. After a sigh,* DURAND-RUEL *follows.]*

INT. EXHIBITION HALL OF THE SALON - DAY

*[*DEGAS, *hands bracing his lower back, rocks slowly on his heels, studying* CASSATT's *"Ida."* DURAND-RUEL *is interested but not nearly so much as* DEGAS. *Then, suddenly pointing…]*

DEGAS: Finally! Someone who sees as I do!

*[*DEGAS *moves closer, focuses on the signature and reads:]*

DEGAS *[CONT'D]*: Mary Cassatt. … That's…
DURAND-RUEL *[checking the form]*: American.
DEGAS: Impossible!

[He snatches the form which CASSATT *filled out, confirms the information, slaps it back in place, then returns to the painting for a closer look.* DURAND-RUEL *studies* DEGAS.]*

DEGAS: She actually seems to care for the old crone. Look at the line of that jaw. … Such a waste. She'll meet a man, get married, lock away her brushes, then spend the rest of her life making babies and needlepoint.

*[*DEGAS *stomps away, shouldering past other gallery hounds.]*

DEGAS: It's despicable! Tragic! Absurd!!

*[*DURAND-RUEL *lingers to study the painting. He shrugs, unimpressed, then follows* DEGAS *out.]*

EXT. STREET NEAR THE CASSATT HOUSE - DAY

[CASSATT *and* LYDIA *with the Mare behind them.*]

CASSATT: I'm sorry if I embarrassed you.
LYDIA: No you're not. But at least we're here and not in Philadelphia.
CASSATT: And what is that supposed to mean?
LYDIA: A woman's reputation is all she has.
CASSATT: The only reputation I care about is what they say about my paintings. The rest is irrelevant.
LYDIA: There are other things in life besides making pictures.
CASSATT: Not to me.

[LYDIA*'s hurt, angry, embarrassed.* CASSATT *tries to soothe.*]

CASSATT: Lydia… I promise to behave if you'll promise not to smother me.
LYDIA: I'm tired. I need to get home.

INT. A STABLE - DAY

[*A STABLE HAND mucks stalls.* CASSATT - *sketch pad and charcoals stashed near the open doorway - grooms the Mare which, having been ill-treated for so long, shies.*]

CASSATT: Shhh. Yes yes, I know how it feels.

[*At the door,* THERESE, *an awkward young woman with a great body, spots* CASSATT*'s art supplies and enters.*]

THERESE: Madame? Do you need a model today?
CASSATT: No. And I'm a Miss not a Madame.

[THERESE, *not noticing the Stable Hand, begins to undress.*]

CASSATT *[CONT'D]*: What are you doing?!
THERESE: They say I have excellent bones. For life study. Two francs an hour.

CASSATT: Please. Put your dress back on.

THERESE: I can hold difficult poses and I never complain.

[CASSATT regards her, then slaps the grooming brush into her hand.]

CASSATT: In that case, I'll pay you three francs to groom my horse. ... I'm sure you're a very good model, but today I need a groom.

[Begrudgingly, THERESE begins brushing the Mare. CASSATT gives some instruction. The girl continues. When THERESE rubs the Mare's leg, the horse rears and whinnies in pain.]

CASSATT: Careful. Her leg's very tender.

[THERESE continues brushing. The girl does indeed have interesting musculature. Sweat glistens on her skin.
Shafts of sunlight, motes of light in the hay dust. The image grabs CASSATT. She begins to sketch the girl at work.]

THERESE: You've cheated me, Miss.

CASSATT: How so?

THERESE: For three francs you've gotten a model and a groom.

CASSATT: You're modeling for me as a groom.

[The girl brightens with the change in job description. CASSATT grins, continues sketching.]

EXT. THE STABLE - DAY

[Later. As CASSATT rushes off, in B.G., we see DEGAS, his back to us, conferring with the Stable Hand who directs him toward the stable. Just as DEGAS turns our way, CASSATT turns the corner. They just miss one another.]

[BACK TO] INT. THE STABLE - CONTINUOUS

[THERESE smoothes a discarded drawing which CASSATT has left

behind, examines it closely, then tries matching her former pose to the one in the drawing, the brush a mere prop. DEGAS *watches from the doorway, amused, then approaches…]*

DEGAS: There is no more perfect line in nature than the curve of a thigh.

[He picks up the drawing. Examines it. Compares drawing and subject. THERESE *pulls her dress taut against her thigh, strokes her leg.* DEGAS's *eye follows her hand.]*

THERESE: They say I have excellent bone structure. For five francs –
DEGAS: A thigh, my dear, is a thigh, regardless of species. And a filly, a filly. I believe this is Miss Cassatt's horse, which makes you…
THERESE: Her model. Miss Cassatt's gone for the day. Who shall I say's called, a painter or a gentleman?
DEGAS: I wasn't aware the two were mutually exclusive. … Both.

*[*DEGAS *lingers a moment longer, then starts to go. With the drawing.* THERESE *gives chase and snatches it back from him.]*

DEGAS: Oh. Yes. Sorry.

EXT. TRAIN STATION - DAY

[A train has just arrived, the platform crowded. Stepping down from a carriage is LOUISE ELDER *(20), a rich young American woman. She scans the platform then spots…*

CASSATT *and* LYDIA *rushing toward her.* LOUISE *rushes to greet them. She gives* LYDIA *a quick hug then, bubbling with excitement, embraces* CASSATT. *(Ad lib greetings) Then…]*

LOUISE: I can't believe I'm finally here!
LYDIA *[scanning the platform]*: Where's your mother?
LOUISE: Still in London. I pestered her so much she finally let me come alone. I want to see everything!
CASSATT: Then we'd better get started!

[CASSATT takes LOUISE by the arm and rushes her off.]

EXT. CARRIAGE - PARIS STREET - DAY

[CASSATT, LOUISE, and LYDIA in an open carriage. LOUISE's luggage is strapped into the boot.]

LOUISE: Lydia's letter said you just got another painting into the Salon.
LYDIA *[with pride]*: Mary's portrait of Madame Clothier.
LOUISE: Congratulations!

[When CASSATT shrugs off the compliment...]

LYDIA: It's an exceptional painting.
CASSATT: It's perfectly acceptable.
LYDIA: Everyone else seems to think it's a major accomplishment.
CASSATT: I'm sick of paintings that look like they've been dipped in brown varnish. Including my own!

[Then, after a pause...]

CASSATT: Now if you want to see some real paintings – Driver!

[SMASH CUT TO] EXT. DURAND-RUEL GALLERY - DAY

[The carriage pulls to a stop. CASSATT leaps out. She hustles LOUISE to the gallery window where DEGAS's "Ballet Rehearsal on Stage" is on display. CASSATT burbles with excitement.]

CASSATT: In the last few months there's been work like this popping up all over Paris. Such light, and color! *[taking LOUISE's arm]* There's more inside.
LYDIA *[from the carriage]*: Mary? Can't we do this some other time? Louise must be exhausted.
LOUISE: I'm fine. Really.
LYDIA: Then I'll wait for you out here.

[CASSATT hurries LOUISE into...]

INT. DURAND-RUEL GALLERY - CONTINUOUS

[CASSATT plants LOUISE in front of MONET's "Sunrise."]

CASSATT: Well? … What do you think?
LOUISE: It's certainly… different.

[CASSATT draws LOUISE along to a landscape by PISSARRO.]

CASSATT: The color simply jumps off the brush, doesn't it?

[DURAND-RUEL, the proprietor, watches from the sidelines. CASSATT seems intoxicated by the paintings, but LOUISE keeps glancing out the window to LYDIA and the waiting carriage.]

LOUISE: Lydia seems… tired.

[CASSATT turns. When she sees LYDIA in the open carriage, shielding her eyes from the sun, CASSATT sobers.]

CASSATT: She tries so hard to keep up. For weeks she'll be fine, then…
[with regret] Maybe we should go.

[CASSATT takes LOUISE by the arm. DURAND-RUEL graciously holds open the door for them as they exit.]

DURAND-RUEL'S *VIEW FROM THE GALLERY WINDOW*

[LOUISE climbs back into the carriage. CASSATT lingers for a moment in front of the DEGAS painting in the window.]

INT. CASSATT HOUSE - CASSATT'S STUDIO - DAY

[CASSATT builds a frame. Her carpentry is precise. LOUISE examines CASSATT's unframed impressionist painting of "Poppies in a Field."]

LOUISE: It almost feels as if you painted this right out in the field.

[CASSATT, *pleased by* LOUISE'*s remark, takes the painting and begins fitting it with the newly finished frame.*]

CASSATT: I've tried painting in the open air but it's not for me. I feel more comfortable here in the studio.

[*After sanding an edge, she hammers home the frame.*]

LOUISE: Since when do you make your own frames?
CASSATT: Since we got the horse. [*off her look*] Long story.

[CASSATT *sets the framed painting on an easel.* LOUISE *admires it while* CASSATT *begins gathering up her drawing supplies.*]

INT. CASSATT HOUSE - FRONT HALL - DAY

[CASSATT *toting her sketchpad and supplies, a smock over her arm, is halfway out the door, impatiently waiting for* LOUISE *to finish putting on her hat.* LYDIA *appears.*]

LYDIA: Mary? Where are you taking her now?
CASSATT: There's a painting of a woman I need to study. You're welcome to come along if you want.
LYDIA: We've got tickets for the ballet.
LOUISE: In that case, maybe we shouldn't –
CASSATT: We'll be home in plenty of time.

[CASSATT *takes off.* LOUISE *gives* LYDIA *a parting kiss then rushes after her. Their energy is exhausting to* LYDIA.]

INT. A GALLERY OF THE LOUVRE - DAY

[CASSATT *- utterly absorbed in her work, mouth tight with concentration - makes a study of the Madonna and Infant in a Baroque Nativity painting by an Old Master.*
LOUISE *strolls off to look at other paintings. Glancing back, she notices A* MAN *sidle up behind* CASSATT *and lean in over her*

shoulder. Through LOUISE's *eyes, we see that the man is…* DEGAS. DEGAS *compares study and original.* CASSATT *feels him there but doesn't acknowledge his presence. Finally…]*

DEGAS: I think the shepherd on the left is a far more interesting subject.

[CASSATT *studiously ignores him.]*

DEGAS: You've found the structure of the face, but the hands…
CASSATT: I'm studying faces, not hands.

[But then, taking up the challenge, CASSATT *turns her attention to the hands. She works, rubs out, tries again.]*

DEGAS *[with a twinkle]*: Now perhaps you can appreciate why we call them Masters.

[When CASSATT *finally turns to him,* DEGAS *is already walking away. She goes back to work, dismissing the interruption.* DEGAS *glances back at her.* LOUISE *rejoins* CASSATT.]

LOUISE: Who was that?
CASSATT: Just another opinionated man offering unsolicited advice.

[They watch DEGAS *walk away.* CASSATT *returns to her study. But she's distracted.]*

CASSATT: Is he still there?

*[*LOUISE *steals a glance.* DEGAS *loiters nearby.]*

LOUISE: Yes.
CASSATT: What's he doing?
LOUISE: Watching us, pretending not to. What do you think he wants?
CASSATT: Offhand I can think of half a dozen things, none worth repeating.

*[*CASSATT's *concentration is shot. When she steals another glance,*

DEGAS *is gone. A flicker of disappointment.]*

EXT. DURAND-RUEL GALLERY, PARIS - DAY

[Later. CASSATT *and* LOUISE, *returning home, lugging* CASSATT's *supplies, stop to look at* DEGAS's *"Dance Rehearsal on Stage" still in the window.* CASSATT *shields her eyes to cut the glare off the glass.* DURAND-RUEL, *locking up, spots them.]*

DURAND-RUEL: Back again?
CASSATT: It's not good for the pigment to be exposed to so much sun.
DURAND-RUEL: It hasn't done much for business either.
CASSATT: You should take it out of the window.
DURAND-RUEL: For five hundred francs I'd be more than happy to oblige you.
CASSATT: If I had 500 francs, I would.

*[*DURAND-RUEL, *noting her supplies, sighs.]*

DURAND-RUEL: Isn't that always the way? Those who know can't buy; those who buy, don't know.
LOUISE *[innocently]*: I have the money.

*[*DURAND-RUEL *is charmed and amused.* CASSATT *holds his gaze. As* DURAND-RUEL *unlocks the door and invites them in...]*

LOUISE: I promised Father I wouldn't bring home more paintings and here I am, three days in Paris!
CASSATT: Just blame it on me.

[Pushing through the DANCERS in DEGAS's *painting, we...]*

[DISSOLVE TO] INT. THE THEATRE - NIGHT

[BALLERINAS on stage, dancing. Music by Tchaikovsky.
IN A LOGE. CASSATT, LYDIA, *and* LOUISE. LYDIA *concentrates on the stage spectacle. (See* CASSATT *painting)* LOUISE's *eyes roam the audience.* MARY *studies her sister's hand gripping the rail. She makes*

a discreet sketch-note on the cover of her program. LOUISE *nudges her. Points below.* CASSATT *leans to the edge of the box and looks down on…* DEGAS, *unaccompanied, sitting near the front of the house, enraptured by the dancers, a small sketchpad on his lap. Glancing up, he's surprised to find* CASSATT *and* LOUISE *staring at him.* CASSATT *averts her eyes.* LOUISE *whispers…]*

LOUISE: Isn't that the man from the Louvre?

*[*LYDIA *overhears. Looks down into the lower seats. Sees…* DEGAS *staring back up at them. He holds his gaze for a long moment before shifting his attention back to the stage.* LYDIA *looks to her sister.* CASSATT *focuses on the dancers.]*

EXT. STAGE DOOR - NIGHT

[After the show. CASSATT, LYDIA, *and* LOUISE *make their way through the crush of people in the alley behind the theatre. Passing the open stage door,* CASSATT *sees…* DANCERS *mingling with their "patrons," gentlemen in evening dress. Among them, she also sees…* DEGAS, *engulfed by a cluster of young Dancers. One of the Dancers playfully chucks* DEGAS *under the chin with the toe of her ballet slipper, then skips off through the open stage door past the three women.* DEGAS *discovers…* CASSATT, LYDIA, *and* LOUISE *watching him.* DEGAS *bows to them. The eye contact between* CASSATT *and* DEGAS *lingers too long for* LYDIA's *liking. Grabbing her sister's arm, she hurries her along.* DEGAS *escapes the clutch of dancers, rushes to the door just in time to see* CASSATT *glancing back at him.]*

INT. CASSATT'S STUDIO - NIGHT

*[*DEGAS's *painting on its easel catches ambient light in the otherwise dark studio. Suddenly, the flare of a gaslight.* CASSATT, *in her nightgown, approaches the painting, studies it for a long moment, then pulls up a chair. Chin on her arms, she loses herself*

in the painting and her thoughts.
LYDIA *appears, in B.G., at the partly open door. She watches her sister for a long moment, then approaches.]*

CASSATT: I couldn't sleep.
LYDIA: Who was that man at the theatre?

*[*CASSATT *hesitates, then points to the painting.]*

LYDIA: Is that why you made Louise buy it?
CASSATT: No.

*[*LYDIA *pulls up a chair, sits. Finally...]*

CASSATT: I always knew that if I wanted to be a serious painter I'd have to be here, in Paris. Now I'm absolutely sure of it. ... My God, he's good.
LYDIA: So are you.

*[*CASSATT *shrugs off the compliment.]*

LYDIA: But I worry that if you don't make time for other things in life...

*[*CASSATT*'s intense focus on the painting shuts* LYDIA *out.]*

LYDIA: Well, I can see that now's not the time to discuss this.

*[*LYDIA *exits.* CASSATT *barely glances at the door.}*

INT. THE CAFE DE LA NOUVELLE ATHENES - DAY

*[*DEGAS, *having already drunk too much too early in the day, holds court at a table filled with his colleagues.]*

DEGAS: No artist who considers himself independent should give a damn what the Academics think!
PISSARRO: No Salon, no sales; no sales, no –
DEGAS: We don't need the Salon, what we need is conviction!

MONET: What we need is more wine.

PISSARRO: And the money to pay for it.

DEGAS: Why must you always think like a Jewish peasant!

[Albeit good-natured, the laughter and remark sting PISSARRO.*]*

DURAND-RUEL *[big entrance]*: Waiter! Two more bottles!

[At the table, he flashes a thick wad of franc notes.]

DURAND-RUEL: Today Degas buys for everyone.

*[*DURAND-RUEL *throws the money in front of* DEGAS. *Explains.]*

DURAND-RUEL *[CONT'D]*: Compliments of his new collectors. Your "Ballet Rehearsal" is gone. Sold!

MONET: If you'd have put mine in the window –

RENOIR: Who bought it?

DURAND-RUEL: Two Americans.

MONET: Americans?

DURAND-RUEL: Young women.

VARIOUS: Who are they? Are they rich?

RENOIR: Besides "young," are they beautiful?

PISSARRO: Renoir only wants to know if they're fat.

MONET *[to* DURAND-RUEL*]*: If they were buying, why didn't you push mine?

DEGAS: Unlike Renoir, Monet only wants to know if their wallets are fat.
[to MONET*]* Perhaps these young ladies simply prefer works of substance.

MONET: Ugly women drinking absinthe or sewing hems? If that's your idea of substance –

DEGAS: Your aversion to humanity is noted, sir, and humanity will, I assure you, return the favor. Come, Paul!

*[*DEGAS, *rising, tosses cash on the table then starts for the street.* DURAND-RUEL *hesitates only a moment before following.]*

MONET: Degas doesn't paint, he draws.

RENOIR: Who cares, as long as he keeps paying for the drinks. I hope he sells everything.

INT. CASSATT'S STUDIO - DAY

[A sun-filled room. Therese, dressed respectably, arranges flowers. CASSATT, *in a paint-spattered smock, readjusts the pose.* DEGAS's *"Dancers" has been hung on the wall;* CASSATT's *"Poppies" sits on the floor beneath it.*
MATHILDE, CASSATT's *maid, enters with* DURAND-RUEL *and* DEGAS.]

MATHILDE: Miss Cassatt?

*[*CASSATT *seems not to have heard. She continues working.* DEGAS *makes a bee-line for his painting.]*

DURAND-RUEL: We didn't mean to interrupt you.
CASSATT *[still painting]*: Of course you did. Otherwise you wouldn't have come.

[When she finally turns, with a disarming smile, she discovers DEGAS *stooped over, studying her "Poppies."]*

DURAND-RUEL: May I introduce my colleague, Monsieur Edgar Hilaire Germain –
CASSATT: Degas. Yes, I know.

*[*DEGAS, *still a little drunk, lifts* CASSATT's *"Poppies."]*

DEGAS: These figures have no hands!
CASSATT: Nor the poppies heads. Yet you see both heads and hands. They are –
DEGAS *[annoyed]*: Impressions. Yes, yes, of course. May I ask where you painted this?
CASSATT: To your left. Under that skylight.
DEGAS: Then there's hope for you yet.

*[*DEGAS *hands the painting off to* DURAND-RUEL, *then turns his attention to* CASSATT's *other works.]*

DEGAS: You studied…

[CASSATT snatches her painting from DURAND-RUEL, setting it aside, face to the wall.]

CASSATT: At the Pennsylvania Academy. When I first arrived in Paris I studied with Gerome. But not for long.

DEGAS: Nor slavishly.

[DURAND-RUEL picks back up CASSATT's "Poppies." As he compares CASSATT's brushwork with that of DEGAS' "Dancers"…]

DEGAS *[CONT'D]*: When I saw you working in the Louvre…

CASSATT: You should have introduced yourself. … Why didn't you?

[No reply.]

THERESE: He came to the stable looking for you. Just last week.

[DEGAS flashes an angry look at THERESE. THERESE begins gathering her things.]

CASSATT: What do you think you're doing?

THERESE: It's been five hours, Miss.

CASSATT: Has it?

[It has. CASSATT "uncramps" her hand.]

THERESE: For a franc I'll wash and iron this dress.

CASSATT: Fine. Tomorrow. Same time.

THERESE *[exiting, happily]*: Thank you, Miss.

DURAND-RUEL: You spoil her.

[CASSATT poofs the idea, sets aside her brush and palette, wipes her hands with a spirit-soaked rag, then extends her hand to DEGAS in greeting – American style.]

CASSATT: Welcome to my studio.

[DEGAS takes her hand. He seems about to kiss it, Parisian style, but then studies it. Almost clinically.]

DEGAS: The human hand is so difficult to render.

[He turns her hand palm-up, tracing a line with a fingertip. She flushes. Turning her hand back over again...]

DEGAS: A great painter could shut himself up for a lifetime and do nothing but indicate fingernails!

CASSATT: I avoid hands - when possible. Too much history in them.

DEGAS: Precisely!

[When she extracts her hand, DEGAS grabs DURAND-RUEL's.]

DEGAS: See these! Maps of avarice! The trademark of a dealer! If you want to avoid history, then paint the hands of infants!

[He releases DURAND-RUEL's hand. A charged silence. DEGAS finally breaks off by turning his attention to CASSATT's easel and her painting-in-progress of THERESE. Finally...]

DEGAS: Drawing, my dear, is everything.

CASSATT: Color is simply drawing in depth. Isn't it?

DEGAS *[slightly flustered]*: Yes. I suppose it is.

[She flashes a smile then busies herself with her brushes. He can't take his eyes off her. When she turns to him...]

DEGAS: Au revoir, Miss Cassatt.

[He bows, then abruptly exits. Once DEGAS is gone...]

DURAND-RUEL: He so rarely drinks that when he does it goes straight to his head.

CASSATT: And tongue. But I suspect he's just as blunt without the wine.

[DURAND-RUEL writes a name and address on the back of one of his

business calling cards.]

DURAND-RUEL: The address of his studio.
DEGAS *[OC]*: Paul!!
DURAND-RUEL *[handing her the card]*: He seems quite taken with you.

[CASSATT moves to the window. DURAND-RUEL bids farewell, then lingers at the door. CASSATT looks down onto the street.]

DURAND-RUEL: Odd, he didn't say a word about his own painting.
CASSATT: Oh, but he did.

HER VIEW – THROUGH THE WINDOW

[DEGAS on the curb, staring back up at her. LYDIA and LOUISE, returning from market, side-step him. DURAND-RUEL joins DEGAS, takes his arm, ushers him away. DEGAS keeps looking back over his shoulder at CASSATT, pontificating exuberantly to DURAND-RUEL. CASSATT leans closer to the glass to keep them in view.]

INT. THE CASSATT DINING ROOM - NIGHT

[MR. PHILLIPS, an American in his late 50s, clearly invited by LYDIA as a potential match for MARY, holds forth. LYDIA seems "enthralled." LOUISE and the other GENTLEMEN at table are politely attentive. CASSATT checks her tongue.]

PHILLIPS: Europe is drowning in a cesspool of moral depravity. Its people are so consumed by the pursuit of fashion and frivolous pleasures, they lack all energy for commerce! I look at Paris and see decadence!

[PHILLIPS takes a moment to chew. Each passing moment brings CASSATT closer to a boil. LYDIA monitors her closely.]

PHILLIPS *[CONT'D]*: An obsession with style at the expense of substance and industry. I tell you, I literally shudder at life in this city!
CASSATT: So do I.

[Though not at all the way he means. LOUISE *stifles a laugh.]*

PHILLIPS: What respectable woman does not?!
CASSATT: Indeed.

[While refilling PHILLIPS' *wine glass...]*

CASSATT: Give me a gray metropolis humming with machines, a city stripped of its poets and painters and its ladies in wonderfully silly hats. A city like...

[Having filled his glass to the rim, she carefully adds one more drop – surface tension alone keeps the wine from spilling. She then abruptly raises her glass...]

CASSATT: Pittsburgh!

[When PHILLIPS *hesitates...]*

CASSATT: Surely Mr. Phillips, you'll drink to your morally robust home town?!

[Shamed into it, PHILLIPS *ever so carefully lifts his glass. Bordeaux sloshes over the rim, down his white shirt, onto the white tablecloth and into his lap.]*

LYDIA: Mathilde?!!
CASSATT: I'll get her.

*[*CASSATT *leaps up, rushes off.* LOUISE *follows her into...]*

INT. HALLWAY OUTSIDE DINING ROOM - CONTINUOUS

*[*LOUISE *can barely control her laughter.* CASSATT, *having barely escaped suffocation, erupts...]*

CASSATT: Dear God, where does Lydia find these people?!!

[CASSATT, *infected by* LOUISE, *starts to grin.*]

CASSATT: Can you imagine being saddled for life with a man like –

[*The pantry door swings open revealing…*]

LOUISE: Mr. PHILLIPS!

[*… in the doorway, daubing wine stains with a napkin.*]

PHILLIPS: Your sister warned me that I might find you a spirited woman.
CASSATT: Moi?
PHILLIPS: Fascinating evening.

[PHILLIPS *turns to leave, passing* LYDIA *in the doorway.*]

CASSATT [*off* LYDIA'*s glare*]: If you'll excuse me….

INT. CASSATT'S STUDIO - NIGHT

[CASSATT *enters, angrily strips off her dinner gown, tosses it over a chair. Draping a smock loosely over her shoulders, she grabs charcoal and paper, finds a spot on the floor and begins working furiously.* LYDIA *enters, rigid with anger.*]

LYDIA: I hope you're satisfied.
CASSATT: For God's sakes, Lydia, I'm thirty-five years old! almost a spinster - which is exactly what I want to be! I do not want to be married!
LYDIA: Don't say that.

INT. CASSATT HOUSE - BOTTOM OF THE STAIRS - CONTINUOUS

[LOUISE *and* MATHILDE *listening to the argument.*]

CASSATT [*OC*]: Why not?! It's true. This charade of hurling me at these vile old -
LYDIA [*OC*]: Alden Phillips –

[BACK TO] CASSATT'S STUDIO - CONTINUOUS

[CASSATT and LYDIA at each other.]

LYDIA: Happens to be a well-respected gentleman of means.
CASSATT: The man's a pompous windbag! The whole thing is ugly and demeaning!

[When LYDIA huffs...]

CASSATT: If he's such a prize, why don't you marry him?!
LYDIA: You know perfectly well why I can't.

[CASSATT instantly regrets what she's just said.]

CASSATT: I'm so sorry. That was thoughtless and cruel. Lydia...

[LYDIA avoids her touch. Her eyes well with tears.]

CASSATT: I just want to be left alone to do my work. Is that so awful?
LYDIA: Other women manage to paint and still maintain respectable lives.
CASSATT: Amateurs painting watercolors on Sunday afternoons! And I do not need a husband to be respectable! Just because you can't marry –
LYDIA: My illness is my burden, not yours.
CASSATT: Then do us both a favor and stop herding these chamber of commerce Americans through our lives!

[LYDIA rushes from the room.]

BOTTOM OF THE STAIRS - CONTINUOUS

[LOUISE and MATHILDE see LYDIA in tears at the top of the stairs. The door to CASSATT's studio slams behind her. LYDIA flees to her own room. Another slam.]

[BACK TO] CASSATT'S STUDIO - CONTINUOUS

[CASSATT *retrieves her sketchpad. Goes back to work. A tear forms. She angrily wipes it away with the back of her hand. She wills herself to concentrate.*]

[DISSOLVE TO] *CASSATT'S STUDIO - LATER*

[CASSATT *has been working for hours trying to capture the details of hands in drawings. Her own fingers have cramped; her hands are black with charcoal. She is stiff, sore, surrounded by sketches: hands, wrists, fingers, nails.*
CASSATT *goes to her stove - the tea has boiled down to a brackish paste. She takes a closer look at her own hands.*
Her eye lands on DURAND-RUEL's *card, still lying on a table. She turns it over. Studies it while wiping her hands…*
A moment of decision.]

INT. CASSATT HOUSE - DOWNSTAIRS HALLWAY - NIGHT

[MATHILDE, *in her nightdress and robe, carrying a taper, looks down the hall at the front door, just clicking shut.*]

INT. LANDING OUTSIDE DEGAS'S STUDIO - NIGHT

[ZOE, DEGAS's *maid, knocks at the studio door. Behind her…*
CASSATT *waits - not altogether sure she should have come - hands still smudged with charcoal, holding* DURAND-RUEL's *card, a thick roll of drawings tucked under her arm.*]

ZOE *[knocking again]*: Sir?
DEGAS *[OC]*: What is it?

[DEGAS *flings open the door - disheveled, face tight with furious intensity, his hands coated with blue plasticine. Behind him…*
The FIGURE OF A DANCER worked in wax. DEGAS *blinks, his vision clears. Seeing* MARY, *his face lights up. He extends his hand in greeting, only belatedly realizing it's covered in plasticine. He wipes it on his blouse.*]

CASSATT: Seems it's my turn to interrupt.
DEGAS: Please, come in.

[He ushers CASSATT *into...]*

INT. DEGAS'S STUDIO - NIGHT - CONTINUOUS

*[*CASSATT *goes directly to the sculpture in progress.]*

CASSATT: Sculpture? I didn't realize you -
DEGAS: It helps me draw.
CASSATT: And drawing is -
CASSATT & DEGAS: Everything.

[A small, shared smile. ZOE *discreetly slips back out. Surveying the studio,* CASSATT *notices a familiar DRESS tossed over the back of a chair near the changing screen.]*

CASSATT: Isn't this...? *[picking it up]* You can come out now, Therese.

*[*THERESE *peeks out from behind the screen.]*

THERESE: Hello, Miss.
DEGAS: I had this idea for a free-standing dancer, I needed a model and...
CASSATT *[mildly teasing]*: Therese volunteered. For a price.

[Sheepishly, THERESE *steps into the room. She is naked except for slippers, a few interesting blue smudges on her skin.]*

CASSATT: Whose slippers?
DEGAS: Mine.
CASSATT: Well, I suppose she has to wear something.
DEGAS: I see you've brought some sketches.

*[*DEGAS *takes them. While he unrolls her drawings...]*

CASSATT: I get furious when I'm interrupted so please - continue your dancer.

178

[As he spreads out the drawings…]

DEGAS: I liked your comment about hands having so much history in them. They're so intricate. Revealing. *[without looking up]* There's coffee on the stove.

[She declines with a shake of her head – her full attention on DEGAS's reactions to her sketches. When he finally looks at her, their eyes meet. CASSATT avoids by turning her attention back to the sculpture. At her side, he reviews his work in progress - MARY's presence making him, if anything even more self-critical.]

DEGAS: She has body - but no soul. She's dancing in a vacuum. … Junk!

[Suddenly, DEGAS hammers a fist into the soft plastic and wax. THERESE gasps – as if struck by the blow herself.]

DEGAS: If you can grow poppies under a skylight, I can make…

[DEGAS grabs a FLANNEL ROBE and flings it on the floor.]

DEGAS: Seascapes! The beach at Trouville!!

[He hands CASSATT a charcoal.]

DEGAS: There's paper - someplace.

[While adjusting lights, DEGAS orders THERESE into a pose.]

DEGAS: You! Sit. Face the lights.

[THERESE sits on the robe on the floor.]

DEGAS: No! The other way. Front leg out. The other up. Lean back on one arm. One, I said! Look at your toe. The big one. Your toe! Not HER!

[CASSATT pours herself a cup of coffee.]

CASSATT: I've never had coffee at the beach.

DEGAS: Just smell that sea breeze!

CASSATT: And the gulls! Listen to them!

> [*Their shared flight of fancy has an air of intimacy about it.* THERESE *finds it all incomprehensible.* DEGAS *slaps a sheet of paper to his board then grabs a stick of pastel.*
> DEGAS *begins to sketch. She watches. Sets aside her cup.*
> *The charcoal in her hand itches.* DEGAS *grins – he knows the impulse. She flips one of her drawings; begins to sketch.* DEGAS *winks at her. Colleagues. As they work side by side...*]

DEGAS: I despise painting in the open air. It's all so... rushed! Quick! catch the light! ... Quick! Lay the blue before the red dries! There's no time left to see!

> [*As* DEGAS *riffs, the full force of his charisma fires* CASSATT. *For her, it's all very sexy. Still drawing...*]

DEGAS: If I were the government I would create a special brigade of gendarmes whose sole task would be to harass these outdoor rogues! [*off her reaction*] Not kill. Just a little buckshot now and then. As a warning.

> [CASSATT *laughs. They work on in silence.*]

EXT. THE DURAND-RUEL GALLERY - NIGHT

> [*Later.* CASSATT *carries an unframed pastel of "Ballerinas" which* DEGAS *has given her. He carries her drawings. In the gallery window the* PISSARRO *landscape is now on display.*]

CASSATT: Most men see ballerinas as sylphs. But you stripped away the romance and showed the sweat, the drudgery and endless repetition.

DEGAS: Remarkably like painting, isn't it?

> [*Both smile.*]

CASSATT: I used to press my nose against this window till it was too dark to see.

[They walk on. Their shoulders brush. A delicate dance.]

DEGAS: A group of independents - most of whom the Salon has rejected - are planning a separate exhibition. I think you should join us.

[CASSATT's excitement builds.]

DEGAS: Our only rule is to refuse to submit to the Salon. A risk, but one worth taking. In my opinion.

[When she doesn't say anything…]

DEGAS: Think about it.
CASSATT: I have. *[Then…]* When, where and how many paintings?
DEGAS: Soon; I have no idea; and as many as you want.

[They walk on, a fresh energy in their steps. Exhilaration.]

EXT. PARIS BOULEVARD - NIGHT/DAWN

[The eastern sky pearls. They stroll on. Almost intimate.]

CASSATT: Can I ask something very personal?
DEGAS: Of course.
CASSATT: Do you dream in color?
DEGAS *[with a laugh]*: No.
CASSATT: I do. Always.
DEGAS: I dream in lines. Perfect lines.

[He takes her arm. They stroll on. Around them the waking city is coming to life.]

DEGAS: The city is the proper and only subject of a modern painter. I want to capture it all! The view of a chanteuse from the orchestra pit, lovers in sordid hotels spied from a closet. Pretense, fear, love!

[Then, as if suddenly struck by the thought...]

DEGAS: Have you ever been in love?
[off her reaction] I am sorry. That was presumptuous.

[But surprisingly, she answers...]

CASSATT: Once. At least I imagined I was.
DEGAS: Without imagination, love dies.

[Impulsively, he puts his arm around her waist.]

DEGAS: One loves what one imagines the other to be. Once reality intrudes... poof! I prefer friendship.
CASSATT: So do I.

[A glance. A smile. Relief. Yet a bit of disappointment.]

[DISSOLVE TO] EXT. THE CASSATT HOUSE - DAY

[They arrive in front of the house.]

DEGAS: It's been years since I've worked alongside another artist. And you?
CASSATT: Not since school. I need to feel I'm on my own, doing something no one else can do, not part of a pack. But I enjoyed tonight. ... And to think I almost didn't come.
DEGAS: Why did you?

[She doesn't answer. Silence. She should go in, he should go. Neither wants the evening to end. Finally...]

DEGAS: Was it difficult? Coming out alone? At midnight? Or don't you care what people think?

[When she doesn't comment...]

DEGAS: You should. I do. I'm actually a very old-fashioned man. I believe in codes of conduct. Honor.

CASSATT: Does that mean you think less of me now?

DEGAS: I think I think too much about you.

[CASSATT *studies his face. He averts his eyes.* CASSATT *is pleased, yet confused. When he finally looks up...*
Their eyes meet. Hold. A long deep look. They should touch, but their hands are full. They should kiss at any moment.
Both are flustered, each drawn to make the first move, each fighting the impulse, waiting for the other. Neither does.
Finally, she takes back her drawings. He bows. She heads for the door, glancing back before going inside. DEGAS *lingers.*]

INT. BREAKFAST NOOK, THE CASSATT HOUSE - DAY

[LOUISE *reads at the table (Vasari, "Lives of the Painters").* MATHILDE *serves breakfast.* LYDIA *enters, sitting down opposite* LOUISE. CASSATT *rushes in, flushed, carrying both* DEGAS' *paintings and her drawings.*]

LYDIA: Where have you been?!

CASSATT: Working. Look what Degas gave me!
[*to* LOUISE] Did you know that he even works in sculpture? He says they're only experiments at this point, but -

LYDIA: You were alone with him?!

CASSATT: I learned more from Degas in two hours than I did in two years of art school!

LYDIA: What kind of teacher conducts his classes in the middle of the night?

CASSATT: We're colleagues, Lydia. Friends!

[CASSATT *rushes off with* DEGAS's *painting, but leaves her drawings behind. When* LYDIA *unrolls them, she's shocked by the sketch of a nude woman (not recognizably* THERESE*), on a... rug? coat? beach?* LOUISE *and even* MATHILDE *squeeze in for a look.*]

LYDIA: That couldn't possibly be...

LOUISE: Mary?... No.

[But she's not sure. Neither is MATHILDE *– who avoids* LYDIA's *questioning look by busying herself at the stove.]*

EXT. CAFE DE LA NOUVELLE ATHENES - DAY

*[*DEGAS *sits at a sidewalk table, pen to paper, utterly absorbed. Behind him we see...*
A very pregnant woman BERTHE MORISOT *(30s) flanked by two well-dressed gentlemen, her husband* EUGENE MANET *(late 30s) and his brother, the painter,* EDOUARD MANET *(late 40s).*
The BROTHERS MANET *peel off to chat with some friends.* BERTHE *slumps into a chair at* DEGAS' *table. He nods a greeting but continues writing. She leans in for a look.*
Then, with a chuckle...]

BERTHE: Poetry?
DEGAS: Some of us haven't used the brush as an excuse to become subliterate.

[When she reads the text...]

BERTHE: Edgar? Is that a love poem?
DEGAS *[folding up the page]*: A sonnet. And not a very good one.
BERTHE: So who is she? One of those part-time ballerinas you're so fond of? I hear they're remarkably flexible.
DEGAS: She happens to be a very bright and talented young lady.
BERTHE: Talented at what?
DEGAS: Painting.
BERTHE: So you see, darling, there are more of us than you suspected! I hope you'll ask her to join our next exhibition. We could share a room.
DEGAS *[rising]*: I already have. Now if you'll excuse me, I have an appointment.
BERTHE: With your new lady-friend?
DEGAS: As a matter of fact, yes.
BERTHE: Good. I'll go with you.

[BERTHE *takes* DEGAS's *arm. As they walk off, she turns to wave goodbye to the* MANETS. *But, up ahead,* DEGAS *spots…*
LYDIA *and* LOUISE *heading their way.* LOUISE, *spotting* DEGAS, *tries to turn* LYDIA *away.* DEGAS *tries to turn* BERTHE *away.*
Too late. LYDIA *has seen* DEGAS *on the arm of a pregnant woman who seems to be flirting with two other gentlemen.*
As they pass, DEGAS *tips his hat to* LYDIA *and* LOUISE.
A few paces on, BERTHE *glances back to find* LYDIA *scowling.* BERTHE *makes a face in reply.* DEGAS *yanks her back in line.]*

DEGAS: I really wish you hadn't done that.
BERTHE: And why not?! If you saw the look -
DEGAS: She happens to be her sister.
BERTHE: Oops.

INT. THE LOUVRE - DAY

[CASSATT *poses, leaning on her umbrella while looking at a fragment of classical sculpture in a case (see* DEGAS *work).* DEGAS *draws. To* BERTHE, *sitting off to the side…]*

CASSATT: So how do you manage it all? Career, marriage, and motherhood?
DEGAS: It helps to marry into a family of painters. Even if it means marrying the wrong brother.
BERTHE: Don't be snide, Edgar.

[CASSATT *rubs her stiffened neck. As she rolls her head, she spots two American women,* BERTHA PALMER *and* SARA HALLOWELL, *watching her and whispering. Breaking the pose…]*

CASSATT *[to* DEGAS*]*: Your turn to pose.
BERTHE: Good luck. As far as I know, Edgar has never posed for anything.
CASSATT: He owes me three hours.
DEGAS: Three?!
CASSATT: And I'm being generous. Let's go.

[*She helps* DEGAS *pack his supplies.]*

INT. THE ACADEMIE SUISSE - DAY

[A MALE MODEL *poses nude on the raised platform at the center of the huge room packed with students at their easels. A loud, chaotic place. The afternoon session is nearly over.*
CASSATT *and* BERTHE *sit side by side sketching furiously.]*

CASSATT: My sister seems to think a woman's life is either scandalous or empty without a man in it. If I believed I could be happy as a wife and mother, I'd do it. But I have this.
BERTHE: Painting makes you that happy?
CASSATT: Of course not. It drives me insane.

[Two small, knowing grins. Only then do we see that their subject is…
DEGAS, *nearby, sketching an ancient Janitor.]*

CASSATT: And only another artist would understand what I meant by that.
BERTHE: Then marry a painter. I did.
CASSATT: If the primary reason to get married is to appear respectable, why on earth marry a painter?!

[Good point. BERTHE *laughs.]*

CASSATT: Besides, in a few years we'll all be famous. And no one cares what famous people do.

[Suddenly a BELL rings to end the session. Most of the students prepare to go. A few linger over their work. As CASSATT *prepares to go,* BERTHE *gently stops her.]*

BERTHE: Wait. There's something you should see.

[They step aside to let the students pass. Then they see…
PISSARRO, MONET, *and* RENOIR *each staking claim to a section, rushing from place to place, scavanging abandoned TUBES OF PAINT which still contain usable amounts of pigment.]*

BERTHE: They can't afford paint, so…

[PISSARRO, *thrilled with his booty, shouts across the room to* BERTHE, *his hands filled with partial tubes.}*

PISSARRO: Prussian blue. Chromium and barium yellow! An entire tube of white!!
CASSATT: Who's that?
BERTHE: Camille Pissarro.

[MONET *and* RENOIR *argue over rights to a tube.* PISSARRO *rushes in to adjudicate the dispute.]*

CASSATT: And the dark-haired one?
BERTHE: Auguste Renoir - excuses his fetish for fleshy women by claiming to be a modern Rubens. Monet, you know, at least he knows you. You made quite an impression on him.
CASSATT: So to speak.

[CASSATT *is deeply saddened by the spectacle.* DEGAS *appears behind them. Then comments…]*

DEGAS: Never pity an artist. No one puts a gun to a man's head and tells him - or her - "You must be a painter." We each pay a price for our independence. This is theirs.

[*Off* CASSATT'*s reaction…]*

INT. DURAND-RUEL GALLERY - DAY

[CASSATT *guides* LOUISE *on a shopping spree of her fellow artists' work.]*

CASSATT: This one's good but that one's -
  [*to* DURAND-RUEL] She'll take it.
LOUISE: But -
CASSATT: You can't possibly return to New York without at least a few of Pissarro's lanscapes or -

[DURAND-RUEL *helps his Assistants remove the painting and add it to the growing pile near the door.* CASSATT *drags* LOUISE *across the room to a pastel by* RENOIR.]

CASSATT: Well?

LOUISE: It's so...

CASSATT: Sensual? ... Think Rubens. Paul! She'll take this one too.

LOUISE: Mary, please...

CASSATT: Your clothes are beautiful, YOU are beautiful. You've already got everything you need and you still have fifteen thousand francs to spend on anything you want.

LOUISE: But -

[*As* CASSATT *drags her toward yet another painting...*]

CASSATT: I know your Father would prefer to see your closets filled with ballgowns. Explain to him that art makes a better dowry than railroad stock.

LOUISE: I have. Repeatedly. He disagrees.

CASSATT: New York's filled with nothing but dull black and white engravings! If you don't surround yourself with color, you'll forget everything. Ah, now this one!

[*Off* DURAND-RUEL'*s look of utter gratitude...*]

INT. MANET'*S DINING ROOM - NIGHT*

[MANET, *at the head of the table.* BERTHE MORISOT *ladles out large servings of her fish stew to the assembled...*
DEGAS, RENOIR *and his mistress* LISE, PISSARRO, *other* WOMEN, MANET'*s brother* EUGENE [BERTHE'*s husband*], DURAND-RUEL, MONET, *and* LOUISE. *The mood is festive, celebratory.*
DURAND-RUEL *taps his glass for a toast to...*
LOUISE *and* CASSATT, *sitting opposite* DEGAS *at mid-table.*]

DURAND-RUEL: A toast! To our new friends who this afternoon saved us all, and especially me, from the poorhouse.

[Cheers, applause, drinks.]

MANET *[to* LOUISE*]*: I'm curious why Miss Cassatt didn't get you to buy any of her own work.

DEGAS: What he's really asking is why she didn't urge you to buy any of his!

PISSARRO: There's certainly no call for her to buy Degas' since he's more than happy to give his masterpieces away as love-offerings.

[Laughter, drinks etc. CASSATT *and* DEGAS *squirm.]*

BERTHE: Edgar? ... Are you blushing? *[off his reaction]* Surely it's not possible that our resident cynic's fallen in love!

DEGAS: I am no stranger to love, Madam. But who could blame me for being circumspect when I am forced to spend my days among such swine. Misses Cassatt and Elder excluded.

MANET: Why not give us a poem, Edgar?

BERTHE: Edouard, please. Don't.

*[*DEGAS *rises to the challenge, locks eyes with* MANET. *Then...]*

DEGAS *[finally]*: I am a line, seeking completion.

[He then turns to CASSATT. *Locks eyes with her. A hush falls.]*

DEGAS: What once was blank, has form.
What once was certain, is not.
Foolish men seek reason,
Wiser men and better men find love.

[After a moment's silence. Applause. Cheers.]

BERTHE *[to* EUGENE*]*: Why don't you ever write me poems?

[Before EUGENE *can stutter a reply...]*

DEGAS: Because, my dear, your husband, dear sweet kind man that he is, ... is an imbecile.

[Howls. Despite the cut, EUGENE is grateful to be off the hot seat.]

DEGAS: And, Eugene, I say that with the greatest affection.
BERTHE: Why do you put up with him, Mary?

[All eyes on CASSATT who after appraising DEGAS, declares...]

CASSATT: Because he's someone who sees as I do.

INT. CASSATT'S STUDIO - DAY

*[CASSATT at her easel, working at fever pitch. Short fuse.
THERESE, in her slip, sews the same dress last seen at DEGAS's studio.
CASSATT has positioned her so that light from the window falls
dramatically across her shoulders. A strap of the dress is torn; a wine
stain on a hip; a cigar burn on a sleeve. THERESE seems distracted.]*

CASSATT: Concentrate on the stitch.
THERESE: Yes, Miss.

*[At the far end of the studio, LOUISE sorts through her recently
acquired collection of impressionist paintings.]*

LOUISE: Father's going to have a seizure when he sees all these.
CASSATT: Then that's his failing, not yours.

[THERESE fidgets.]

CASSATT: Dammit, Therese!

[CASSATT physically and a bit roughly re-positions her.]

CASSATT: What is wrong with you today?! And what in God's name have
you been doing in this dress?!

[Before THERESE can answer, MATHILDE enters.]

MATHILDE: Miss?

CASSATT: Now what?!

MATHILDE: You have visitors, Miss. Two women. A Mrs. Palmer and a Miss Hallowell. From Chicago in Illinois.

CASSATT: Ask my sister to give them tea and find out what they want.

MATHILDE: Your sister's out. It's you they want to see.

CASSATT: I don't care what they want! This exhibition's only two weeks away and I'm already three weeks behind! Now if you don't mind, I'd actually like to get some work done today!

MATHILDE: Yes, Miss.

[MATHILDE *exits.* LOUISE *wanders to* CASSATT'*s side, watches what she's doing. She's in the way. Finally...]*

LOUISE: Did Lydia say where she was going?

CASSATT *[too sharply]*: No.

[LOUISE *and* THERESE *exchange a look.]*

INT. DEGAS'S STUDIO - DAY

[LYDIA *sits stiffly in a chair, teacup and saucer in her lap.]*

LYDIA: As you may or may not know, I'm not in the best of health. My kidneys are failing which means... I may only have a few good years left. My sister knows but I've been careful to hide from her the full extent of my condition. And with our parents in America, I've made it my responsibility to see that she is properly situated. With an American.

[DEGAS, *uncomfortable with the situation, fusses with the tea service.]*

DEGAS: I come from two generations of bankers. Like yours, my family doesn't altogether approve my choice of professions.
[pacing] I have a modest income. I may be a painter, but I am also a gentleman. And my family's reputation is impeccable.

LYDIA: Excuse me, but are you offering -

DEGAS: Miss Cassatt, I love your sister. I regard her as my equal, in all things. I'd ask her to marry me if I didn't already know the answer. Mary's already wedded. To her work.

[LYDIA *is at first taken aback by this admission, then softens.*]

DEGAS: In my heart, I consider myself silently engaged.
[*off her reaction*] I said, silently. Mary knows nothing of this. So I beg you to keep this conversation absolutely confidential.

[LYDIA *sets aside her cup and rises.*]

LYDIA: Mister Degas, you have my word. I will not share this with anyone. Least of all my sister.
DEGAS: Please, call me, Edgar.

[*After a long moment,* LYDIA *extends her hand.*]

LYDIA: Edgar.

[*He takes it. Kisses it. She's charmed. But cautious.*]

INT. DURAND-RUEL GALLERY - DAY

[*The Impressionist Exhibition. In a room of their own...*
CASSATT *and* BERTHE *sit, surrounded by their paintings.*
BERTHE *holds her infant* JULIE *while* CASSATT *scans a tabloid for reviews. In the adjoining room, artists easily outnumber spectators, and those who've come, came to mock.*]

CASSATT: Damn the critics!
BERTHE: What did you expect?
CASSATT: Still, it's infuriating to be reduced to an afterthought!
BERTHE: Did they at least spell our names right?
CASSATT: This one dropped my second "T" and gave it to you.
BERTHE: Shows how closely he looked at our paintings. Then again, he may be illiterate.
CASSATT: Likely.

[She begins to read…]

CASSATT: "And of the two women in the group, Berthe Morisott" - two 't's' - "a pupil of Manet, and a Miss Cassat - no given name, one 't' - "pupil of Degas, at least show some feminine charm."

> *[CASSATT angrily tosses the papers aside. In the adjoining room, they see…*
> PISSARRO *trying to restrain* MONET *from physically attacking a particularly obnoxious trio of young men;*
> DURAND-RUEL *flitting from painter to painter, smoothing feathers, stroking egos;*
> DEGAS *touring the room with* LOUISE *on his arm, followed closely by an ill-at-ease* LYDIA.*]*

CASSATT: When they say "pupil" what they really mean is "camp follower." As if we can't learn from a man without sharing his bed.
BERTHE: Or vice versa. It comes from having posed for them, you know.
CASSATT: Manet posed for Degas and no one's suspected them of a liaison.

> *[They laugh.* JULIE *begins to squall.* BERTHE *dandles her.* CASSATT *studies Mother and Child closely – obviously moved by the image. But the reverie's broken when, in B.G. …*
> MONET *breaks free from* PISSARRO *and begins driving the obnoxious trio from the gallery.]*

DEGAS: That's it! Drive the Philistines from our temple!

> *[*LYDIA *and* LOUISE *retreat to the comparative calm of the Women's Room.* DEGAS *leans in room and declares the event…]*

DEGAS: A great success! The fools have stayed away in droves and the idiots are swarming like flies! We've finally proven the general public's total ignorance!

> *[… then returns to the fray.]*

LYDIA: He can't possibly be serious.
CASSATT: It's either that or slow suicide.

[LYDIA, *showing her frailty, heads for the divan.* CASSATT *and* BERTHE *make room. Louise homes in on one of Berthe's works.*]

BERTHE: So, Lydia, what do you think?
  [*off her look*] Of our paintings?
LYDIA: I think…

[*After scanning the room…*]

LYDIA: I think they're glorious. And anyone who doesn't, is either a fool, a Philistine, or a horsefly.

[*Smiles. Even* JULIE *seems to agree, and reaches for* LYDIA.]

LOUISE: Berthe? Is this one for sale?
BERTHE: That one? No. Sorry.

[DURAND-DUEL, *smelling "sale," suddenly materializes.*]

DURAND-RUEL: But all the rest are.

EXT. THE CASSATT HOUSE - DAY

[*A CARRIAGE is packed with luggage, crates, and paintings.* LOUISE *is leaving. Among those to see her off, besides* LYDIA *and* MATHILDE, *are* DEGAS, DURAND-RUEL, *and* BERTHE *with* JULIE. CASSATT *hugs and holds* LOUISE.]

CASSATT: No matter what your parents say, don't you dare marry some boring man. Show him your paintings and if he starts talking about the stock market, drop him. Promise me.
LOUISE [*wiping away a tear*]: I promise.

[CASSATT *ushers* LOUISE *to the carriage. With a glance at* DEGAS,

LOUISE *whispers to* MARY…]

LOUISE: Follow your heart.
CASSATT: You too.

[LOUISE *breaks away to the waiting carriage under a shower of warm farewells: "Bon voyage. Come back soon. Must you go?" As the carriage rolls off,* CASSATT *turns to…*]

CASSATT: Edgar?

[*But he's slipped away.* LYDIA *places an arm around her sister.*]

EXT. THE STABLE - DAY

[*With* LYDIA *and the* STABLE HAND *looking on,* CASSATT *inspects the Mare's condition. When she presses a foreleg, the Mare whinnies in pain and rears. Gently drawing the bridle, she strokes the Mare's head, calming her.*]

CASSATT: If only I'd found you sooner…

[*Sadly turning her over to the* STABLE HAND…]

CASSATT: There's nothing more to be done.
STABLE HAND: I'll see to it, Miss. I'll make sure it's done right and quick.

[*The* STABLE HAND *leads away the hobbling Mare.*]

CASSATT [*after a pause*]: I think I'll go for a walk.
LYDIA: I'll come with you.
CASSATT: No. You need to rest.

[CASSATT *walks off.* LYDIA *watches her go.*]

EXT. PARIS PARK - DUSK

[As darkness falls, CASSATT *sits alone on a bench in a park, her head bowed. Without her sketchpad to occupy her hands, she is carefully tearing a LEAF, shaping a silhouette.]*

INT. DOOR OUTSIDE DEGAS'S STUDIO - NIGHT

*[*CASSATT *and* ZOE, DEGAS's *maid, outside the locked door, unnerved by the shouts and crashing inside.]*

MARIA *[OC]*: And I'm telling you it's filth!

DEGAS *[OC]*: And who are you to tell me what is or isn't an appropriate subject?!

MARIA *[OC]*: I have modeled for masters! There are thirty-six of me in this year's Salon!! Twenty the year before!!

DEGAS *[OC]*: Had I known I was in the presence of such an authority I would have given you the brush!!

[The sound of things - brushes? palette? paint pots? - being thrown. Crashes. MARIA's *yelps.]*

ZOE: They've been screaming like that for hours.

DEGAS *[OC]*: Where are you going?!

MARIA *[OC]*: I'm leaving.

DEGAS *[OC]*: I've paid for five hours!

MARIA *[OC]*: Keep your damn money!

[Tussling on the other side of the door.]

MARIA *[OC]*: Let go of me!!

[Banging, crashing. The door flies open. MARIA, *a young model, her clothing in disarray, shoves past and flees.* DEGAS *appears.]*

DEGAS: Maria!!

[Seeing CASSATT, DEGAS *retreats back into his sudio. After a moment's hesitation,* CASSATT *goes into…]*

INT. DEGAS'S STUDIO - NIGHT

[A shambles. DEGAS, *slumped on a divan, surrounded by sketches of* MARIA *washing herself in a small flat tub.*
CASSATT *closes the door behind her, then surveying the room's disorder, notes the tub, the sponge and towel.]*

DEGAS: The nerve of that, that…
CASSATT: Poor ignorant girl?
DEGAS: Poor? Yes. Girl? Debatable. Ignorant? An understatement!

*[*CASSATT *stands behind him at the divan and massages his shoulders. He takes one of her hands and presses it to his cheek. She sees the sketches littering the floor.]*

DEGAS: Two centuries ago, I would have done "Susannah Bathing." Now I paint "A Woman in a Tub" - same subject! - and my model calls me depraved! *[leaping up]* I ask you, what is so disgusting about a woman washing herself? You bathe. I bathe.

*[*DEGAS *rages, snatching up sketches.]*

DEGAS: Is this depraved? Pornography?! Why must the nude always be presented as if she's posing for an audience?
CASSATT: Why is Susannah always the one being oggled by the old men?
DEGAS: There is nothing provocative about a woman at her toilet! Nothing!!
CASSATT: Edgar, please. I agree with you. But these women seem concerned with nothing but their bodies. They're like animals cleaning themselves. Seen through a keyhole.
DEGAS: Exactly! YOU see! But try to get THEM to!

[Fixated on his sketches…]

DEGAS: I've been through six models in two days – they talk to one another, you know. Dammit. I was so close.

CASSATT: To...

DEGAS: A line. Pathos. A fleeting moment of humanity - there, see it? From the lower back across the buttocks, the tension in the calf, the -

[He crumples a drawing and hurls it at the tub. She strokes him, trying to soothe, comfort, reassure. Then...]

DEGAS: Pose for me? *[off her reaction]* You've posed for me before.

CASSATT: At the Louvre. In a hatmaker's shop. On - I couldn't possibly...

DEGAS: Why not?

CASSATT: Because.

DEGAS: Don't you think I know what you look like without your bustle and boots? I thought we'd gotten past such delicacies in art school!
[undoing his shirt] Do you want me to pose nude for you?

CASSATT: No, not at the moment, thank you.

DEGAS: Of course. You are interested only in your modern Madonnas and Childs.

CASSATT *[with a wry smile]*: Children. And you, my friend, are neither. Besides, I am quite aware of what you must look like.

DEGAS: And I, you.

[Long pause. Finally...
CASSATT *goes to the studio door and locks it.]*

CASSATT: Stoke the fire. If I catch cold and can't work, I'll never forgive you.

DEGAS: Thank you.

Still standing at the door, her eyes locked on his, CASSATT *begins to unbutton her blouse. Finally, she approaches. He reaches out to hug her, she holds him back.*

CASSATT: One condition. I don't want you to draw my face.

DEGAS: It's not your face I want.

CASSATT *[with a grin]*: No wonder you can't keep models.

[She gives him a playful kiss on the cheek, then lifts the dressing screen back in place. He feeds the stove.]

DEGAS: You know the line I'm after?

[As she disappears behind the screen…]

CASSATT *[OC]*: Yes.

ON CASSATT – DISROBING BEHIND THE SCREEN

CASSATT: Do you have a robe?
DEGAS *[OC]*: Do you need one?
CASSATT: Temporarily.

*[Nearly unclad, she waits… and waits. Finally…
A robe flops over the top of the screen./*

CASSATT: Thank you.

[After pulling on the robe, she removes her undergarments. Then, drawing the robe tight, she steels herself before stepping back into the studio. DEGAS is at his easel, materials ready. Professional. She moves to the tub-basin. Matter of factly…]

DEGAS: The sponge is over there someplace. Maria threw it at me.

[CASSATT finds the sponge and steps into the basin.]

CASSATT: Are you ready?
DEGAS: Whenever you are.

*[After a long moment, CASSATT tentatively loosens the robe then lets it slip. A bit. She hesitates, then drops it.
Moving slowly from close on her bare back, we track slowly around to her face - her eyes are clenched shut.]*

DEGAS *[OC]:* You are alone, in the privacy of your own room, in your own home. The house is empty. Your sister, mother, guests, Mathilde, everyone is gone. The water is very warm.

> *[SOUND of water pouring into the basin.* CASSATT*'s eyes open.*
> DEGAS *is right next to her, pouring water from a pitcher into the basin. He takes the sponge from her hand, soaks it, then gently washes her back - a parent bathing his child.*
> *She takes and holds his hand, then takes the sponge. As she begins sponging herself, he returns to his easel.]*

A SERIES OF QUICK DISSOLVES AND CUTS

> *[*DEGAS *sketching.* CASSATT *adjusting her pose.* DEGAS *repositioning her.* CASSATT *stretching, then resuming a pose.*
> DEGAS *massaging a stiff tendon in her neck.*
> CASSATT *glancing at a sketch. Then stroking him.*
> CASSATT *shifting poses. Flushing. His hand on her neck, rearranging her hair. A stroke of his fingertips.*
> CASSATT*'s positions becoming increasingly less studied, more comfortable with her nakedness and his penetrating gaze.*
> DEGAS' *sketches becoming freer, coming faster. His shirt now fully open. Perspiration. He switches to red chalks and red pencil - the room's light warms, a subtle shift to reds and ambers and golds. Her skin seems to glow.* CASSATT*'s eyes meet his with greater directness, her gaze more honest, less hidden, revealing more, stating desire.*
> *Then, suddenly... They are together, embracing.*
> *She slides the shirt from his shoulders. His hands, almost trembling, caress. Hers trace lines, curves, planes.*
> *Quickened breath, a staccato of small cries. Hands, fingers, stiffening, clutching, grasping. ... Then release.]*

[DISSOLVE TO] DEGAS' STUDIO - LATER - NIGHT

> *[The fire in the stove glows - the only light in the room besides the spill from gaslights outside. Fresh drawings litter the studio.* CASSATT*, in the robe, curls up with* DEGAS *on the divan as they study the drawings together.]*

DEGAS: I've failed.

CASSATT: I think they're glorious.

DEGAS: Is that the painter talking or the model?

CASSATT: I'm not a vain woman.

DEGAS: You should be.

CASSATT: Nonsense.

[She just looks at him, then kisses him. They kiss again, caressing, making love. Instinctively, she leads.]

INT. FRONT DOOR - CASSATT HOUSE - DAY

[The door creaks open. CASSATT peeks in, listens for any stirring, then carefully recloses the door behind her.
She tiptoes down the hall toward the stairs, her antennae on full alert. The first step creaks. She quickly backs off. Strategizes. Tries again. Freezes. Listens. Then moves on.]

INT. HALL OUTSIDE CASSATT'S STUDIO - CONTINUOUS

[CASSATT creeps down the hall, her breath shallow and heart pounding. So intent on the distant sounds of muffled voices, she doesn't notice... MATHILDE coming up behind her with a tea service. MATHILDE observes. Very curious. Then...]

MATHILDE: Miss?

[CASSATT jolts. Stifles a yelp. Nearly knocks over a vase.]

CASSATT: Oh God, Mathilde! You scared me.
    [then with urgency] You've got to tell Lydia that I was working late and that I spent the night in my studio.

[MATHILDE tries to stop her, but CASSATT's already through the door and into...]

INT. CASSATT'S STUDIO - CONTINUOUS

[CASSATT *stops dead when she discovers...*
BERTHA PALMER *and* SARA HALLOWELL *oohing and ahhing over
her paintings.* LYDIA *flashes her a hot, critical look.]*

PALMER: Miss Cassatt! Bertha Palmer. And my associate...
HALLOWELL: Sara Hallowell. From Chicago.
CASSATT: In Illinois. Yes, I know.

[The two women aren't quite sure what to make of CASSATT.]

PALMER: You've been a devilishly difficult woman to find.
LYDIA: Lately my sister's been keeping unusual hours.
MATHILDE: Working night and day.
LYDIA: That will be all, Mathilde.

[CASSATT *uses* MATHILDE'*s exit as cover to discreetly rebutton her
dress and smoothe her hair. Palmer catches her at it.]*

PALMER: Well. I can see you're busy, so we'll get right down to it.
HALLOWELL: Bertha's been named director of the Women's Building for
    the Chicago World Exposition. Only the work of American women will
    be shown.
PALMER: We're both great admirers of your oeuvre. It's a disgrace you're so
    unknown in your own country.
CASSATT: So at this exhibition, the women will have their own building?
HALLOWELL: The only men on the premises will be visitors!
CASSATT: And once again "women's art" will have been set apart.
    [Off their reaction...] I prefer to celebrate women, not segregate them.
PALMER: In a perfect world, I'd agree. Given our limitations, I'm prepared
    to offer you a sizable commission to paint a mural for the East Wall.

[Clearly, the offer comes as surprise to CASSATT. *Equally evident is
her interest. She goes to a window. Her mind racing, she barely hears*
PALMER. *To herself...]*

CASSATT: A mural.

[PALMER *removes papers from her carrying case.*]

PALMER: The committee has given a great deal of thought to the message that this mural should convey.

HALLOWELL: The theme is Modern Woman.

PALMER: Regarding the fee, if you'd rather I negotiate with your dealer -

CASSATT: What are the dimensions?

[*It takes a moment for* CASSATT'*s implied acceptance to register. The two Chicago women bubble with excitement.*]

INT. DURAND-RUEL GALLERY - DAY

[DEGAS *examines one of his "Dancers." He squints, pinching the bridge of his nose. He covers when* CASSATT *rushes in.*]

CASSATT: I've been asked to present a major work in an American exhibition.

DEGAS: That's wonderful! Congratulations.

CASSATT: A sixty foot mural.

DEGAS: A mural? [*suddenly suspicious*] Will you have to go to –

CASSATT: I'll have to get out of the city. Find a place with a barn or a -

DEGAS: Just how long will you be away?

CASSATT: No more than a year.

DEGAS: You can't! [*catching himself*] It's insane! Losing an entire year just to plaster some absurd fresco! A waste of your time and talent!

CASSATT: Was Michelangelo's ceiling a waste?

DEGAS: You, my dear, are no Michelangelo and some warehouse is no Sistine!

CASSATT: You're acting as if this commission is some kind of personal attack!

DEGAS: Since when have you become an authority on cowboys and Indians?!

CASSATT: The subject is modern women!

DEGAS: Parisians aren't modern enough for you?!

[DURAND-RUEL *approaches from his office.*]

CASSATT: I'm going to do it.
DURAND-RUEL: Do what?
DEGAS: Decorate the inside of a garage!

[DEGAS *storms out, shielding his eyes.*]

DURAND-RUEL: A garage?
CASSATT: A commission. Never mind. Damn him.

[CASSATT *starts to go.* DURAND-RUEL *pulls out an envelope.*]

DURAND-RUEL: Give this to Degas. The damn fool even forgot why he came. [*explaining*] Proceeds from his latest sales less my commission.

[DEGAS *reenters.*]

DURAND-RUEL: Forget something?

[DURAND-RUEL *flags the envelope.*]

DURAND-RUEL: This perhaps?

[DEGAS, *ignoring him, marches to his painting, tears it off the wall and starts back out with it under his arm.*]

DEGAS: This needs work. It cannot be shown in this condition.
DURAND-RUEL: Degas?! Your cash!

[*But* DEGAS *is already gone.* CASSATT *grabs the envelope and follows* DEGAS. DURAND-RUEL *follows her out the door to…*]

EXT. DURAND-RUEL GALLERY - CONTINUOUS

[*They watch* DEGAS *stomp off with his painting.* DURAND-RUEL *nearly spits with anger.*]

DURAND-RUEL: That man - One week after Rouart bought one of Degas' pictures, Degas went to his house and ran off with it, said it needed more work. That was six years ago! Why do we put up with this madman?!

CASSATT: Sometimes I wonder.

[CASSATT *goes after* DEGAS, DURAND-RUEL *goes back inside.*]

EXT. SIDEWALK NEAR THE CAFE NOUVELLE ATHENES - DAY

[CASSATT *finally catches up with* DEGAS, *the painting still under his arm.*]

DEGAS: Go. Move. Paint your damn buffalo if that's what you want. Just leave me alone.

[She shoves the envelope into his pocket.]

CASSATT: With pleasure.

[DEGAS *continues a few more steps, then stops suddenly. He holds out his picture, examining it, disgusted with it.*]

DEGAS: Wrong. All wrong! Hideous!

[CUT AWAY TO]
EXT. CAFE DE LA NOUVELLE ATHENES - CONTINUOUS

[*From the Cafe,* MANET, MONET, PISSARRO, *and* BERTHE *with* JULIE *watch the scene between* CASSATT *and* DEGAS *unfold.*]

PISSARRO: Lover's quarrel?
MANET: Depends whose picture he's carrying, hers or his.
BERTHE: Hers.
RENOIR: His.

[When DEGAS *flings his painting into the street…]*

MANET: His.

[*They watch* CASSATT *march off, clearly upset.*]

EXT. STOREFRONT - A NEARBY STREET - DAY

[CASSATT *stands in front of the window as strangers pass by. She seems to be window-shopping. But as we pull in closer, we see that she is struggling to bring her emotions back under control, angrily wiping away frustrated tears. Then...*
In the window's reflection, she sees A WAGON loaded with manure being drawn by a single painfully limping horse – her old Mare.
CASSATT *turns. The wagon is being driven by the same bestial* DRIVER *who first owned it.* CASSATT *charges in an absolute rage. Grabbing the reins...]*

CASSATT: Where did you get my horse?!
DRIVER: Not you again.
CASSATT: This horse was supposed to have been destroyed.
DRIVER: For thirty francs she's yours.

[CASSATT *starts to unhitch the animal. The* DRIVER *tries to shove her away. The Mare whinnies in pain. The Men and Women from the sidewalk gather for the show. A* GENDARME *rushes up.]*

GENDARME: What's going on here?!
DRIVER: I paid good money for this bag of bones.
CASSATT: Not to me you didn't!
DRIVER: You gave it away!
CASSATT: To be put down not driven to death!
DRIVER: Then you should have done the dirty work yourself! What?! Afraid to dirty those pretty little gloves?!

[CASSATT *grabs the* GENDARME's *PISTOL from his holster. Before the* GENDARME *can do anything to stop her...*
CASSATT *pulls back the hammer – CLICK! – grips the pistol firmly in both hands and turns to the* DRIVER.
With one look at the look in CASSATT's *eyes and the gun in her hand, the* DRIVER *dives for safety - into the manure.]*

CASSATT *turns quickly to the Mare, plants the muzzle right against her skull. Then pulls the trigger.*
The report is ear-shattering, and at such close range, BLOOD splatters back onto CASSATT'S *face.*
The Mare, instantly dead, collapses to the pavement.
Silence. When CASSATT *turns, passersby duck for cover.*
CASSATT *returns the pistol to the stunned* GENDARME.
CASSATT *feels the blood on her face. Wipes at it with her fingers, streaking her cheeks. The* GENDARME *offers her his handkerchief.*
CASSATT *stares at her fingertips.]*

GENDARME: Miss?
CASSATT: I'm… I have to leave now.

[The crowd parts for her as she walks away.]

[FADE OUT & BACK UP ON]
EXT. CHATEAU BEAUFRESNE - DAY

[A rustic country estate, not far from Paris: long-neglected grounds, a barn just off from the main house in front of which trunks and crates are being unloaded from wagons. LYDIA *and* MATHILDE *supervise. We follow* CASSATT *to…]*

EXT. THE BARN AT BEAUFRESNE - CONTINUOUS

[She lingers a moment at the open barn doors, then enters…]

INT. THE BARN - CONTINUOUS

[Despite the open doors, the place is gloomy. Workmen are raising a large - 58 feet long, 12 feet high, three panel canvas with a curved top edge.]

CASSATT: Careful!

*[*CASSATT *rushes to make sure the canvas is properly secured.* LYDIA *enters behind her and watches.]*

*[*CASSATT *steps back, next to* LYDIA, *to take in the full sweep of the blank surface.]*

CASSATT: I'll need to install a skylight. And a window over there.

LYDIA: It's so... huge.

CASSATT *[slightly daunted]*: And empty.

[DISSOLVE TO] INT. THE BARN STUDIO - WEEKS LATER - DAY

[A skylight has been installed. CASSATT *stands on a make-shift scaffold trying to sketch a rough outline at a high point in the center panel. The scaffolding wobbles.*

CASSATT's *hair and clothing are disheveled. There is a distinct lack of authority in her hand and line. So used to working in smaller, more manageable scale, for the first time we see a* CASSATT *unsure of herself and tentative.*

Straining to reach, she nearly falls.

LYDIA, *having brought a tea tray and sandwiches into the barn and set them out on a rough small table in the middle of the room, gasps.]*

[DISSOLVE TO] THE BARN - LATER THE SAME DAY

[Mid-lunch. CASSATT, *a half-eaten sandwich in her hand, stares at the panels.]*

CASSATT: In the center I see three groups. Mixed ages. In an orchard. Three there... four... and another group of three to their right - Picking fruit and passing it, elder to younger.

*[*LYDIA *refills her sister's cup.* CASSATT *doesn't notice.]*

CASSATT: Women plucking the fruits of Knowledge and Science.

[Pointing her sandwich at the half-sketched right panel...]

CASSATT: That one will celebrate the arts: drawing, music, and dance. And over there *[left]*...

[The left panel, unlike the other two, is still totally blank.]

CASSATT: Women pursuing fame.
LYDIA: Something which you, of all people, should understand.

[LYDIA plants the teacup in her sister's hand.]

CASSATT: But the problem is how to show it, to others. Up there.

[With MARY still staring at the blank panel, LYDIA clutches her free hand.]

LYDIA: I have total confidence in you.

[CASSATT accepts the gesture without sharing the sentiment.]

INT. DEGAS' STUDIO - DAY

[DEGAS, wretched with self-neglect, self-pity, and brooding, sits dishevelled in the brightest, most intensely sunlit spot under the window. In his hands is a lump of wax which he molds and presses, shapes and flattens.]

BERTHE *[OC]*: Do you mean to tell me that you haven't even written to her?

[Only then do we see that BERTHE has been surveying his madly disordered studio – sketches and unfinished work, many of them images of CASSATT, lay strewn about.]

BERTHE: She's been gone for six months!
DEGAS: I'm not the one who left.
BERTHE: Don't be childish.

[He pokes the wax. Pulls, flattens. Holds it up in the bright light, close to his face, yet squints to see. He's in pain.]

BERTHE: Edgar? What's wrong?

[No answer. When BERTHE's *shadow falls across the shape...]*

DEGAS: Do you mind?

*[*BERTHE *backs off.]*

DEGAS: Thank you.

[He readjusts to recapture the light. Then...]

DEGAS: Has she written to you?

[When BERTHE *hesitates...]*

DEGAS: Well? Has she or hasn't she?
BERTHE: A few letters. Just notes really.
DEGAS: Well there you are. Her and that damned mural.

*[*DEGAS *jabs violently at the wax.]*

DEGAS: Who cares what a pack of prairie-trotting barbarians think?! The only thing they're good for is building railroads and flinging their money at banal pictures in the vain hope that, if they spend enough, it will make them into something other than a race of scrubbed-up land-grabbers!

[He hurls the lump of wax. Despite herself, BERTHE *laughs. Tries to smother it.* DEGAS *doesn't seem to have noticed – any more than he's noticed that his fly is open. Finally...]*

BERTHE: We're all going out for a weekend. You're welcome to come along.
DEGAS: Did she invite me?
BERTHE: I'm inviting you.
DEGAS: In that case, I decline.
BERTHE: The fresh air will do you good. You always loved the country at Mesnil.
DEGAS: Nature is passé.

[He roots around the clutter looking for the lump of wax.]

DEGAS: I would rather spend my Sundays sniffing locomotives in Gare St. Lazare than some pseudo-bucolic dung heap! And you can tell Miss Cassatt that when she's ready to resume her career, I'll be here.

[Groping, he finds the lump - impaled on a paint brush.]

EXT. CHATEAU BEAUFRESNE - DAY

[Two carriages pull up in front of the house. A flurry of activity as CASSATT, LYDIA, *and* MATHILDE *greet…*
BERTHE *and* EUGENE *with their toddler daughter,* JULIE…
PISSARRO; RENOIR *and* LISE; MONET *and his mistress* CAMILLE;
MANET, *leaning heavily on a cane, fussed over by* DURAND-RUEL *done up for his notion of a stylish country get-away.*
Hugs, kisses, warm greetings.]

CASSATT: So good to see you. What a lovely dress! And Julie! Look at you!

[Finally, a third carriage rolls up and groans to a halt.
DEGAS *descends from the carriage. Bows to* LYDIA. LYDIA *nods greetings, then herds the group inside.*
DEGAS *hangs back. So does* CASSATT.*]*

CASSATT: I'm glad you've come.
DEGAS: Berthe left me no choice.
CASSATT: Aren't you coming in?
DEGAS: First, I'll walk for an hour. Then a nap. A temporary reprieve from their incessant chit-chat. I hate all this talk about art!
CASSATT: For someone who hates the subject, I've never known you to lack an opinion. … I'll walk with you.
DEGAS: You have guests.

[DEGAS gives her a slight stiff bow before walking off.]

CASSATT: Dinner's at six.

[CASSATT *heads for the house. When she glances back, she sees...* DEGAS *straining to read the face of his pocket watch, tilting it at a variety of odd angles.]*

INT. BARN STUDIO - DAY

[A huge table constructed of planks and sawhorses occupies the middle of the room, underneath the mural-in-progress.
CASSATT *is at the head of table.* MANET *is at the foot, his leg propped up on a stool. All the others have taken their places with the exception of* DEGAS *whose chair sits empty.*
A distinctive centerpiece of LILACS (see Cassatt's still-life "Lilacs in a Window") graces the table.
DEGAS's *Ballerina painting - the one he gave her - hangs on a side wall. While* MATHILDE *serves the soup, the others assess the mural - the panel on the left, still empty.]*

CASSATT: Even though it will be raised sixty feet from the floor, I've decided not to play games with perspective.
BERTHE: What exactly do modern women in an allegorical painting wear?
CASSATT: Allegorical haute couture, of course.

[Her wit garners applause.]

PISSARRO: What does Degas say?
CASSATT: Precious little.
RENOIR: A miracle.
BERTHE: Between his walk and exactly sixty-five minute nap has he even found time to take a look?
CASSATT: No.
DURAND-RUEL: All the way from the station he did nothing but lay down his conditions for civilized dining.
MANET: Don't tell me. Dinner must be served promptly at six!
BERTHE: No brandy or cigars -
RENOIR: No women with plunging necklines or insistent perfume. Both of which he claims distract the senses.
PISSARRO: And above all, no flowers on the table.

LYDIA *[reaching for the lilacs]*: Then perhaps I should -

CASSATT: Leave it.

PISSARRO: He told me that flowers belong in the garden not on the table.

MANET: The man is becoming more impossible every day.

BERTHE: How can you tell?

MANET: The pain in my leg increases whenever he's around.

[A CLOCK begins to strike six. On cue, DEGAS enters.]

DEGAS: Good evening.

MANET: You see, six o'clock, and dinner is served!

CASSATT: With or without the guests.

[DEGAS glares at the centerpiece (or is he trying to focus?)].

RENOIR: I love a large bouquet, don't you?

PISSARRO: The bigger the better.

RENOIR: As intoxicating as a heady perfume on a beautiful full-chested woman. Lise, darling, show Degas your splendid bosom, would you?

[Everyone at the table snickers.
LISE, RENOIR's model/mistress, pulls her dress down over her shoulders, teases, then pops a button. DEGAS, rarely a good sport, and especially not tonight, fumes. BERTHE offers...]

BERTHE: Cigar?

[Everyone, but especially the women at table chuckle.]

DEGAS: I've come to the conclusion that women are incapable of appreciating anything but Switzerland and lemonade! When it comes to art, they have no style!

BERTHE: I beg your pardon?

DEGAS: Madam, you make paintings as if you were making hats!

BERTHE: If I were a man, I'd choose pistols and ask you to name your seconds!

DEGAS: See! No style! Even at duelling!

CASSATT: You want a duel? Very well.

[CASSATT *rises and faces off with* DEGAS.]

CASSATT: I challenge you to present the ugliest, plainest, most ill-begotten girl in Place Pigalle and within two weeks I will give you a painting of such style and poignant truth you will beg me to lend it to you! Name your medium! Oil, pastel, print, charcoal, or Swiss lemonade!

DEGAS: Finally! A duellist with style!

[*After a self-dramatizing pause...*]

DEGAS: Oil! A portrait. And I must see at least one hand, her teeth and - if she has them - an ear!

CASSATT: Done!

DEGAS [*grinning wickedly*]: I met a charming young creature crossing your field. I will deliver her tomorrow morning at ten!

CASSATT: Fine. Now for God's sakes, sit down before Mathilde's soup congeals.

[DEGAS *"feels" his way into his chair, reaches for his napkin, subtly groping - the white on white is hard for him to "read."* CASSATT *notices. Once* DEGAS *is in place, he realizes that the centerpiece of lilacs is right in front of him. He glares at it.* BERTHE *nudges it closer to his plate. All SNIFF loudly.*]

DEGAS [*pushing away*]: I've lost my appetite.

CASSATT: Along with your sense of humor.

[DEGAS *picks up the centerpiece.*
CASSATT *rushes to the window, flings it open, then waits for* DEGAS *to march across the room and drop the vase outside.*]

CASSATT: There. Now the lilacs are back in the garden where they belong and you are safely in the barn with the other animals.

[DEGAS *glares at her. She stares right back. He then spots his "Ballerina" on the wall behind her.*]

DURAND-RUEL: I think it needs work, don't you?

[*General giddy assent.* DEGAS *shoots them a look then reaches up to take down the painting. The frame has been chained to the wall of the barn. Peals of laughter.* DEGAS *walks out. The laughter trails off. Silence. Then…*]

CASSATT: How's your leg?
MANET: Improving.

[*Another burst of laughter at* DEGAS' *expense.*]

EXT. THE GROUNDS OF CHATEAU BEAUFRESNE - NIGHT

[*After dinner. Moonlight.* CASSATT *and* BERTHE *walk arm in arm.* BERTHE *smokes a thin cigar. After a puff…*]

BERTHE: Obnoxious, isn't it? Started as an affectation, now it's a habit.
CASSATT: As vices go these days, smoking's minor. When did Degas suddenly become a gourmand?
BERTHE: A week ago Tuesday. Last month it was Roman Catholicism. Tomorrow he may be a vegetarian or a Hindu!
CASSATT: For such an eccentric man, he's surprisingly conventional.… If only he wouldn't change his conventions so often.
BERTHE [*after a few more paces*]: You still love him, don't you?

[CASSATT *shrugs.*]

CASSATT: Do you still love Manet?
BERTHE: Which one?
CASSATT: I suppose that answers my question.
BERTHE: Poor Eugene, I don't know why he puts up with me. Still, marriage suits me. Unlike you. Or Degas. Even so, we all expected the two of you to be married by now.
CASSATT: Us? Married?! Half the time we're not even speaking!
BERTHE: In that case, maybe he'd make a better husband than I thought.

[Knowing smiles. BERTHE *flips her cigar into a stream.]*

CASSATT: Thank you for bringing him.

EXT. CHATEAU BEAUFRESNE - DAY

[A beautiful country morning. No sign of CASSATT *or* MANET.
RENOIR *and* MONET *paint* LISE *and* CAMILLE *in a field near a tree.*
PISSARRO *plays tag with* JULIA *while* BERTHE *looks on from a bench
where she sips her morning coffee. She sees...*
DEGAS *and a VERY PLAIN YOUNG WOMAN coming down the road.]*

INT. THE BARN STUDIO - CONTINUOUS

*[*CASSATT *confers with* MANET *about her mural.]*

MANET: You know what's always struck me most about working a big canvas?
CASSATT: Composing the space?
MANET: The incredible amount of paint.

[At first, CASSATT *just blinks at him, then realizing the joke, starts
to laugh. It's a relief to finally laugh freely in the shadow of the mural.*
MANET *laughs with her. They're yucking it up when they discover...*
DEGAS *standing silently at the open barn door, ushering in a rather
homely Young Woman with slightly bucked teeth and big ears. (see
"Girl Arranging Her Hair") After a stiff bow,* DEGAS *departs.]*

[BACK TO] EXT. THE BARN - CONTINUOUS

[As DEGAS *walks off,* BERTHE *and the others watch him go.]*

INT. THE CHATEAU KITCHEN - DAY

*[*CASSATT *checks on preparations for dinner.* MATHILDE *and her hired
help are frantic.* DEGAS *pokes around, critically sniffing dishes, checking
the firmness of vegetables, tasting sauces. When he sticks a finger into
one of* MATHILDE'S *sauce pans,* MATHILDE *smacks his hand.]*

MATHILDE: You will please wait until it is properly reduced!

[Elbowing DEGAS *aside, she tastes the sauce herself.* CASSATT *hauls* DEGAS *out of* MATHILDE's *way.]*

MATHILDE: There is no white pepper! How am I supposed to make a credible sauce when I have no white pepper?!
CASSATT: Use black.
MATHILDE: My sauce will look like soot!!

*[*CASSATT *and* DEGAS *retreat to the kitchen door.]*

DEGAS: How's the model I brought you?
CASSATT: Challenging.
DEGAS *[too sharply]*: That's what makes it a duel.
CASSATT: Why are you always so angry?
DEGAS: Me? Angry? Why should I be angry?

*[*DEGAS, *turning, accidentally knocks a bowl from the counter.]*

MATHILDE: Out! Out of my kitchen! Both of you! Get out!

*[*CASSATT *is already down on her hands and knees cleaning up the mess.* MATHILDE *takes over. When* CASSATT *looks up at* DEGAS, *she finds him rubbing his eyes. She leads him out.]*

EXT. OUTSIDE THE KITCHEN DOOR - CONTINUOUS

*[*DEGAS *tries to focus on* CASSATT's *face but can't.]*

CASSATT: Did something fly into your eye?
DEGAS: No. I'm fine.

[Holding his face, she studies his eyes. He tries to avoid.]

DEGAS: I just told you I'm fine!

[CASSATT reaches back inside the kitchen door, picks up THREE FORKS from the counter, then holding them up...]

CASSATT: How many forks am I holding?
DEGAS: Will you stop these parlor games?! I just had too much sun.
CASSATT: How many? Answer me!
DEGAS: Four.

[CASSATT puts down the forks, gently takes DEGAS by the arm and leads him away from the house.]

EXT. CHATEAU BEAUFRESNE - SUNSET

[DEGAS averts his eyes from the setting sun. The glare is obviously painful to him. CASSATT observes. Then...]

DEGAS: Mary... I'm going blind.
CASSATT: It may just be a temporary -
DEGAS: I've seen three different doctors. They all agree. My eyes have always been weak, but this is...

[He takes a deep steadying breath. She braces herself.]

CASSATT: Go on. Tell me.
DEGAS: I can't see without bright light. But the brighter the light, the more it hurts. It's like having hot needles stabbing my eyes. Sometimes I'm fine, but then, just when I think I've gotten better...

[He starts to break.]

DEGAS: Oh God, what am I going to do?

[She holds him. Comforts. Then, after a long moment...
He reaches out, finds and takes her hand. Kisses it. Then presses it to his face, covering his eyes. When he finally removes her hand, he blinks.]

DEGAS: Maybe it's best that I can't see the expression on your face.

[She takes his hand. Grips it tightly.]

CASSATT: Is there anything I can do?

*[He shakes his head, no. When he finally pulls away…
He pulls out a device – an eyeglass frame with one lens covered in
opaque material, the other with a narrow slit.]*

DEGAS: One of the doctors gave me this absurd contraption.

*[He turns away, puts it on, then turns back to face her. It looks
ridiculous. But CASSATT doesn't laugh.]*

DEGAS: If you say it becomes me…

[She kisses him. Tenderly.]

[DISSOLVE TO]   EXT. THE MESNIL TRAIN STATION - DAY

*[The weekend guests are leaving - except for BERTHE and her daughter,
JULIE. CASSATT, LYDIA, and MATHILDE have come to see them off.
CASSATT holds DEGAS's hand.]*

CASSATT: Stay.
DEGAS: You have your work and I have…
CASSATT: If you don't have the good sense to stay here with me, at least
take care of yourself. And if you need me, write. Promise?

[He nods. An awkward embrace. Then, covering emotion…]

DEGAS: Four days in the countryside with these devotees of natural
sunlight and I am reminded why I infinitely prefer life in the city.

[The train starts to move. The others shout to DEGAS to board the train.]

DEGAS: I have not forgotten our duel.
CASSATT: Neither have I.

[DEGAS *"feels" for the entryway and climbs aboard. The train pulls out of the station.* BERTHE *goes to buy a newspaper.* CASSATT *watches the train go. When she turns, she finds…*
LYDIA, *pale, gasping, and on the verge of fainting, clutching* JULIE's *hand, frightening the child.]*

CASSATT: Lydia?

[CASSATT *rushes to her, supports her.* BERTHE *rejoins them.]*

LYDIA: Just exhausted.
BERTHE: After four days with that pack of hynenas, it's no wonder.

[*They start back to the Chateau.]*

INT. LYDIA'S ROOM - CHATEAU BEAUFRESNE - NIGHT

[LYDIA, *propped in bed, afgan pulled to her chest, rides out the pain and bone-weary fatigue.* CASSATT *intercepts* MATHILDE *at the door, takes the tray, and comes to* LYDIA's *bedside.]*

CASSATT: Mathilde's made you some soup.

[LYDIA *waves it off.* CASSATT *urges a spoonful on her.* LYDIA *finally takes it - for her sister's sake. Refuses more.]*

CASSATT: Any better?

[*The lack of an answer alarms* CASSATT. LYDIA *clutches her hand.]*

LYDIA: Was it really worth it?
CASSATT: Having guests? *[Off* LYDIA's *annoyed look…]* Ah. The big "it." *[pause]* There's no simple answer to that. If I'd had a say in the matter, I would live at least two completely different lives. Still, I wouldn't trade my life for anyone else's, if that's what you mean.
LYDIA: More or less. How much longer before you finish the mural?
CASSATT: I have to be done by April to meet the deadline.

LYDIA: When I think of you, all alone, all winter long, in that drafty old barn… *[slight pause]* Isn't there some way you could finish it in Paris?

CASSATT: A studio that size would cost a fortune. Besides, I think I'd rather use the money to buy this place. What do you think? A home of our own? A garden. Horses.

LYDIA: I think you'll do exactly as you please regardless. You always have.

CASSATT: Have I really been such a burden?

LYDIA: A challenge. Like Edgar's duel.

[Off CASSATT's *reaction…]* He's really not a bad man - not my first choice, but all things considered… acceptable.

[From the doorway…]

BERTHE *[gently teasing]*: Lydia, are you still trying to marry off your sister?

CASSATT: Old habits die hard.

LYDIA: I've given up. For better or worse, she's married her work.

BERTHE: And married well. If you ask me. Then again, no one did.

[When LYDIA *catches* BERTHE's *wink at* CASSATT *and her sister's grin, she launches into a self-parody of an old complaint…]*

LYDIA: That's it! Laugh at me! Thumb your noses at society! I know what you think. Poor, fussy, pathetic Lydia. But I have done my duty, Miss Mary!

CASSATT *[sadly]*: And done it brilliantly.

[then with mock firmness] Now eat your soup.

*[*LYDIA *takes the spoon. But just as she starts to reach for the bowl, she falters, quickly setting aside the spoon.]*

LYDIA: Mary, I need to…

[She struggles out of bed. CASSATT *and* BERTHE *help* LYDIA *across the room toward the shielded chamber pot. As* LYDIA *disappears behind the screen…]*

LYDIA *[OC]*: Oh God, it's so humiliating.

[CASSATT *and* BERTHE *exchange a worried look.*]

EXT. THE GARDEN AT BEAUFRESNE - DAY

Crisp autumn. CASSATT *paints* LYDIA, *seated alone on a bench. ("Lydia Crocheting")* LYDIA *is pale and drawn.* BERTHE *smokes, scans a letter from* LOUISE. JULIE *plucks flowers from a bed.*

BERTHE: Louise's new husband sounds simply delicious.
CASSATT: I reserve judgment.
LYDIA: Why aren't you working on your mural? First that hideous buck-toothed girl, now this.
CASSATT: I'm sick of crawling around that scaffold. I needed a change. And you've always been my best subject.

[LYDIA, *flustered, begins ripping at the crochet.*]

LYDIA: Look what you've made me do! I'll have to pull five rows!
BERTHE: What's the matter, Lydia, can't stand a compliment?
LYDIA: Hush.

[CASSATT *smiles. Continues painting.* BERTHE *gives* LYDIA *an affectionate little kiss on the temple before going off to supervise* JULIE *who's now tearing up whole plants with glee.*
CASSATT *looks up from her painting to find the needles and crochet in* LYDIA'*s lap, her sister's eyes closed, head back.*]

CASSATT: Tired?

[LYDIA *nods her head, yes.*]

CASSATT: Then just close your eyes and rest.
LYDIA: But -
CASSATT: I've got plenty more to work on.

[LYDIA *naps.* CASSATT *continues painting, totally absorbed. Her sister seems very much at peace.*

After a long moment, BERTHE *and* JULIE *return. With only slight urging from her mother,* JULIE *presents her ratty bouquet to* LYDIA. CASSATT *observes, filled with emotion.]*

JULIE: Aunt Lydia?
BERTHE *[whispered]*: I think she's asleep, honey.

[Before BERTHE *can lead her away,* JULIE *nudges* LYDIA. *No response. Then tugs at her sleeve. The crochet and needles fall to the ground.* CASSATT *turns suddenly alert. Then…* LYDIA *slumps heavily.]*

CASSATT: Oh God! Lydia! Lydia!!

*[*CASSATT *rushes to her aid.* JULIE *watches, frightened.]*

CASSATT: Lydia!!

[DISSOLVE TO]   EXT. A CEMETERY - PARIS - DAY

*[*LYDIA's *funeral.* CASSATT's *fellow painters have gathered. After* MARY *tosses a last handful of earth onto* LYDIA's *grave, the mourners begin to slip away.* BERTHE *lingers.*
Scanning faces, CASSATT *spots* THERESE *- surprisingly well-dressed. After a moment's eye contact,* THERESE *rushes off.* MARY *and* BERTHE *remain at graveside until they are alone.]*

CASSATT: I can't imagine life without her. She was always there - managing, nagging…
BERTHE: Matchmaking.
CASSATT: Lydia made marriage her mission because she didn't think I could live alone. Maybe she's right.

*[*CASSATT *searches the dwindling crowd for some sign of* DEGAS.*]*

BERTHE: I can't believe he's not here.

[CASSATT, tight-lipped, says nothing. Then sadly...]

CASSATT: Lydia never quite made up her mind about Edgar. Or me. She knew that to get where I'm going, I needed steadiness - a smooth straight uphill road. And she knew that life with Edgar would be a twisting, pitted, boulder-strewn path. It's a wonder our paths ever crossed. And when they did, I always had Lydia to go back to. *[slight pause]*

CASSATT *[CONT'D]*: Whenever I tried to imagine the three of us living together, I'd remember who I am and who he is.
[slight pause] He's not a cruel man, or even insensitive. Just insecure.

BERTHE: And willful.

CASSATT: No more than I. Lydia would have understood why he's not here and forgiven him. ... But I can't.

[CASSATT abruptly turns away.]

INT. CASSATT'S STUDIO, PARIS - DAY

[CASSATT, still in her black mourning dress, sits in her unheated studio surrounded by a gallery of Lydias in oil, chalk, ink and pastel. On an easel is CASSATT's "GIRL ARRANGING HER HAIR" - her response to DEGAS's challenge.
DEGAS enters unannounced, bearing a bunch of LILACS - very much like those in the centerpiece at Beaufresne. CASSATT barely acknowledges him. Then, after an awkward silence...]

DEGAS: My eyes - knowing they would be seeing you - have granted me a reprieve. You are my elixir!

[He presents the lilacs. Finally, after another silence...]

CASSATT: Where were you?
[when he doesn't answer] Lydia's funeral! I needed you.

DEGAS: And I am here.

[As he moves from one painting of LYDIA to the next...]

DEGAS: This is how I want to remember your sister, not as -
CASSATT [*flinging the lilacs*]: Go away! Please. Just go.

[*She begins covering the paintings with dropcloths.*]

DEGAS: Unlike your sister, I will die alone; unknown, unmourned. And yet just yesterday, I bought two portraits by Ingres!

[CASSATT *just gapes at him in disbelief.*]

DEGAS: I shall give them to the nation, then go to the Louvre to sit with my bequest and think of the noble deed I've done. I will have nothing yet I will have owned a few sublime objects. That will be my chic.

[*She ignores him. Only then does* DEGAS *see the painting of the "Girl." He's stunned. Lifting the painting…*]

DEGAS: I am defeated. Such style! The glitter of the earring alone elevates the subject to a higher -

[CASSATT *grabs her bag.*]

DEGAS: Where are you going?
CASSATT: Beaufresne. I have work to do.

[*She exits. He pursues, with the picture.*]

EXT. STREET OUTSIDE THE CASSATT HOUSE - CONTINUOUS

[DEGAS *chases* CASSATT. *When he darts in front of her, she tries to get around him. He counters.*]

DEGAS: If I were a cavalier in a plumed hat -
CASSATT: You'd look like a cheap actor in a suburban theatre.

[*She breaks past* DEGAS. *He dogs her heels.*]

DEGAS: I would pledge my life to yours, ask forgiveness for my many faults, and beg you to grant me the honor of your hand in holy matrimony.

[She quickens her pace.]

DEGAS: Would you? If I asked?
CASSATT: Forgive or marry you?
DEGAS: Either. Both.
CASSATT *[walking away]*: Neither.

INT. BARN-STUDIO AT CHATEAU BEAUFRESNE - DAY

[Winter. The room is cold. CASSATT's breath steams as she digs a narrow TRENCH in the earth near the mural's base.
The upper supports of the panels have been slung by block and tackle from the rafters. The right panel has already been lowered into the trench so that upper portions of the painting can be reached. The scaffold is off to the side.
Much work has been done on the mural since last seen, but all of it on the lower portions, and none at all on the left panel. The hands, arms, and faces of the few figures blocked in are still undefined and featureless.
MATHILDE enters with the mail, holding one letter apart.]

MATHILDE: Another one from Degas.

[CASSATT takes it to a spot under the skylight. When she opens it - a single spray of pressed lilac. MATHILDE, her age and frailty showing, leaves. As CASSATT reads...]

DEGAS *[V.O.]*: "My dearest Cassatt, flowers in the garden last only a season, blossoms in a vase, mere days, but you are in my heart, a perpetual bloom, and in my brush forever."

[CASSATT stares at the letter, then crumples it into a tight ball and throws it into the trench.]

INT. DEGAS'S STUDIO - DAY

[DEGAS *sits, hands grimed with pastel, shielding his eyes. The* YOUNG MODEL, *covered with a towel and standing near a wash basin, seems unsure of what to do.*]

MODEL: Master?
DEGAS: There is no master here. Just go.
MODEL: Will you want me tomorrow?
DEGAS: Yes. … No. I don't know. No.

[ZOE *enters, a LETTER in her hand.*]

DEGAS: What?!
ZOE: This was just delivered.
DEGAS: From Cassatt?

[*He grabs the letter, tears it open. Having trouble reading it, he shoves the note back to* ZOE.]

DEGAS: Well what are you waiting for?! Read it to me.
ZOE: It's from your brother.
DEGAS [*suddenly deflated*]: Oh. Just leave it. Thank you.
MODEL: Sir?
DEGAS: Tomorrow. Three o'clock. Now go.

[ZOE *and the* MODEL *leave.*
DEGAS *stumbles through his studio, upsetting easels and open jars of paint. He goes through his "store" of paintings until he finds his "Miss Mary Cassatt at the Milliner's." Touching its surface very very lightly, his hand trembles.*]

INT. THE BARN AT BEAUFRESNE - DAY

[*Mid-winter.* CASSATT *feeds wood into the stove. She's down to her last few logs. Despite the fire the room is freezing.
Her cough begins to sound ugly. Her nose runs. Shivering, she pulls*

an old blanket around her shoulders and tries to warm herself at the stove, staring up at the mural...
Details of trees, geese, and dogs have been completed in the center panel but the women's features still haven't been worked. The left panel sports a few lines but nothing more.
She goes to the table for a pot of paint. When she tries to remove the brush, she finds the paint congealed. Frozen.
Taking it to the stove, she tries to heat it. The paint softens. She stirs. The pot cracks. Paint pours out, hissing on the hot metal, filling the air with a harsh toxic steam. In trying to save it, she burns her hand. A total loss.
CASSATT *sits on the cold dirt floor and fighting tears, beats the ground.]*

INT. A BROTHEL - PARIS - NIGHT

[At the draped door to the salon, MATHILDE *hands a few coins to a YOUNG BOY who then heads for the corridor leading to the back rooms.* MATHILDE *suffers the stares of the lounging PROSTITUTES, the smirk of a passing PATRON. Then...*
Therese, led by the Boy, draped in a loose robe, emerges from the corridor. Her eyes meet MATHILDE*'s.]*

EXT. THE TRAIN STATION AT MESNIL – DAY

[A cold gray winter's day. An empty platform. From the train, one cloaked passenger (a woman) disembarks, carrying a single small cheap bag. She seems lost. Moving to the far end of the platform, she asks directions of the Station Manager.]

INT. THE BARN AT BEAUFRESNE - DAY

*[*CASSATT *- pale, haggard, wracked with fever, blanket drawn tight - sits on the floor, her back against the nearly cold stove, her woodpile reduced to woodchips and crumbled bark.*
The barn door opens. Snow drifts in. A Woman enters.]

THERESE: Miss?

[CASSATT doesn't stir. THERESE approaches, finding CASSATT barely conscious - fingers blue, cheeks flushed but the rest of her strangely bloodless.]

THERESE: Miss! Miss!

[THERESE tries to warm CASSATT's fingers by rubbing them between her own, blowing on them, pressing them to her cheek and neck. CASSATT barely responds. THERESE checks the stove. Dying embers. THERESE quickly undoes CASSATT's dress - CASSATT half-heartedly resists - then undoes her own. She then hugs CASSATT, pulling the blanket around them both.]

EXT. CHATEAU BEAUFRESNE – DAY

[Weeks later. Near the barn, THERESE chops wood. Judging from the pile, she's been at it a while.]

INT. THE BARN – DAY

*[Despite her still "iffy" condition, CASSATT is hard at work on her mural. All the faces and hands have been worked – they're all obvious variations on one model… THERESE.
THERESE enters with an armful of wood. She feeds the woodstove. CASSATT glances at her. Smiles. THERESE smiles.]*

CASSATT: Another week and it's done.

[THERESE steps up next to her. THERESE glories in her image.]

INT. CASSATT'S STUDIO, PARIS - DAY

*[Left in the same condition as last seen – paintings covered with dropcloths, an empty easel, slanting winter light.
The door lock turns. The door creaks open on unused hinges, MATHILDE – now quite decrepit – enters, followed by…
DEGAS, who feels his way past the threshhold.]*

DEGAS: Thank you for...

[MATHILDE *dismisses his thanks, then withdraws, leaving* DEGAS *alone in the lifeless studio. After a long moment, he lifts a cloth, revealing* CASSATT's *"Girl in an Armchair."]*

EXT. THE BARN - CHATEAU BEAUFRESNE - SPRING - DAY

[Huge wooden crates for shipping CASSATT's finished mural to Chicago *lay open, two of its three sections lean against the barn. Steadying herself against the doorjamb,* CASSATT *watches* THERESE *supervise the* THREE WORKMEN *pack the mural. Though much improved,* CASSATT *is still noticeably pale and haggard. She turns as...*
A CARRIAGE *rolls around the corner of the barn and pulls to a stop next to the freight wagons.* BERTHE *leaps out, brandishing two bottles of champagne.]*

CASSATT *[brightening]*: Berthe?

[BERTHE *rushes to* CASSATT. *Embraces her. Spins her.]*

BERTHE: Congratulations! You did it!

[THERESE, *bursting with pride, rushes up and grabs* BERTHE *just as the Workmen tote the once-problematic left panel (Women Pursuing Fame) past them.]*

THERESE: Look! They're all me!

[The faces and hands of the mural figures are, indeed, all variations on *one model...* THERESE.]

THERESE: Miss Cassatt says that once they're sixty feet in the air, no one will notice.
CASSATT: I don't know what I would have done without her.
THERESE: And vice versa. Let me get some glasses.
BERTHE: No need.

[BERTHE *pops a bottle, then hands it to* CASSATT.]

BERTHE: First drink to the artist!

[CASSATT *takes a tiny sip, then hands the bottle back to* BERTHE.
BERTHE *heads for the crates.* CASSATT *and Therese follow.
AT A WAGON,* BERTHE *taps one of the already sealed crates. She
offers the unopened bottle to* CASSATT.]

BERTHE: You do the honors.

[CASSATT *takes the bottle, steadies herself…
The Workmen stop to watch as* CASSATT *winds up, swings…
But* CASSATT'*s blow is too weak. The bottle bounces off the wood.*]

CASSATT: I think you'd better.
BERTHE: We'll do it together.

[BERTHE *takes* CASSATT'*s hand and together they wind up…*]

BERTHE & THERESE: One, two… Three!

[*The bottle smashes onto the crate, blessing its journey.*]

INT. KITCHEN – CHATEAU BEAUFRESNE – EVENING

[THERESE *finishes preparing their supper.* BERTHE *begins bringing
bowls to the table.* CASSATT *sits. She looks weary and drawn.*]

CASSATT: How is…
BERTHE: Degas? He keeps to himself. Rarely goes out. And when he does…
CASSATT: And his sight?
BERTHE: Comes and goes. A terrible thing.

[CASSATT *coughs nastily, steadying herself against the table.* THERESE
rushes over with a glass of wine. BERTHE *watches closely.*]

CASSATT: I don't feel nearly as badly as I must look.

BERTHE: Liar. But, not to worry, I just found this incredibly handsome young doctor - a few doses of his magic potions and you'll be back in action.

INT. A DOCTOR'S OFFICE - DAY

[CASSATT refastens her bodice after a "modest" examination. The DOCTOR, preparing a solution with a granular gray powder in a flask, explains the treatment he's prescribed.]

DOCTOR: This procedure works wonders for physical and nervous exhaustion.

[He heats the flask over a flame, trapping the gasses in a bubble.]

DOCTOR: Quite new, only been in use a year - still experimental. I think we'll find dramatic improvement.

[He brings her the flask and a primitive inhalator mask.]

DOCTOR: All you have to do is inhale the warm vapors. I personally find it quite soothing and invigorating.

CASSATT: That gray powder...

[Holding flask and inhalator to CASSATT's face...]

DOCTOR: New element... called Radium.

[After a moment, we go in close on CASSATT as she inhales the vapors deeply. She coughs. Waits moment, then inhales again.]

DOCTOR *[OC]*: You may experience some nausea. Not to worry, that's to be expected.

[CASSATT holds in the inhaled vapors. When he removes the flask we see that his hands are covered with a vicious rash.]

EXT. A PARK, PARIS - (MAGIC HOUR)

[Strollers on promenade. CASSATT, fresh from the DOCTOR, suddenly veers toward a bench. Nearly collapses. Though the evening is cool, she's flushed and sweating.
She mops her brow with a handkerchief. A look of panic crosses her face. She starts off, then clutches a tree. Hiding behind the trunk, she retches. Recovering, she daubs at her lips with the hankie, straightens her spine, taking a deep breath.
A twinge of pain. She balls her fists. Then…
CLOSE ON - CASSATT's hand poised to knock at…]

INT. THE DOOR OUTSIDE DEGAS'S STUDIO - NIGHT

[CASSATT doesn't knock. The door is slightly ajar. She hesitates, then quietly enters…]

INT. THE DOOR OUTSIDE DEGAS'S STUDIO - CONTINUOUS

[We follow CASSATT's eyes as she surveys the room. The studio is a shambles. There are sketches, incomplete paintings and pastels, partly sculpted figures, props for models, remnants of partly eaten meals, empty wine bottles, and…
DEGAS, sound asleep on the divan, his rumpled week-old clothes symptomatic of his current emotional state.
On an easel she finds her painting "GIRL IN AN ARMCHAIR" (also known as "The Blue Room") "borrowed" from her studio.
CASSATT touches the painting's surface - her familiar signature in the lower right corner.]

DEGAS *[OC]*: The arm of that chair is magnificent.
CASSATT *[turning to him]*: You reworked it for me.
DEGAS *[knowing full well he did]*: Did I? We worked so well together.

[Finally, after a long pause…]

DEGAS: Did the prairie-hoppers enjoy your allegory of the modern woman?

CASSATT: One reviewer called it "impudent, the work of an uncompromising and uncooperative personality."

DEGAS: Did they at least return it in good condition?

CASSATT: Unfortunately...

[DISSOLVE TO]   EXT. (INSERT) CHATEAU BEAUFRESNE - DAY

[Spring. CASSATT *and* THERESE *stand outside the barn. Huge shipping crates containing the MURAL PANELS have just been removed from the wagons. Shipping labels are prominent.*
CASSATT *hands a DELIVERY MEN a crowbar with which he pries open the largest of the crates, revealing the center panel – "Women Plucking the Fruits of Science & Knowledge."]*

CASSATT: It really is dreadful, isn't it?

THERESE: Maybe if it'd been hung lower...

CASSATT: They might've been truly disgusted.

[As the Workmen climb back into their wagons, CASSATT *roots around in her tool box.]*

THERESE: The Americans are idiots! I don't mean you, Miss. I meant...

*[*CASSATT *has found what she's looking for... MATCHES.]*

THERESE *[alarmed]*: What are you doing?

CASSATT: It's served its purpose.

*[*CASSATT *strikes the match.* THERESE *knocks it from her hand.]*

THERESE: You can't! That's me!

*[*CASSATT *searches* THERESE*'s face for a long moment, then reaches back into the tool box.]*

THERESE: Please. I'll buy it from you. I'll work for you for free, for as long as it takes, just don't -

[CASSATT *pulls out a carpet knife, then turns to the mural.*]

THERESE: No!!

[*While slashing the canvas, cutting out a painting-sized portrait…*]

CASSATT: The president [*cut*] of the Women's Christian [*cut*] Temperance Union [*cut*] called it undignified [*cut*]!

[CASSATT *rolls the extracted fragment, hands it to* THERESE, *then starts cutting out another.*]

CASSATT: Frivolous [*cut*]! Degrading! [*cut*] Forbidden fruit! [*cut*] Cynical!

[*She extracts another "portrait," drops it.* THERESE *retrieves it while* CASSATT *attacks what's left of the mural.*]

[BACK TO]   INT. DEGAS'S STUDIO - CONTINUOUS

[CASSATT *has just finished telling the tale.*]

DEGAS: So you finally agree that it was a mistake?
CASSATT: In some ways, I suppose it was. Then again, without mistakes, we'd learn nothing.
DEGAS: Without you, I'd cease to exist.
CASSATT: I see you're still a slave to exaggeration.
DEGAS: I love you.
CASSATT: As I said, we learn from our mistakes.
DEGAS: Falling in love was a mistake?
CASSATT: Pretending we're not who we are, is. I'm feeling quite old, Edgar.
DEGAS: Safely ancient and sufficiently famous to abandon celibacy?
CASSATT: Soon, Edgar. Very soon.

[*Finally, she sits beside him. They hold hands, studying "their" "Blue Room." Finally…*]

CASSATT: I've used the commission money to buy Beaufresne.

DEGAS: I see.

CASSATT: There's plenty of room for… You could stay as long as you like.

[DEGAS *pulls away.*]

DEGAS: The city is my subject, not trees.

CASSATT: Mesnil's not that far from Paris. You could come and go whenever you felt like it.

DEGAS: So could you.

CASSATT: I have to. For my printmaking.

DEGAS *[returning]*: Good. For a while there I thought you'd converted to landscapes!

CASSATT: Still a slave to my Madonna and Childs.

DEGAS: Children.

[*It takes a moment for her to remember. When she does, she smiles, then, patting his hand…*]

CASSATT: Yes. Children.

INT. A PRINTMAKING STUDIO (1890S) - DAY

[CASSATT, *now fifty, is striking a print. The work is hard, dirty, mechanical.* DEGAS *works right alongside her, but with his eyes bothering him, he finds* BERTHE, DURAND-RUEL - *also in their fifties - and* JULIE, *now a lovely but bored teen, especially irritable.*]

BERTHE: This is industry, not art! We might as well all be in a kettle factory!

[CASSATT *and* DEGAS *focus on striking the print.*]

BERTHE: If this is about making money -

CASSATT: This is about printmaking.

BERTHE: Finally, after all these years, our paintings are selling and you two decide to open up a print shop!

CASSATT: Since when have artists ever let the market decide their medium?

DURAND-RUEL: Ever since the pharaohs decided to decorate their tombs.

[CASSATT hands DURAND-RUEL a freshly-struck print ("Woman Bathing"). DURAND-RUEL invites comment from BERTHE and JULIE. JULIE shrugs her indifference; BERTHE lights up a cigar.]

JULIE: Can I have one?

BERTHE: No. Aunt Mary doesn't approve.

DEGAS: Neither do I.

[With a sharp glance at BERTHE, DEGAS exits. CASSATT slams down the plate. DURAND-RUEL reconsiders the print.]

DURAND-RUEL: On the other hand, what with Japanese prints all the rage…

BERTHE: Uh oh. I think Paul's just smelled something.

CASSATT: What?

BERTHE: Money.

[Off DURAND-RUEL's hungry grin…]

INT. DURAND-RUEL GALLERY - DAY

[CASSATT sits glumly. In her hands, a catalog labeled "An Exhibition of Paintings and Prints by Mary Cassatt," with a reproduction of her "Woman Bathing" on its cover.
PISSARRO sits beside her, tugging at his long white beard. The few patrons sniff with unsubtle condescension.]

CASSATT: They hate my work.

PISSARRO: No more than mine.

CASSATT: That's a comfort.

[When DURAND-RUEL joins them…]

CASSATT: Have any other painters come?

DURAND-RUEL: A few. Most are working in the countryside or in the South.

PISSARRO: Where I should have stayed.

DURAND-RUEL: I'm thinking of organizing a show in New York and I'd like to include these, if you'll permit me.

CASSATT: Why restrict the ridicule to one continent? Take 'em on the road! Australia, Africa, Asia!

PISSARRO: Don't forget Antarctica.

CASSATT: All the "A" places!

DURAND-RUEL: You have friends in America.

CASSATT [rising]: I thought I had friends here.

[When she turns, she discovers DEGAS standing just inside the gallery door, catalog in hand. He says nothing. Finally...]

CASSATT: Well?

DEGAS [after a pause]: Your "Bathing Woman" is worth some comment.

CASSATT: Surely nothing the critics haven't already said.

DEGAS: Have the critics pointed out that the single line which gives volume to her back manifests such supple skill and grace that I am forced to confess... I never imagined you could draw so well. I stand silent in the presence of greatness.

[He bows deeply – too deeply – and stays down.]

DEGAS: I salute you, Mademoiselle Cassatt. You are... an accidental American.

[He remains bent over for an embarassingly long time. Finally CASSATT, pleased, pulls him back up.]

PISSARRO: So, have you seen my prints?

DEGAS: Yes.

PISSARRO: And?

DEGAS: As a printmaker, you're a superb painter.

[She playfully slaps DEGAS's arm. He nudges her right back. They stroll off together.]

INT. RESTAURANT - PARIS (1890S) - DAY

[CASSATT, her hair now sprinkled with gray, enters on the arm of THERESE. CASSATT scans the room, squinting. She dons a pair of

eyeglasses and sees…
LOUISE, *now in her late 30s, waving from a distant table.*
After dismissing THERESE, CASSATT *navigates the room on her own.*
LOUISE *rushes to meet her. They embrace.]*

LOUISE: How I've missed you!

[As they move on, HENRY HAVEMEYER *(40),* LOUISE'*s husband, rises and extends his hand to* CASSATT *in greeting.]*

LOUISE: Henry, Mary Cassatt.
HAVEMEYER *[warm handshake]*: I've heard so much about you.
CASSATT: So how's the Stock Market?
HAVEMEYER *[puzzled]*: Booming when we left New York. Why?

*[*LOUISE *laughs.* CASSATT *grins at the private joke. Then she notices a painting, half-uncovered, leaning against the wall next to their table - *PISSARRO'*s "The Orchard."]*

CASSATT *[to LOUISE]*: I see you've been shopping.
HAVEMEYER *[lifting the painting]*: Not her. Me.

*[*CASSATT *and* LOUISE *exchange a knowing smile.]*

LOUISE: So? Has he passed the test?
CASSATT: With honors.

*[*DURAND-RUEL, *running late, rushes to join them.]*

DURAND-RUEL: Louise! You look marvelous. And, Mary…

[Huggy/kissy with the ladies then a warm handshake for HENRY, *teasing him about the painting…]*

DURAND-RUEL: My God, Hank, don't tell me you've been lugging that picture around with you all morning?!!
CASSATT: "Hank?"

LOUISE: Whenever Paul comes to New York, he stays with us.

[Settling at the table, HAVEMEYER pulls out his checkbook.]

HAVEMEYER: First things first.
DURAND-RUEL *[discreetly]*: Six hundred seventy-five thousand, three hundred twenty francs. For the Monet and the Pissarro.

[CASSATT raises an eyebrow at the sum. While HAVEMEYER nonchalantly writes out the check...]

LOUISE: We've even convinced Father that art's a good investment.

[A WAITER pours champagne. HAVEMEYER slips the check to DURAND-RUEL. When DURAND-RUEL glances at it...]

DURAND-RUEL: Excuse me, Hank, but this is -
HAVEMEYER: I've decided to keep the Cassatt and Degas as well.
DURAND-RUEL: Splendid.
HAVEMEYER: My pleasure.
DURAND-RUEL: In that case, lunch is on me!

[When he notices CASSATT is watching him with suspicion...]

DURAND-RUEL: Unless Mary would like to treat.

[CASSATT hammers back her champagne.]

INT. DEGAS'S STUDIO - DAY

[While DEGAS fusses, setting up a camera on a tripod...]

CASSATT: It doesn't bother you that work we once sold for hundreds now changes hands for hundreds of thousands?
DEGAS: I am like the racehorse which has just won the Grand Prix. ... I am satisfied with my ration of oats.

[While checking focal length with a string...]

DEGAS: Lately you've been thinking more like a dealer than an artist. You know what they're saying about you?

CASSATT: Spare me.

DEGAS: That you're just a pimp for your rich American friends - buying up paintings for pennies, looting the national heritage.

CASSATT: Works that the Salon rejected!

[CASSATT fumes. DEGAS doesn't seem to notice, or care.]

CASSATT: It's Monet, isn't it? Now that he's rich and "a national treasure" he forgets he once traded paintings for food! I arranged his sales and now he calls me a pimp?! Americans got bargains because your country-men chose to laugh up their sleeves rather than part with their sous!

DURAND-RUEL *[entering]*: Knock knock!

[He ushers in HAVEMEYER and LOUISE. CASSATT still fumes.]

DURAND-RUEL: Edgar, I'd like you to meet -

DEGAS: Yes, yes, later.

[DEGAS immediately grabs the arrivals and poses them.]

DEGAS: Please, over here. You, sir, stand behind her and look... over there.

[Unlike the others, CASSATT is not amused.]

DEGAS: Mary, look at Louise!

LOUISE: After all these years, you still remember me.

DEGAS: Of course I do, Miss Elder.

HAVEMEYER: Missus Havemeyer. And I am Mister Havemeyer.

DEGAS *[distractedly]*: Congratulations. Now hold your positions.

[DEGAS rushes back to his camera, and then while ducking under and popping back up from under the hood...]

DEGAS: The problem with all photography is slavery to nature! The photograph needs artifice! Great art requires as much cunning as the perpetration of a crime! For God's sakes, Mary, stand still!

[DEGAS *exposes the plate. The flash pan has not ignited. He steps out from under the hood to check.* CASSATT, *annoyed, breaks rank. Just as she steps next to* DEGAS...
The PAN flashes. FLASH TO...
A SUN FLARE. Then reveal CASSATT *shielding her eyes. She blinks. Rubs. Blinks again.*]

LOUISE *[OC]*: Mary? Are you all right?

[*We are in...*]

INT. A NURSERY (LATE 1890S) - DAY

[CASSATT, *in the middle of painting* JULIE *with a baby (see any of* CASSATT'*s mature Mother-Child paintings or pastels), scans the faces of* JULIE, *the baby,* LOUISE *and* BERTHE. *All are a blur - coming near but never into focus, haloed with frosty light.*
CASSATT *once more blinks and rubs.* LOUISE *examines* CASSATT'*s eyes.*]

LOUISE: What's wrong?
CASSATT: Nothing. I'm fine. Just need a break. Sorry.
BERTHE: Try a cold compress.

[CASSATT *nods agreement.* BERTHE *tosses aside her newspaper and herds everyone out.*]

CASSATT: Berthe? I promised Edgar I'd pick him up some supplies.
BERTHE: Let him wait. Just get some rest.

INT. A SITTING ROOM - DAY

[CASSATT *sits alone in the sun-flooded room, wringing a damp cloth in her hands. Finally, she gets up and crosses to the window. She blinks. Tries to focus. When the image "frosts" beyond her cataracts, she bunches the drape tightly in her fist. After a long moment she dons hat, coat, and gloves.]*

EXT. AN ARTISTS' SUPPLY HOUSE - DAY

[CASSATT exits, carrying a parcel. The newspaper stand next door is doing a brisk business. All along the street, men and women devour the reports of the Dreyfus Affair. Extreme reactions. Loud arguments break out. Up ahead, a fistfight.]

INT. DEGAS'S STUDIO - DAY

[CASSATT enters to find DEGAS viciously grilling a MODEL who's in the process of undressing behind the screen. He smacks a newspaper against the screen for emphasis.]

DEGAS: I asked if you think Dreyfus is innocent!

[When the intimidated girl doesn't answer...]

DEGAS: Do you have opinions on anything?! Are you stupid or just illiterate?

CASSATT: What she thinks has nothing to do with her ability to pose.

DEGAS *[to the MODEL]*: Until you answer my questions you will not pose for me.

[While CASSATT has seen DEGAS in such rages before, she's never seen one never quite like this. She monitors him closely while removing her coat, hat, and gloves.]

DEGAS *[CONT'D]*: Whose side are you on? The Jews? Or the military's? Answer me, dammit!

CASSATT *[intervening]*: I happen to think that Captain Dreyfus has been unfairly accused. Does that mean I'm not welcome?

DEGAS: Spoken like a true expatriate. If you find the French so disagreeable why don't you go back to Pittsburgh or Philadelphia or wherever it is you still insist on calling home. At least I know who I am.

CASSATT: A nouveau-riche Gaul with social pretensions, weak eyes, and an even weaker bladder. Dear God, this is the kind of simple-minded prejudice you always railed against! It's so... common!

[DEGAS bristles. Boils. Trying to bring down the heat...]

CASSATT: Look, this is an issue on which reasonable people can disagree -

DEGAS: We are not talking about some idle opinion - a preference for beef over pork! We are talking about treason! The National Honor! Which naturally means nothing to you since you're no more French than that ludicrous Jew, Pissarro.

CASSATT: Camille Pissarro -

DEGAS: Was born in the Indies.

CASSATT: The French Indies.

DEGAS: Not good enough.

[DEGAS obnoxiously begins to hum the Marseillaise.]

CASSATT: This is absurd! Nationalism is a disease! A cruel hoax perpetrated on otherwise innocent people!

[DEGAS wheels on the dark-complexioned young MODEL who's just stepped out from behind the screen.]

DEGAS: Look at her!

CASSATT: She's lovely. What of it?

DEGAS *[with venom]*: She is a Jewess! And she can leave!

MODEL: But I'm a Protestant!

DEGAS: Equally bad! Get out!!

[When the MODEL retreats, DEGAS hurls his newspaper at her. She ducks. CASSATT holds open the door. The MODEL grabs her clothing and splits. CASSATT closes the door.]

CASSATT: There. Are you satisfied?

[DEGAS *glares at her. His hostility is palpable. Hateful.*]

CASSATT: Are we going to work or are you going to spend the entire afternoon defending the lies of these pompous pot-bellied generals?

[*His gaze turns, if anything, even more hateful. He has just crossed some dangerous line for her.*
CASSATT *removes the tubes of paint from the bag and tosses them on his sofa.*]

CASSATT: Two tubes of ultramarine lemon. One of viridian. Two maddar lake. And vermillion. As requested.
DEGAS: The Jews have taken over the banks, the government, the -
CASSATT: Do you have any idea how ugly this makes you?
DEGAS: When truth is ugly -
CASSATT: Stop it! Just stop it! My God, listen to what you're saying! Sometimes the truth is ugly. But just because a thing is ugly doesn't make it true! Think! Pissarro is a Jew and you've been friends for almost thirty years!
DEGAS: Not any more.

[CASSATT *is dumbstruck. Finally...*]

CASSATT: You're willing to destroy a friendship over this nonsense?
DEGAS: With pleasure and without so much as a twinge. Dead. Done. Gone!
CASSATT: Then I pity you.
DEGAS: And for that, I detest you.

[*After a beat,* CASSATT *begins to gather up her things. She starts for the door, opens it. Stops.*]

CASSATT: Until you apologize to that girl, to Pissarro, and to me, I will have nothing more to do with you.
DEGAS: Apologize? ... Never.
CASSATT: In that case, goodbye.

[She leaves, slamming the door behind her. He huffs, then drops onto the sofa - right on top of the tubes of paint.]

EXT. DEGAS'S BUILDING - DAY

[CASSATT is about to cross the street when...
A window on the second floor opens. DEGAS leans out.]

DEGAS: Cassatt!

[She turns, fully expecting that he's come to his senses.]

DEGAS: The money for the paints.

[He flings a fistful of franc-notes out the window. The bills flutter down around her and swirl in the wake of a passing horse and carriage. CASSATT stares back up at DEGAS until he slams his window shut.]

INT. DURAND-RUEL GALLERY - DAY

[The walls are hung with what are now impressionist and post-impressionist masterpieces, among them works of both CASSATT and DEGAS. Prominent is CASSATT's "Woman and Child with Oval Mirror." DURAND-RUEL is "working" a prospective buyer when he spots...
CASSATT bulling her way through the crowd, lugging a framed but unwrapped painting. She rudely inserts herself between DURAND-RUEL and the Buyer, shoving the picture at him.]

CASSATT: Dispose of this for me.

[It's DEGAS's portrait of "Mary Cassatt with Cards in the Louvre." The Buyer is intrigued. DURAND-RUEL is shocked.]

CASSATT: Frankly, I'm tempted to destroy it.
DURAND-RUEL: But Degas gave this to you. As a gift. It was his way of saying –
CASSATT: I'm well aware of its provenance.

[Before the Buyer can speak, DURAND-RUEL *draws* CASSATT *aside.]*

DURAND-RUEL: Is it something he said or -

CASSATT: Edgar Degas is a vicious, narrow-minded bigot! And any suggestion that he was anything to me besides a former colleague, I will regard as a slander. If you won't handle this, I'll take it to someone who will.

*[*DURAND-RUEL *clutches the painting, unwilling to give it up.]*

DURAND-RUEL: Of course, I'll handle the sale, but if you ask my opinion –

CASSATT: I've asked for a professional service, not advice. I'm willing to sell at any price... on one condition. I want it sold to a stranger, someone who knows nothing about me or Degas. I want my name and my connection to this piece kept out of it. Understood? Paul?

[He nods his head, yes. CASSATT *starts to walk away.]*

DURAND-RUEL: Degas thinks your new work is -

CASSATT: I no longer care what Mister Degas says about anything.

[She finds DEGAS *at the other end of the gallery, bouncing excitedly in front of her "Oval Mirror."]*

CASSATT: I need to use your back door.

[Too late. DEGAS *hears her. Rushing toward them...]*

DEGAS: Cassatt! You have given us the greatest painting of this century! The line and color, the modelling of the hands! Such hands!

[In front of her...]

DEGAS: My God, you've given us the Infant Jesus and his English Nanny!

CASSATT *[offended]*: What is that supposed to mean?

DEGAS: You have secularized one of the great religious themes! Made us see the cult of the Madonna with modern eyes!! And you have no idea what you have done! Such humility! I love you for that! To hell with our differences! I forgive you! I forgive me! I forgive everybody! I've even forgiven Dreyfus!

CASSATT [to DURAND-RUEL coldly]: Sell it.

[CASSATT walks away.]

DEGAS: Mary? Where are you going? Mary!

[FADE OUT & BACK UP ON]
EXT. CHATEAU BEAUFRESNE (1915) - NIGHT

[The porch. CASSATT, now 71 and almost blinded by cataracts, stands beside JULIE MORISOT, now a mature young woman. To the northeast, LIGHT flashes on the horizon accompanied by what sounds like thunder. An approaching storm?]

CASSATT: And I haven't seen him since.

[Flash and thunder - the distant thud and boom of cannons.]

JULIE: Come back inside.

[Another rumble of artillery fire and long guns.]

CASSATT: That's what comes of national honor, Julie. Cannons and boys dying. Damn him. Damn them all.

[Cassatt turns to go into the house, guided by JULIE.]

INT. KITCHEN - CHATEAU BEAUFRESNE - NIGHT

[THERESE fixes tea at the stove. On the table between CASSATT and JULIE lies an official-looking document.]

JULIE: The War Department's ordered you to leave! With the Germans advancing -

CASSATT: Let them come. This has been my home for twenty years.

JULIE: But, Aunt Mary -

CASSATT: Your mother and I came of age in a different world. You're too young to understand. I gave some of my best years and sold some of my best work to buy this place. For me Beaufresne is independence. My sister died here. And so will I.

[A rumble outside. Julie goes to the window. Explains…]

JULIE: Trucks. And soldiers. Heading for the front.

THERESE *[serving the tea]*: Miss?

CASSATT: Since everyone else is telling me what to do, you might as well too.

THERESE: Now that Julie's here… I'm leaving. Tomorrow morning. I've volunteered. As a nurse.

[CASSATT nods her head, sadly.]

INT. CASSATT'S ROOM - BEAUFRESNE - DAY

[CASSATT stands at a window. Though she cannot see, over her shoulder we see swirling smoke. Behind her, at the bureau, JULIE goes through a drawer in which she's just found…
A pack of letters. A love poem in DEGAS's hand. A cameo of LYDIA. A strange photo of CASSATT and DEGAS - the one from the HAVEMEYER session. And a Legion of Honor Medal. Bringing it to her…]

JULIE: Aunt Mary, what's this?

[CASSATT reaches out. JULIE places the Medal in her hand. It only takes an instant for CASSATT to recognize it. A complex reaction – irony, years of exclusion, eventual but belated acceptance. She finally explains…]

CASSATT: The Legion of Honor Medal. To commemorate my service to France.

JULIE: I didn't know they gave these to foreigners.

CASSATT: It just depends who's in charge. And whose art they own. Awards like these add value to a collection. We all got one. Eventually.

[Another shell hits nearby. The concussion rattles the pane. CASSATT *doesn't flinch.* JULIE *snaps shut the drapes and pulls* CASSATT *away from the window, leading her to the bed.]*

JULIE: Aunt Mary, I'm afraid. I can't help it. I wish I weren't but I am.

*[*CASSATT *motions her to come sit beside her.* JULIE *does.]*

JULIE: How can you be so brave?

CASSATT: Force of habit. Hardly a virtue. There've been very few things in my life that frightened me. Actually, only two. One was –

JULIE: Going blind?

CASSATT: That's an accident of fate. If I hadn't taken that damned radium... But at the time, who knew?

JULIE: So what were you afraid of?

CASSATT: Failure.

JULIE: And... ?

CASSATT *[with a small grin]*: The disapproval of Mister Degas.

[Silence. Then...]

JULIE: Mother always wondered why the two of you never married.

CASSATT: He never asked. At least never in the right circumstances. The man had the worst timing of anyone I have ever known. He was impossible.

JULIE: If he had asked, at the right time, would you have said "yes?"

CASSATT: I don't really know. In so many ways we were married, or at least it felt that way. No matter how angry we got, it seems we always ended up back together. I suppose it was the work.

JULIE: Maybe it wasn't.

CASSATT: Anyway, that's all past.

[Another explosion outside which rattles the house. When CASSATT *senses* JULIE's *terror...]*

CASSATT: Since you won't leave without me, I think it's time we took a vacation. We'll start packing tomorrow.

JULIE: What about your paintings?

CASSATT [half-teasing]: What else is there to pack?

[slight pause] Now fetch me a shawl, would you? I'd like to tour the garden one last time before they blast my lilacs to smithereens.

[Another blast. CASSATT hurls the Medal at the window.]

INT. THE BARN-STUDIO - DAY

[CASSATT stands in the open door, shawl drawn tight around her, looking without seeing, onto the grounds. Behind her we see JULIE remove DEGAS's Ballerina painting from the wall.]

JULIE [bringing it to her]: When'd you buy this one?

[CASSATT tilts the picture into the full sunlights, strains to see but can't make it out. But when she feels the frame's distinctive edge, lightly touching the surface of the pastel itself... A secret smile.]

CASSATT: Most men, when they woo a lady, give them flowers and jewels...

[A pause. Then a sigh.]

CASSATT: I do wonder how he is.

[She hands the painting back to Julie who packs it in a crate. CASSATT wanders back into the barn.
From a storage rack, JULIE lifts down...
CASSATT's "Girl Arranging Her Hair." Absorbed by it, she doesn't realize that CASSATT is right behind her until...]

CASSATT: Julie?

JULIE: Yes?

CASSATT: What are you doing?

[CASSATT gropes closer, then, finding the frame, runs her fingers over the wood. She recognizes it immediately.]

CASSATT: She was such an ugly child. Degas hired her. I painted her. She never realized how she was being used.
[slight pause] Put an extra layer of wrapping on it, will you?

EXT. THE GARDEN - CHATEAU BEAUFRESNE - NIGHT

[CASSATT feels her way down the dark gravel path to the bench where LYDIA once sat crocheting. She sits. Remembers.]

EXT. CHATEAU BEAUFRESNE - DAY

[The wagons are loaded. It's time to go. CASSATT lingers for a long moment – listening, remembering faded images, then, taking JULIE's arm, climbs aboard the coach.]

INT. DEGAS'S STUDIO - DAY

[DEGAS (81) is working on another wax sculpture of a dancer, his hands slathered with blue plasticine. The MODEL poses nude. He blindly follows the lines of her body with his fingers, memorizing the shape and line, leaving traces of blue wax on her skin.
The years have not been kind to him. He is now an old man with a white beard, almost totally blind.]

MODEL: Sir?
DEGAS: You are here to pose, not to engage in repartee.
MODEL: But your toast is burning!
DEGAS: I know. I like the smell.

[He heads for the stove and removes the smoldering bread.]

DEGAS: It reminds me of…
MODEL: Reminds you of what?
DEGAS *[after a pause]*: Oh hell, I'm so old, I can't remember.

[He munches at the burnt toast, then tosses it. He wipes his hands on a rag then begins searching for his jacket.]

DEGAS: Get dressed. That's enough for today. Lock the door when you leave. I'm going out.

[*The* MODEL *hands him his rumpled jacket and walking stick.*]

EXT. DEGAS'S BUILDING - DAY

[CASSATT *and* JULIE *stand on the sidewalk across the street from* DEGAS'S *house. Automobiles pass.* JULIE *is carrying a painting wrapped in muslin. After a long pause…*]

JULIE: Do you want me to go in with you?
CASSATT: I think this is something I need to do alone. Just get me across the street. I'll manage the rest.

[JULIE *takes her arm. Just as they start across the street…*
DEGAS *emerges from the door of his building wearing his dark rumpled suit, his tie askew, supporting himself on a stick, "feeling" his way toward the street.*
JULIE, *for whom* DEGAS'S *face tickles a memory, is about to say something when an approaching* DRIVER *honks his horn and swerves around them.*]

CASSATT: Horrible things. [*then a shared secret*] I love them.

[*Just as* CASSATT *and* JULIE *have nearly crossed the street…*
DEGAS *turns away to follow the curb.*
Since neither CASSATT *nor* DEGAS *can see…*
They pass, a meter apart – he, feeling his way up the sidewalk; she, feeling her way to his front door.
As DEGAS *continues on his way in BG…*
CASSATT *knocks at the door. Waits. Knocks again.*
A NEIGHBOR WOMAN *from next door leans out.*]

NEIGHBOR WOMAN: He's not in. You one of his models?
CASSATT: What? … Oh. No. Though years ago I did pose for him.
NEIGHBOR WOMAN: Terrible the way he treats them. They show up and

he's off, walking. Spends whole mornings following funerals. It's mad. When I see him, who should I say called? Ma'am?

[CASSATT *doesn't answer. She gropes her way down the sidewalk.*
JULIE *rushes up and takes her arm. But then...*
Heading back toward them is DEGAS. *He stops.*
CASSATT *stops. Julie suddenly realizes what's happening.*]

JULIE: Aunt Mary?
CASSATT: Shhh.

[*On her own, without* JULIE's *assistance,* CASSATT *starts down the sidewalk toward* DEGAS *just as* DEGAS *starts toward her.*
The sightless gaze of each floats off-target until they are almost within touching distance. Both grow still. Until...]

DEGAS: Mary?
CASSATT: Hello, Edgar.

[*He reaches out. When his fingertips find her face, his expression changes, softens. So does hers.*
He begins feeling the lines of her face.
Then, she too begins to feel his face.
Big close-ups of them both as his fingers trace her lips and her fingers trace the lines of his face.
JULIE, *a sentimental soul, chokes back a sob.*]

DEGAS: Is there somebody with you?
CASSATT: Julie Morisot. Berthe's daughter. We've brought something for you. Julie!

[JULIE *approaches.* CASSATT *takes the painting and presents it to* DEGAS.]

DEGAS: What's this?
CASSATT: Open it.

[He carefully removes the muslin. DEGAS *feels the frame, then adjusts the painting so it catches the brightest possible light. It's* CASSATT'*s "Girl Arranging Her Hair."*

He puts his face inches from the canvas, trying first one eye, then the other, then finally delicately touching its surface, "reading" the brushstrokes. He starts to smile.]

DEGAS: Ah.

CASSATT: Recognize it?

DEGAS: Seared in my memory. My God she was an unattractive girl, wasn't she?

CASSATT: Not after I finished with her.

DEGAS: You always managed to bring incredible beauty out of ugliness.

CASSATT: Did I bring beauty out of you?

DEGAS: Kicking and screaming.

[After a pause…]

DEGAS: Can you still work?

CASSATT: I see the pictures in my head.

DEGAS: In my dreams I see you so clearly.

CASSATT: Lines or color?

DEGAS: Both.

[Facing one another, smiling, each holds a side of the painting's frame. Then with great animation and vitality…]

DEGAS: Would you like to come up to my studio? I've just started a new sculpture. … The models hate the way I grope and poke, but what can I do?! I'd ask you to pose but –

*[*CASSATT *throws her arms around him and kisses him, holding him tight. He tries to hand the painting off to* JULIE.

When JULIE *finally takes it,* DEGAS *clings to* CASSATT.

Over their embrace…]

END CARDS:

EDGAR DEGAS DIED SIX MONTHS LATER

MARY CASSATT LIVED ANOTHER TEN YEARS

SHE DIED IN 1926 AND WAS BURIED
AT CHATEAU BEAUFRESNE

THE BEAR

&

HIS MONKEY

———◆———

Or, The More or Less True Account of a
Venturesome Twelve Week Journey to
Scotland and the Hebrides With Doctor
Samuel Johnson and James Boswell, Esq.

LIST OF CHARACTERS

(in order of appearance)

DR. SAMUEL JOHNSON	WOMAN, BAREFOOT
JAMES BOSWELL	EUAN MACRAE
BENJAMIN FRANKLIN	MALCOLM MACRAE
EDMUND BURKE	HUGH MACRAE
OLIVER GOLDSMITH	PA MACRAE
MARGARET BOSWELL	MA MACRAE
SERVANT GIRL	NORMAN MACLEOD
JOSEPH	FLORA MACDONALD
SCOTSMAN	ANNIE MACLEOD
TAVERN-MAID	LITTLE GIRL
DRUNK PATRIOT	LITTLE BOY
EAGER WOMAN	PRETTY ANNIE
OTHER WOMAN	COLIN
LADY ALISON MACINTYRE	A LASS
MALE GUEST	AUCHINLECK
CLERIC	STEP-MOTHER
WOMAN WITH THICK ACCENT	MARY
SCAMP	BETSY BOSWELL

INT. THE TURK'S HEAD TAVERN – (LONDON, 1773) – NIGHT

[From the head of a long table, DR. SAMUEL JOHNSON (63) – a big bear of a man – presides over the weekly gathering of his "Club." His voice booms.]

JOHNSON: Americans, sir, are felons and fanatics living among savages! To the moral detriment of each!

[JAMES BOSWELL (33), the Club's newest and by far youngest member, hangs on his every word, taking notes on the conversation. Anticipating a reaction...
We follow BOSWELL's gaze down the table, past the others who've also turned to the evening's special guest...
BENJAMIN FRANKLIN (67) - wearing his distinctive fur cap. FRANKLIN leans across a huge pile of books on the table in front of him, and with a playful twinkle...]

FRANKLIN: This America which you imagine exists only at its most remote frontier. Philadelphia, I assure you, is as civilized as London.
JOHNSON: Then why, sir, do you wear that "pelt" on your head?
FRANKLIN: For the same reason, sir, you wear that wig. A concession to taste. Though, in my case, it also keeps my bald head warm. Here, try it.

[FRANKLIN offers his "cap" to JOHNSON. JOHNSON removes his wig, revealing a headful of short, wiry, uncoifed hair. They exchange head-pieces; then don them. Laughter.]

FRANKLIN: Now that you are suitably attired, perhaps you will return with me to Pennsylvania. One week among us and your prejudices will disappear.

[EDMUND BURKE *(44), the famed Anglo-Irish statesman, seated at mid-table, interjects...]*

BURKE: What, and let facts wreck opinions which have taken Johnson a lifetime to acquire?! Never!
FRANKLIN: Bravo, Burke!

[OLIVER GOLDSMITH *(45) – the playwright, chimes in...]*

GOLDSMITH: For all his talk of other peoples and places, the furthest Johnson has been from London is Streatham.
JOHNSON: All that life can afford is to be found in London. Any man who tires of London is tired of life! Yet...

[After a huge and hurried slurp of lemonade – his end of the table is littered with empty cups...]

JOHNSON: I am in no way adverse to travel. On the contrary, my dear Goldsmith, I relish its prospect.
GOLDSMITH: Then why have you never taken Boswell up on his offer to tour Scotland?!
JOHNSON: I've been busy earning my living.
GOLDSMITH: Pah! With the King's pension your living is secured. If you don't want to go rambling with Bozzy or Franklin, say so!

[On the spot, JOHNSON *changes the subject...]*

JOHNSON: I must inscribe those books for Doctor Franklin before I forget.

[As FRANKLIN*'s pile of books is shunted down the table, and* JOHNSON *snatches the pen right out of* BOSWELL*'s hand...]*

JOHNSON *[CONT'D]*: Though I still think that no place demonstrates the vanity of human hopes more than a public library.
FRANKLIN: Why compile a Dictionary, if not to advance general learning?

*[*JOHNSON *grumbles and inscribes.* BOSWELL *hovers at* JOHNSON*'s*

shoulder to see what he's writing.]

JOHNSON: For God's sakes, man, give me room!

[BOSWELL quickly backs off, covering his embarassment with...]

BOSWELL: Unlike America, the libraries of Scotland, public and private, are well stocked with Doctor Johnson's works. Now if I can just entice him to come to Edinburgh to inscribe them, as he seems willing to do for the Philadelphians, we may yet get the great man out of his lair and into the wild!

JOHNSON *[still scribbling]*: In due time, Bozzy, in due time.

BOSWELL: I remember Voltaire's response when I invited him to Scotland.

[Groans, grins, and asides – they've heard this story many (too many) times.]

BURKE: And Voltaire said he'd rather be boiled alive. Accept it as foregone, my friend, you'll never get Johnson to accept an invitation to do that which any French philosopher has declined.

[Laughter. After slamming shut the cover of the last book in FRANKLIN's pile, JOHNSON suddenly announces...]

JOHNSON: I shall arrive in Edinburgh, by coach, Tuesday after next.

[BOSWELL is dumbstruck. JOHNSON hands him back his pen. Then, with a loud grunt, JOHNSON hoists the heavy pile of books.]

JOHNSON: Unless you have suddenly withdrawn your invitation.

BOSWELL: Uh, no. It's just that, well, I'm -

[As he lugs the books back to FRANKLIN's end of the table...]

JOHNSON: Stunned? Delighted? Dismayed? What?

BOSWELL: Sir, I am honored.

[Off the thud of the books landing on the table...]

[SMASH CUT TO] *"TWO WEEKS LATER"*

[THE WHEEL OF A POST-CHAISE bouncing hard, fighting ruts, slashing through puddles, spanking stones, skidding. Hooves thunder, the abused frame and axles scream. A whip cracks, drivers shout, a woman yelps, a gentleman curses. A cacophonic salad.]

[CUT TO] TWO DULL SHEEP standing in the middle of...
EXT. A ROAD - THE BORDERS, SCOTLAND – NIGHT

[THE SHEEP – just two old mates out for a gambol in the moonlit hills – stare tensely down the long road south to London. There's something in the air, something coming – THE POST-CHAISE AND TEAM OF SIX explode over a rise.
THE SHEEP levitate. Then bolt, each for the other's side of the road, absurdly colliding, barely managing to get out of one another's and the COACH'S WAY. THEIR VIEW as the hell-bent COACH roars off, climbing a bumpy grade.
THE POST-CHAISE crests the hill. Stretched out below is...
THE ANCIENT CITY OF EDINBURGH in moonlight, a warm twinkle from its many candles and lanterns, wisps of smoke from cooking fires and hearths.]

INT. THE BOSWELL HOME - PANTRY – NIGHT

[BOSWELL is tearing through cupboards looking for...]

BOSWELL: What's happened to the lemons?! Peggy?! ... Peg!

[MARGARET BOSWELL (35) his wife, enters, already annoyed.]

BOSWELL: Doctor Johnson must have lemonade. I've explained fifty times –
MARGARET *[under her breath]*: Aye, and then some.
BOSWELL: If we can't find the lemons –
MARGARET: Then the great man will just have to drink tea like the rest of us.

[He doesn't like her tone, but before he can respond, a SERVANT-GIRL *flounces in with a BOWL OF CITRUS.]*

MARGARET *[with mock relief]*: Saved!!!

*[*MARGARET *marches out. The* SERVANT-GIRL'*s dangerously loose and low-cut neckline, peevishness, and familiar demeanor around* BOSWELL *are such that we suspect that her "duties" have expanded beyond household chores. Drawing himself up…]*

BOSWELL: Since Doctor Johnson labors under the impression that all Scots are crude savages…

[She slams the fruit bowl on a counter and stomps out.]

FOLLOWING HER - DOWN THE HALL

BOSWELL: I insist that while he is under our roof, we behave impeccably.

INT. THE DINING ROOM - CONTINUOUS

[The GIRL *ducks in and pouts near a WALL CLOCK while* MARGARET *double-checks place settings, re-adjusting silver.* BOSWELL *follows the* GIRL *in…]*

BOSWELL: There must be no mention of politics, religion, anything French, and especially not –
BOSWELL & MARGARET: Macpherson's translations.
BOSWELL: As a matter of fact, yes.

*[*BOSWELL *dogs her heels, triple-checking, readjusting what she's just arranged. The last straw.* MARGARET *wheels on him.]*

MARGARET: James!! If you don't – *[then continuing sweetly]* Perhaps you should go down to the High Street and wait for his coach.
BOSWELL: There's plenty of time.
MARGARET: What with fine weather and clear roads, it may arrive early.

[When BOSWELL *glances at the* GIRL, MARGARET *notices.* BOSWELL *covers by re-adjusting a glass.* MARGARET *grabs his hand.*
The SERVANT GIRL *snickers.* MARGARET *wheels on her. Caught, the* SERVANT GIRL *covers by picking up a spoon. She LICKS it, then gives it a robust polish on her skirt.* MARGARET *snatches it from her hand.*
The GIRL *curtsies and scurries from the room.*
BOSWELL *straining for dignity under his wife's glare, isn't aware of* JOSEPH (40s), *his man-servant – a tall, droll multilingual Bohemian – who materializes right behind him.*]

JOSEPH: Sir?

[BOSWELL, *startled, yelps, and turns.*]

BOSWELL: For God's sakes, stop lurking!
JOSEPH: Yes, sir. Anything else, sir?
MARGARET: That will be all, Joseph.
JOSEPH: Yes, Ma'am.

[JOSEPH *doesn't move. Then, after a slight pause, with a refined but very distinct Germanic accent…*]

JOSEPH: If I might be so bold, the fish forks might be more appropriately placed at the far left.

[*A bow. He exits. Beat.* BOSWELL *and* MARGARET *dash around the table rearranging the fish forks.*]

JOSEPH [*reentering silently*]: Sir?

[*Again,* BOSWELL's *startled. He discreetly sets down a fork.*]

BOSWELL: What now?
JOSEPH: That clock, sir. It's been running approximately one half hour slow.

[*Beat. Blink.* BOSWELL *bolts.*]

[SMASH CUT TO] EXT. STREETS OF EDINBURGH – NIGHT

[BOSWELL races up a hill… takes a shortcut through an alley… nearly slips on something slimy as he rounds a corner… then sprints flat-out down a steep, ankle-twisting cobbled street which debouches on…]

PARLIAMENT SQUARE - HIGH STREET

[BOSWELL runs up just as… THE POST-CHAISE COACH is pulling out. A few PASSENGERS sort through the pile of luggage, OTHERS are getting into waiting carriages. But no sign of JOHNSON. BOSWELL takes off at a dead run, shouting…]

BOSWELL: Doctor Johnson!!

[Just as BOSWELL disappears around a corner…
JOSEPH strolls into the Square. Approaches the luggage, calmly surveys it, then leans over a TRUNK with AN ENGRAVED PLATE identifying the trunk as the property of…
"Sam. Johnson. 7 Johnson's Court, Fleet Street, London."
Off JOSEPH, hoisting the heavy trunk with surprising ease…]

EXT. EDINBURGH STREETS - OLD TOWN – NIGHT

[BOSWELL presses on, shouting JOHNSON's name. He ducks down a dark alley only to find himself in a dead-end courtyard. He staggers to a halt. Despondent, self-flagellating, almost in tears.
But then he hears the distinctive roar of the BIG MAN'S VOICE. With the freakish acoustics of tall tenements and narrow alleys, JOHNSON could be anywhere.]

EXT. A COURTYARD - OLD TOWN – NIGHT

[JOHNSON in a splotched coat over a plain but seriously distressed shirt, the spouts of his TRI-CORNER HAT dripping effluent, screams at A WOMAN leaning from an open third-story window, empty bucket in her hand.]

JOHNSON: For fifty years, I've roamed the streets of London, you fishwife!

[Overlapping him, the Woman gives just as good as she gets, but does so in a Glaswegian accent so thick it's impenetrable to English ears – though we gather it has something to do with equating baby's piss and England.
BOSWELL *rushing into the courtyard, discovers* JOHNSON *shouting…]*

JOHNSON: Fifty years! And not once have I been doused!! But fifteen minutes among you troglodytes and –

*[*BOSWELL *runs up, so breathless, he's almost mute.]*

BOSWELL: I went to the square and…
JOHNSON: Bozzy!!

[Then, to the shrieking Woman above…]

JOHNSON: For God's sakes, stop your mouth!

[The Woman stokes her flow to even greater volume.]

BOSWELL: When I didn't find you, I…
JOHNSON: Did you at least pick up my bags?

*[*BOSWELL *blanches. Beat. Then…]*

BOSWELL: Don't move!

[SMASH CUT TO] PARLIAMENT SQUARE - HIGH STREET

*[*BOSWELL *dashes to the spot where the luggage had been piled.* JOHNSON'*s trunk is, of course, long gone.* BOSWELL *takes off.]*

[BACK TO THE COURTYARD] – BOSWELL, *a marathoner hitting "the wall," staggers into the now empty and eerily silent courtyard. He pipsqueaks…*

BOSWELL: Doctor Johnson?

[Then, seemingly out of nowhere, JOSEPH materializes behind him, JOHNSON's trunk perched casually on his shoulder.]

JOSEPH: Sir?

[BOSWELL leaps like a startled cat. Once he's recovered, they hear LOUD VOICES coming from… A brightly-lit TAVERN beyond the courtyard arch.]

[SMASH CUT TO] A THICK HEAVY HAND slamming onto a table with such force the cups jump, ale slopping over rims of tankards. We are in…

INT. A TAVERN/INN – NIGHT

[JOHNSON leans across the table into the face of a large, red-faced, and sputteringly enraged SCOTSMAN (30s).]

JOHNSON: The Scots, sir, are incapable of producing anything greater than plump sheep, thin cattle, and sheaves of thistle!

[Fighting words. Mutterings among the clientele. JOHNSON lifts his heavy WALKING STICK, a veritable bludgeon.]

JOHNSON: Finegal, sir, is a fraud!
SCOTSMAN: Our great and ancient Scots epic –
JOHNSON: Macpherson's Finegal is neither ancient nor epic. Its so-called heroic lines, the doggerel of a third-rate poet with as little learning and poetical talent as this stick!!

[With which, JOHNSON hammers the table. Then, taunting…]

JOHNSON: Come, sir! Have you no rebuttal?!

[A dangerous silence. A few rough-looking characters begin to reach

inside their coats for weapons. Then, the STREET DOOR CLICKS OPEN. All eyes turn to…
BOSWELL *who enters, followed by* JOSEPH. BOSWELL *senses the tension in the air, the imminent possibility of violence.]*

BOSWELL *[blowing very Scots]*: Well, lads! I see you ha'taken me boon companion under yer wing!!
JOHNSON *[delighted]*: I thought I'd lost you, Bozzy!

[As BOSWELL *crosses, careful not to step on too many toes…]*

JOHNSON: Pull up a chair and order a punch for my fellow scholars! They need more spirits if they're to sustain such spirited literary discussion!

[A TAVERN-MAID *who's "known"* BOSWELL *on an occasional basis for years, intercepts him.]*

TAVERN-MAID: Is this one a friend of yours?!
BOSWELL: Aye. And a bit of a rascal too. But Dr. Johnson also happens to be *[loud enough for all]* the world's pre-eminent man of letters… At least in England.

[At mention of "England," half a dozen Scotsmen spit.
BOSWELL *takes* JOHNSON *by the arm, turning him to the door.]*

BOSWELL: Time to go, sir. Supper waits.

[As BOSWELL *hustles him out, past his countrymen's glares…]*

DRUNK PATRIOT: Mock if you must our Macpherson, but you'll find more poets in the Highland hills of Scotland than in all the alleyways of London.

*[*JOHNSON *stops, turns to the crowd, then…]*

JOHNSON *[quoting Horace]*: "Parturiunt montes, nascetur ridiculus mus."

[Uh-oh. BOSWELL *tenses.* JOSEPH *translates for the puzzled…]*

JOSEPH: "The mountains labor; a silly mouse is born." Horace. Ars Poetica.

JOHNSON *[clapping him on the back]*: Excellent, sir!! A Scotsman and a scholar, who'd have thought it?!

[The crowd erupts.]

JOSEPH: Actually, sir, I am a native of Bohemia.

*[*BOSWELL *hustles* JOHNSON *out the door, just as hurled tankards come sailing their way.]*

EXT. JUST OUTSIDE THE TAVERN/INN – CONTINUOUS

[With cups and cutlery clattering the door behind them…]

JOHNSON: We can't leave. I've booked a room.

BOSWELL *[hustling him off]*: You're staying with us.

JOHNSON: Then I'll be meeting your wife.

BOSWELL: Wives generally live with their husbands, even in Scotland.

JOHNSON: I had better change my shirt then.

JOSEPH *[from behind them]*: Excellent plan, sir.

INT. DINING ROOM - THE BOSWELL HOUSE - LATER - NIGHT

[Dinner's winding down for everyone but JOHNSON. MARGARET *observes in stunned silence as* JOHNSON *gorges himself with utter disregard for acceptable table manners, slurping down oysters with gusto, barely interrupting his flow of speech…]*

JOHNSON: A man of sixty-three who's labored forty years with his pen has earned the right to a vacation. I've long dreamed of travel to exotic lands, and where do I go?! … Scotland!

[A fact which JOHNSON *finds uproariously ironic and funny. Polite, forced smiles from the OTHERS. Johnson guzzles a tumbler of lemonade.]*

SERVANT-GIRL *[flirtatiously]*: More lamb, sir?
JOHNSON: Excellent!!

> *[*JOHNSON *slides enough meat for three onto his plate.* BOSWELL *squirms under the look in* MARGARET's *eye – chilly enough to bring on winter. A socially desperate middle-aged* WOMAN *pipes up...]*

EAGER WOMAN: I simply must ask, why, in your Dictionary, you define "pastern" as the "knee" of a horse?
JOHNSON: Ignorance, madam. Pure ignorance.

> *[She reinvestigates her vegetables.* ANOTHER WOMAN *chimes in.]*

OTHER WOMAN: I, for one, am most grateful that you left out all the naughty words.
JOHNSON: Does this mean, madam, that you went looking for them?!

> *[The* WOMAN *wilts. But from across the table comes a burst of bright laughter. All eyes turn to* LADY ALISON MACINTYRE *(30s) a young, rich widow. Bright and beautiful, she aims her complete battery of charms at* DOCTOR JOHNSON. *He loves it.]*

MALE GUEST: Has anyone informed Doctor Johnson that his so-called definition of "oats" is insulting to Scotsmen?
BOSWELL: You, sir, are the first.
MALE GUEST: Then you, sir, have been too long in London.
BOSWELL: Only a fool could take umbrage at a reference to grains.

> *[At which the Gentleman takes umbrage with* BOSWELL. *A* CLERIC *discreetly asks* MARGARET...]*

CLERIC: How did Dr. Johnson define "oats"?

> *[*LADY MACINTYRE, *overhearing, quotes...]*

LADY MACINTYRE: "Oats are a grain, which in England are generally given to horses, but in Scotland support the people."

[The CLERIC, *the* MALE GUEST, *and both* WOMEN *bristle.]*

MALE GUEST: I assure you that we feed oats to horses just as you do in England.

JOHNSON: Then, sir, I congratulate you on treating your horses as well as you do your people.

*[*LADY MACINTYRE *laughs brightly. The* MALE GUEST *harummphs.]*

LADY MACINTYRE: We must work on bringing Doctor Johnson to Edinburgh. Permanently.

BOSWELL: It's taken ten years to convince him to visit. To convince him to stay might take thirty.

LADY MACINTYRE: Sir, there will always be room in my house for you. And if my books or company prove inadequate, my estate is within an easy stroll of the University, which is just as ancient as the one at Paris!

JOHNSON: As in so many things, Lady, age is rarely an improvement.

LADY MACINTYRE: Then you, sir, are the exception.

*[*JOHNSON *is utterly captivated. When she leans across the table and presses his arm, her bosom heaves with a wistful sigh.* JOHNSON *glows. REACTIONS as* JOHNSON *pats her hand. Sweetly. Then, with an extra little squeeze of his arm, she adds…]*

LADY MACINTYRE: If only I could keep you here. *[then quite softly]* We could spend our days roaming my garden and our evenings with you instructing me in philosophy.

JOHNSON *[not hearing]*: What's that, my dear?

BOSWELL *[a bit too loud]*: She says she'd like to spend her days trotting you 'round her shubbery and her nights in logic.

[The guests are shocked. MARGARET *is secretly pleased.* LADY M., *however, shoots a nasty glance* BOSWELL's *way, flashing her claws. What is it about these two?]*

EXT. THE BOSWELL HOUSE – NIGHT

[BOSWELL, MARGARET, *and* JOHNSON *see off the dinner guests. Ritual formalities.* LADY MACINTYRE'*s carriage waits.*]

LADY MACINTYRE [*on* JOHNSON'*s arm*]: You must promise to call on me before you set off on your odyssey.
BOSWELL: We leave tomorrow at dawn.
LADY MACINTYRE: Then I shall see you off, like Penelope bidding her sweet Ulysses a fond farewell and a swift return.
JOSEPH: We sail from Leith Harbour.
JOHNSON: Until then, m'Lady.

[JOHNSON *helps* MACINTYRE *into her carriage. With a look at* BOSWELL, MARGARET *goes back inside.* JOSEPH *follows her in.* BOSWELL *slips around to the other side of the carriage. He leans in to* LADY MACINTYRE *and in a rushed whisper...*]

BOSWELL: Do not see us off.
LADY MACINTYRE: And why not?!
BOSWELL: If you do, we may never go.
LADY MACINTYRE: I'll take that as a compliment.
BOSWELL: He thinks he's in love with you!
LADY MACINTYRE: You once imagined the same thing.
BOSWELL: He's an old man on his first vacation, Alison. Be kind.
LADY MACINTYRE: Don't worry, "Bozzy," I won't steal him away from you.

[*Her carriage pulls out. As she waves gaily to* JOHNSON...]

JOHNSON: Alison MacIntyre is a blooming rose in a weed-congested wilderness! Her love of learning, her wit, her –
BOSWELL [*with sarcasm*]: Long neck and heaving bosom?
JOHNSON: I hardly noticed.

[BOSWELL, *starting to go back inside, mutters...*]

BOSWELL: Alison MacIntyre is much more and far less than she seems.

JOHNSON: What's that?

BOSWELL: Nothing, sir. Touch of indigestion.

[BOSWELL stops in the doorway to study JOHNSON, who is still watching LADY MACINTYRE's carriage roll off into the night. Beat. BOSWELL goes in. JOHNSON follows.]

INT. BEDROOM - BOSWELL HOUSE - LATER – NIGHT

[The SERVANT-GIRL unpacks JOHNSON's trunk. Buried among the carelessly packed clothing, linen, books and papers, she finds…
TWO PISTOLS along with a POUCH OF SHOT and a HORN OF GUNPOWDER.
Picking them up, the unsecured top of the horn pops open. Black powder spews like Vesuvius over JOHNSON's shirts. BOSWELL, passing, sees what's happening.]

BOSWELL: My God, look what you've done!!

SERVANT-GIRL: Well he might have bothered to tighten the stopper!

[As they jostle one another, trying to flounce the black gunpowder from the shirt…]

SERVANT-GIRL: For God's sakes, let go of me! I'll get it off quicker without your clumsy fingers in the way!

MARGARET'S VIEW – from the open doorway. It appears that her husband is trying to undress the maid and that she is doing everything in her power to help him.

[MARGARET charges in, a nasty set to her jaw. BOSWELL jumps back, hands raised in innocence. MARGARET snatches the pistol from the GIRL's hand and wheels on BOSWELL.]

BOSWELL: Margaret, darling, I swear –

MARGARET: Why's he got pistols?!

[JOHNSON enters, face dripping from the washbasin, toting his wig like a scruffy cat, his hair standing in wild spikes.]

JOHNSON: To defend myself from Highland savages and Highwaymen!! Though I doubt I'll need them here in Town. *[snatching back the PISTOL]* Unless one of your doctors of divinity takes exception to my articles of faith. In which case, I may just have to shoot him!

[In pantomime of a duel, JOHNSON spins wildly and suddenly, forcing MARGARET to dodge and duck out of his way.]

JOHNSON: Bozzy will be my second!!

[With which he tosses the pistol back into his trunk and turns to MARGARET. With surprising gentleness and grace...]

JOHNSON: A marvelous supper, Madam. And as for your giving up your own bed to such an undeserving guest, I am deeply moved, forever in your debt.

[His awkward bow eases her fears.]

JOHNSON: And where will you sleep, my dear?
MARGARET *[with a nod at BOSWELL]*: With him. If he behaves.

[JOHNSON grins. Then with startling abruptness...]

JOHNSON: I rarely sleep before Three in the morning. Therefore, I shall read.
BOSWELL: My library's downstairs.

[MARGARET yanks a book from her shelf...]

MARGARET: Here, try a bit of Finegal!

[She shoves it into JOHNSON's hands and before BOSWELL can object, she flashes him an impish look of defiance.]

MARGARET: A grand book, don't you think? *[exiting]* Candles are in the cabinet.

[Once she's gone, BOSWELL *turns to* JOHNSON, *somewhat sheepishly.* JOHNSON *bursts out laughing.]*

JOHNSON: By God, I like her spirit! You're a lucky man, Boswell. Damned lucky!!

[He flips open the offensive book. While riffling pages…]

JOHNSON *[CONT'D]*: But as for the wench…
BOSWELL: Sir?

*[*JOHNSON *tosses "Finegal" into the trash, then goes to the window. He bangs the frame, trying to open it.* BOSWELL *tries to help.]*

JOHNSON: Do all Scots nail their windows shut? We need fresh air!!

*[*JOSEPH *enters behind them, yet again startling* BOSWELL. JOSEPH *joins them at the window, taps the frame… Once, twice, thrice… then lifts it easily open.* JOHNSON *looks at him – How'd you do that?* JOSEPH *shrugs.* BOSWELL *bids them goodnight. Exits. Before* JOSEPH *leaves…]*

JOHNSON: Tell me, Joseph, do you find your master to be…
JOSEPH: He's a good employer. He treats me well. And we have an understanding. He overlooks my oversights –
JOHNSON: And you overlook his.

[The faintest of faint smiles flickers on JOSEPH's *lips.]*

JOHNSON: Is there a woman in Scotland he hasn't tried to bed?
JOSEPH: Thousands, sir. Then again, he's never been north of Aberdeen or west of Glasgow.
JOHNSON: And Lady MacIntyre?
JOSEPH: Sir?
JOHNSON: Has he… ?
JOSEPH: Sir?
JOHNSON: Nothing.

[A breeze lifts the curtains at the open window. JOHNSON takes a deep lusty lungful. JOSEPH withdraws, leaving the household's honored guest to his breathing.]

INT. UPSTAIRS HALLWAY - LATER – NIGHT

[MARGARET now in nightdress and cap, carrying a lit taper, stops when she hears strange mumblings from JOHNSON's room. The door down the hall is ajar. Candlelight glows within. She tiptoes closer, stealing to the door. She discovers...
JOHNSON reading, occasionally muttering lines aloud. He holds the book an inch from his nose and leans so close to the candles, which he's laid on their sides, that flames singe the front of his hideously matted wig. But what truly appalls MARGARET is the HOT WAX dripping and puddling on her precious carpet.]

[QUICK CUT TO] INT. BOSWELL'S BEDROOM – NIGHT

[MARGARET shakes BOSWELL. He wakes with a start.]

MARGARET: He's turned the candles upside down!!

BOSWELL: Who?! What?!

MARGARET: Your distinguished guest!

BOSWELL: Oh, Johnson... yes. He needs light, for his poor eyes. The candles burn brighter that way.

MARGARET: He's dripping wax all over my rugs!

BOSWELL: It peels right off.

MARGARET: He'll burn the house down! Between that and his pistols – The way he eats! And when was the last time he washed that disgusting wig?!! It's like having a bear loose in the house! And you prance along in his wake like some dancing, awestruck monkey! Why on Earth did you ever bring him here?

BOSWELL: He's an important part of my life.

MARGARET: Your London life.

BOSWELL: And I want him to be part of it all. I want him to love you as much as I do. I want him to –

[Suddenly, they hear heavy footsteps in the hall. JOHNSON, *with a bundle of burning candles and talking rather loudly to himself (in Latin), passes, leaving a trail of wax droppings in his wake.]*

BOSWELL: For ten years I've had to share him, but for the next twelve weeks I shall have the lion of English letters all to myself! Can you just imagine him among the Highlanders?!

*[*BOSWELL *laughs. Even she grins at the idea. Then, a sobering thought…]*

MARGARET: What if he shoots someone?
BOSWELL: Before we go, I promise to lift the pistols from his trunk. By the time he discovers they're gone, it'll be too late.

[He hugs her, holds her. Kisses her.]

INT. BOSWELL'S LIBRARY - NIGHT

*[*JOHNSON *peruses the shelves, leaning close to the spines, the candles threatening to ignite a book. Behind him* JOSEPH *emerges from the gloom, then lights A LAMP.]*

JOSEPH: You'll find the Romans on your left, sir. The Greeks above them.
JOHNSON: Ah, a fellow literary prowler. Excellent, excellent. Any man who takes to his bed before midnight is a scoundrel!
JOSEPH: As you wish, sir.
JOHNSON: How came you to Scotia, Mr. Ritter?
JOSEPH: I am a souvenir of the master's latest tour of the Continent. Like many things, a complicated story.

*[*JOHNSON *waits.* JOSEPH *prefers not to elaborate.]*

JOHNSON: Will you be traveling with us?
JOSEPH: That is Mister Boswell's intention.

*[*BOSWELL, *in nightshirt, enters with one genus of "nightcap" on his head and another of the liquid variety in his hand.]*

BOSWELL: Unlike me, Joseph understands Erse, the native Highland speech. Without an interpreter, we risk possible... misunderstandings.

[Again, clapping JOSEPH heartily on the back...]

JOHNSON: Welcome aboard, sir! "It grows as it goes" shall be our motto! Crescit eundo!
JOSEPH: Very good, sir.

[After Joseph withdraws...]

JOHNSON: Let's go for a ramble!
BOSWELL: But it's –

[As JOHNSON hustles BOSWELL out the door...]

JOHNSON: I have come to these wild Hebrides for adventure! Vale, Bozzy! Vale!!

[SMASH CUT TO] EXT. STREETS OF EDINBURGH - NIGHT

[BOSWELL and JOHNSON dive for the wall when they hear...]

WOMAN'S VOICE *[OS] [impenetrably thick accent]*: Gardy-loo!!!

[A BUCKETFUL of waste-water, flung from an upper story window, SPLASHES onto the very spot where they'd just been standing, splashing BOSWELL's pant leg.]

JOHNSON: What the devil did she say?
BOSWELL: "Gardy-loo." The local equivalent for "Gardez l'eau." The same as in London. The sole difference being that here in Scotland –
JOHNSON: It not only doesn't sound French, it barely sounds human!

[JOHNSON tugs his tri-corner tighter to his skull for protection and suspiciously scans the upper stories of the tenements. BOSWELL starts off, leaving JOHNSON behind. When JOHNSON starts to follow, he

can't find BOSWELL. *There's a moment's panic when he stumbles. Then he hears…]*

BOSWELL *[OFF]*: This way, sir. Take my hand.

*[*JOHNSON *gropes, a bit pathetically, our first glimpse of the old and sometimes fragile man behind the bear. Off* JOHNSON*'s hand clasping* BOSWELL*'s…]*

EXT. NEAR THE BOSWELL HOUSE – NIGHT

*[*BOSWELL *and* JOHNSON *returning home.]*

JOHNSON: Such wondrous eyes don't you think?
  [off BOSWELL*'s look, explaining]* Lady Alison's.

BOSWELL: Ah. … Many's the man who, having fallen in love with a lady's eyes, has compounded his first mistake by seeking to marry the whole woman.
JOHNSON: Well put, sir, well put indeed.
BOSWELL: Merely quoting the master.
JOHNSON: You mean to tell me I said that? *[he knows he did]* To quote oneself is both boorish and redundant. To hear oneself quoted both well and apt is enormously satisfying. I thank you, sir, for the compliment.

INT. BOSWELL'S BED-CHAMBER - DAY

*[*BOSWELL *at a desk, making JOURNAL entries. Beyond the window, DAWN is breaking. He's so absorbed he doesn't notice that* MARGARET *has entered behind him. She watches for a long moment, then approaches. Leaning over him, she massages his shoulders.]*

MARGARET: He's up. And roaming.
BOSWELL: Already?
MARGARET: I've put out a breakfast. If you hurry there may even be some left.

[She reads over his shoulder as he finishes the entry. The more she

reads, the broader her grin becomes.]

MARGARET: " … it barely sounds human!" … Nicely done, James.

[As he completes a sentence, MARGARET takes one of the other pages and reads by the pale morning light. She smiles.]

MARGARET: You've captured him exactly!

[When he finally glances up at her, he finds her regarding him with curiosity, tinged with admiration. She leans down and kisses him. Warmly. But the tenderness of the moment is shattered when the SERVANT-GIRL bursts into the room – her face, hair, chest and bodice dripping with congealed oatmeal – fighting back tears.]

SERVANT-GIRL: He threw his porridge at me! Then called me an insolent little piece of undisciplined sauce!
MARGARET *[under her breath]*: Good.

[QUICK CUT TO] EXT. LEITH HARBOUR - SOUTH SHORE, FIRTH OF FORTH - DAY

[A glorious day. Sun sparkles the waters of the firth, a fresh breeze whips the cloaks and coats and hats of the GROUP at water's edge. JOSEPH hands luggage to BOATMEN. Johnson keeps scanning the roads for some sign of LADY M..
BOSWELL and MARGARET make their farewells, very tender and touched with humor.]

MARGARET: Be careful among those Highlanders. And try to control your "weakness."
BOSWELL: Ah, Peg, you know that you're…

[She presses a finger to his lips. A quick kiss then…]

MARGARET: Off you go! Tide's changing!

[BOSWELL *tiptoes quickly through the shallows and boards the boat.* MARGARET *watches the Boat pull out and head for deeper water.* ON THE BOAT BOSWELL *takes a seat at* JOHNSON'*s side.* JOHNSON *keeps searching the shore for some sign of* LADY MACINTYRE.]

BOSWELL: Seems Lady MacIntyre had a prior engagement.

[*A cruel stroke. Then, after a long silence…*]

BOSWELL: I've something to confess. I took the liberty of removing the pistols from your bag.

[JOHNSON *hoists his STICK, brandishes it over his head, then thumps it sharply on the gunwale.* BOSWELL *shies away.*]

JOHNSON: Then we'll just have to work with what we have!

[JOHNSON *grins, then jostles him.* BOSWELL'*s relieved.* JOSEPH *taps* JOHNSON'*s shoulder, pointing back toward the shore.*]

JOSEPH: There, sir! On the hill!

[*THEIR POV –* LADY MACINTYRE, *in a long white billowing dress, waves a handkerchief, her farewells lost in the wind.* JOHNSON *beams, taking perhaps as much pleasure in* BOSWELL'*s discomfiture as in* LADY MACINTYRE'*s appearance. He rises, waving his stick, rocking the boat, and shouting…*]

JOHNSON: AHOY! MY FAIR PENELOPE!!

[*He nudges* BOSWELL. BOSWELL *half-heartedly waves.*]

EXT. HILL ABOVE THE FIRTH - CONTINUOUS

[LADY MACINTYRE *waves merrily.* MARGARET *climbs up to join her.* LADY MACINTYRE *laughs at* JOHNSON'*s dangerously exuberant demonstration.*]

LADY MACINTYRE: Men can be such children.

MARGARET: And it's often the most troublesome that inspire the deepest affection.

LADY MACINTYRE: Is that how it is with your Jamie?

MARGARET: For all his many faults, he's never boring. A dull husband would drive me mad.

LADY MACINTYRE [smiling]: Dull he's not.

[The color drains from MARGARET's cheeks, a faint wobble.]

LADY MACINTYRE: Mrs. Boswell? Are you all right?

[MARGARET's hand flies to her mouth. Sudden nausea. LADY MAC-INTYRE takes her shoulders, supporting her. Finally...]

MARGARET: I'm three months with child; longer perhaps. Sometimes the sickness...

[She almost spews. Doesn't.]

LADY MACINTYRE: Does Jamie know?

[MARGARET shakes her head, no. LADY MACINTYRE helps MARGARET back to her feet. They turn to look at the BOAT far out on the sparkling Firth, heading north.]

EXT. A VERDANT HILL - FIFE - DAY

[We hear men's voices SINGING. Then, coming into view, is a DONKEY CART with BOSWELL, JOHNSON, JOSEPH, and a grizzled, ill-clad DRIVER. BOSWELL leads them in a version of "Over the Sea to Sky" the most popular tune of its day.
BOSWELL's is a surprisingly good voice; JOHNSON's, about what you'd expect. JOSEPH instinctively adds harmony in a restrained baritone. The Driver's teeth clamp on his pipe. BOSWELL, eager to make this trip perfect, prods the Driver to join in. But the more BOSWELL prods, the more stubbornly silent the Driver becomes. Finally...]

JOHNSON: I order you to sing with us. *[off his look]* I – and I think I speak for all – would rather walk to Aberdeen than further tolerate your silence!

[Judging from the reactions of BOSWELL *and* JOSEPH, JOHNSON *clearly does not speak for them. But* JOHNSON's *on a roll.]*

JOHNSON: Either sing or find another fare!

[The cart's creaks punctuate the ensuing silence until...
THE DRIVER *bursts into the refrain. A pyrrhic victory – the Driver's voice is even worse than* JOHNSON's. *But uncorked, there's no stopping it. He roars in a hideous tuneless caterwaul.* BOSWELL *snidely joins in.* JOSEPH *broods in silence. Off his look,* JOHNSON *shrugs, sorry. A moment later,* JOHNSON *bursts out laughing – his fun-loving side in full evidence.]*

JOHNSON *[nudging* BOSWELL*]*: So, sir, after all these years, we're voyaging in Caledonia!

[Off BOSWELL's *grin,* JOHNSON *makes it a merry trio.]*

[DISSOLVE TO] FURTHER ALONG - MUCH LATER - GLOAMING

[Only the Driver is still singing. JOSEPH *is ready to kill him;* JOHNSON *has grown noticeably cranky. Then...]*

JOHNSON: You said ten miles, fifteen ago! Or do Scots measure their roads by emotion instead of miles?!
BOSWELL *[concealing a smirk]*: It won't be long now, sir.

[Though you'd never guess it from the vast and void of the landscape. The road ahead seems to go on forever to nowhere. After a few more bumps of the wheels, a few more jolts to the spine, another verse of "Over the Sea to Skye," then, a diversion!]

BOSWELL: Look, sir, an angler!

[THEIR VIEW – A FISHERMAN works a trout stream.]

JOHNSON *[grumbling]*: A fishing rod is nothing but a stick with a hook at
one end –
BOSWELL *[quoting from Johnson's Dictionary]*: "And a fool at the other."

*[A look between them. A nasty pothole nearly dislocates JOHNSON's
hip. He glowers at BOSWELL as if he had personally dug the hole. It's
gonna be a long trip, kids.]*

[FADE TO] ESTABLISH - THE INN AT ST. ANDREWS - NIGHT

*[Beauty shot. The gloaming reduced to a thin reed of light along the
horizon throwing the inn's roof into silhouette.]*

INT. THE INN'S TAVERN - CONTINUOUS

*[AT A TABLE The three men are dirty, tired, and testy. And hungry.
JOHNSON could eat two horses instead of his usual pony. The Inn's
CLIENTELE stare openly at these exotic creatures.]*

JOHNSON: What's taking them so long?!

*[As if on cue, the STAFF descend, eager to please. A WAITRESS
brings soup and bread for JOSEPH. A SAUCIER WAITRESS brings
the drinks: lemonade for JOHNSON, whiskey for BOSWELL, beer for
JOSEPH. The PROPRIETOR, in his own peculiar imitation of a great
maitre d', presents two platters, the first to JOHNSON:
Granny Fries - a plate of grilled sheep testicles; then to BOSWELL,
Jellied Brawn - cold sheep brain, halved, and served in a puddle of
what looks like jaundiced aspic.
The PROPRIETOR hovers. Beams.
JOHNSON pokes at a Granny Fry with the tip of a knife.]*

JOHNSON: What is it?
PROPRIETOR: Granny Fries and Jellied Brawn. Specialties of the house. Enjoy.

[The man's accent is even more opaque than Ms. Gardy-Loo's. As the PROPRIETOR *walks away…]*

JOHNSON: What did he say?

[Not a clue. The food looks very strange and barely edible.]

BOSWELL: One can't go too far wrong ordering the cook's specialty.
JOHNSON: What the devil is a granny fry?
BOSWELL: Local cuisine.

*[*JOSEPH *raises his glass and toasts…]*

JOSEPH: "Crescit eundo!"

*[*BOSWELL *sips – his whiskey is nectar of the gods!* JOSEPH'*s beer, on the other hand, is as evilly flat as bog water.* JOHNSON'*s lemonade is nastily sour. Now to the food…*
JOHNSON *tries a bit of Granny Fry.* BOSWELL *tries a small taste of jellied brawn. To their surprise, they're not bad.* BOSWELL *and* JOHNSON *eat.* JOSEPH *watches.* BOSWELL *shares some of his brawn with* JOHNSON, JOHNSON *offers* BOSWELL *a fry.* BOSWELL *munches happily on his Granny Fry until…]*

JOSEPH: Impressive what an inventive cook can do with a sheep's testicle, isn't it?

*[*BOSWELL'*s jaws now work much more slowly and methodically, his imagination far too much in play. Then…]*

JOSEPH: Or congealed brains.

*[*JOHNSON'*s spoon stops halfway to his mouth. A faint flicker of a grin from* JOSEPH *– or is that just the way his mouth turns up when he chews heavy bread?]*

EXT. A SPARSE BUT GRASSY SEA-SIDE FIELD - DAY

[TWO SHEEP graze placidly on a small hillock. Suddenly, they freeze. Then bolt. Behind them a SPRAY OF SAND flies, accompanied by a loud human grumble.
JOHNSON *and* BOSWELL *in a deep sandy bunker on The Old Course at St. Andrews. With* BOSWELL *coaching and* JOSEPH *watching over them from the bank above,* JOHNSON *lashes at the golf-ball with an ancient wooden-shafted niblick.]*

BOSWELL: Head down, left arm straight.

*[*JOHNSON *does neither. He pounds the sand approximately a foot behind the ball, burying the clubhead.* JOHNSON *slowly looks up at* BOSWELL *with homicidal intensity.]*

BOSWELL: A trip to Scotland wouldn't be complete without a turn on the King's royal links. Scotsmen have played here since –

*[*JOHNSON *lashes at the ball again. Thwack!!* JOHNSON, *near-sighted as a mole, squints into the gray horizon, looking for his ball. A proud man in triumph. Meanwhile...*
THE BALL *trickles slowly down across the sand from the lip of the bank, back to* JOHNSON's *feet.]*

JOHNSON: Well? Where did it go? Have I reached the putting surface?!

[Off a warning look from JOSEPH, BOSWELL *opts for...]*

BOSWELL: Excellent shot, sir! Smashing!
JOHNSON: Hah!!

[As JOSEPH *helps* JOHNSON *up out of the deep bunker,* BOSWELL *snatches up the ball.]*

[WIPE TO]   FURTHER ALONG ON THE LINKS

[JOHNSON *roams, searching for his ball.* BOSWELL *drops the ball down the side of his leg and announces…*]

BOSWELL: Ah! Here you are, sir!

[JOHNSON *marches up and with barely a moment's hesitation and without taking aim, swings mightily. The* BALL *soars!* BOSWELL *and* JOSEPH *gape.*]

[QUICK CUT TO]   TWO SCOTSMEN – *on an adjoining hole. One is lined up over a putt, deep in concentration, when* JOHNSON'S BALL *smacks him soundly in the buttocks. They turn to see Johnson gesticulating wildly and enthusiastically as the threesome approaches.*]

EXT. THE BEACH - LATER - DAY

[BOSWELL *stands over his shot. His ball is a few yards from the edge of the wavewash. He is distracted by* JOHNSON *and* JOSEPH *standing nearby,* JOHNSON *speculating.*]

JOHNSON: The natural flight of the human mind is not from pleasure to pleasure, but from hope to hope.

[BOSWELL, *satisfied that Johnson has stopped talking, is about to swing when…*]

JOHNSON *[CONT'D]*: Take Bozzy, here. He hopes that this shot will carry him home in triumph. He takes no pleasure in how he came to such a pass. And even if he should smack the ball soundly, wisely and well, he will, I assure you, be dissatisfied by the result. And if he should –
BOSWELL: Sir, if you don't mind.

[JOSEPH *puts a finger to his lips. They are to be silent.*]

JOHNSON: Ah! My apologies. Please. Proceed.
BOSWELL: Thank you.

[BOSWELL settles over his shot. But just as he begins his backswing, a swell of SEA-WASH pours past his ankles, over his ball, sweeping it out to sea. Off BOSWELL...]

[DISSOLVE TO] EXT. COASTAL ROAD - NEAR ST. ANDREWS - DAY

[The THREE in a horse-drawn cart. BOSWELL massages his bare feet. JOHNSON surveys the landscape, then declares...]

JOHNSON: How go the blisters, Bozzy? The best thing is to keep them dry!

[With which, it begins to rain. Hard. JOHNSON loves it.]

JOHNSON: By tomorrow, lads, we shall be in Macbeth country, riding the Bard's heroic verse through blasted heaths to the very threshold of Cawdor!

[DISSOLVE TO] EXT. A MOOR - NEAR CAWDOR CASTLE - DAY

[The ugly weather hasn't damped JOHNSON's spirits. He's in the land of Macbeth and Macbeth means Shakespeare.]

JOHNSON: "When shall we three meet again, in thunder, lightning, or in rain?!"

[He turns to BOSWELL and JOSEPH slogging through the muck and brambles. Miserable.]

JOHNSON: "Be lion-mettled, proud; and take no care Who chafes, who frets, or where conspirers are!" Come, sir, feed me lines!

[BOSWELL wraps himself tighter in his cloak.]

BOSWELL *[mumbling flatly]*: All hail, Macbeth, thane of Cawdor.
JOHNSON: With passion, Bozzy! And fire! Screw your courage to the sticking place and we'll not fail!
JOSEPH: If it were done, then 'twere well it were done quickly.
BOSWELL: Hear, hear.

[BOSWELL and JOSEPH head back to the castle, leaving JOHNSON roaming in the driving rain, thundering lines. When JOHNSON catches up with them...]

JOHNSON: Let's do the murder of Duncan. You play the Lady, I'll do Macbeth.

[This is getting old very fast. BOSWELL bites his tongue.]

JOHNSON: Are you so ashamed of your blood-thirsty ancestors that you refuse to honor him on his own ground?!

[That's it. BOSWELL explodes...]

BOSWELL: Shakespeare, sir, had him wrong!! He was not some bloodthirsty fiend!

JOHNSON: Then who was it who killed good King Duncan? And Banquo? And all Macduff's chicks?! Macbeth, sir, was a foul and ruthless regicide!

BOSWELL: Macbeth was a native Highland King. And after disposing of Duncan and his gang of Irish interlopers, Macbeth ruled, with his loving wife at his side! for 17 years! Inaugurating two decades of peace and prosperity! Name me a Tudor or Hanoverian who's done half that!!

[Beat. Then, with a bow to BOSWELL...]

JOHNSON: All hail the Thane of Auchinleck!

BOSWELL *[testily walking away]*: My father is still very much alive.

[JOHNSON's hit a raw nerve. He looks to JOSEPH. Oops.
They slog on through puddles and brush, following BOSWELL.
JOHNSON falls behind. His cloak gets tangled in briars. Then...
JOHNSON experiences a sudden sharp pain to his chest. Angina. His breath turns labored. He's frightened.
BOSWELL glances back and discovers JOHNSON struggling with his cloak, hands at his chest. BOSWELL and JOSEPH race back to JOHNSON, who covers his fright and struggles for composure with the attack passed.]

BOSWELL: Are you well, sir?

JOHNSON: Perfectly so.

[After BOSWELL *helps* JOHNSON *extricate himself from the brambles, they start off again. The castle's parapet and walls loom beyond in the swirling mist. Finally...]*

JOHNSON: If a great king's world can be so soon and thoroughly forgotten, who will know or care or even remember that a pamphlet poet named Johnson ever turned a phrase or walked from Temple Bar to the Strand, or spent an evening in conversation at the Turk's Head Tavern with a young and clever Scotsman named – what was his name? ... Bobsill? Ballswell? Wallsabob? ... No, it was Buyswell!

[As they continue on toward the castle...]

JOHNSON: Does the ephemerality of fame frighten you?

BOSWELL: Unlike you, I have no fame to lose.

JOHNSON: Yet you hunger for it. And lacking it, attach yourself to those who do. Having cast yourself as a moon to the blazing suns of our age, your glory is but reflected.

BOSWELL: And your point, sir?

JOHNSON: No point. Mere observation. *[pause]* I assume you're keeping a journal of our travels. In which I am, no doubt, featured.

BOSWELL: We are traveling together.

JOHNSON: I fear I often make more sound than sense.

BOSWELL: Rarely.

JOHNSON: Since your prose will likely outlive me, be kind, but fair. You carry my lasting reputation in your pen. *[slight pause]* I would very much like to see what you've written.

[Off BOSWELL's *mildly alarmed reaction...]*

EXT. A STREET - INVERNESS - DAY

*[*JOHNSON, BOSWELL, *and* JOSEPH *in their cart, roll into town. They're dismayed by the apparent poverty of the place and its sparse*

population. As they pass a decrepit hovel with barefooted men…]

JOHNSON: A decent provision for the poor is the only true test of civilization. And with privilege, comes duty. *[slight pause]* So, my boy, what will you do when you inherit the Auchinleck estates?

BOSWELL: It's not certain I shall ever inherit the estates or the title.

JOHNSON: Will your father be waiting for us in Auchinleck?

BOSWELL: So he says.

JOHNSON: How long has it been?

BOSWELL: Years.

JOHNSON: How much better we'd all be if we could pick our fathers, and sons.

[A look between them. After rumbling along…]

JOHNSON: When I was a lad, my father used me as parlor entertainment. I had such a precocious memory for poetry, he'd stand me on the dinner table and make me recite. Horrifying.
[to JOSEPH, trying to break the mood] And how was childhood in Bohemia?

JOSEPH: Very… Bohemian.

[More poor people pass. Ragged children. Suddenly…]

JOHNSON: Stop the cart!

[JOHNSON leaps from the still-moving cart, digs into his purse and begins leaving pennies in the hands of children sleeping in doorways and to those loitering on the street.]

JOSEPH: Sir, if I might be so bold, these children, unlike the paupers of London, are not abandoned, they have homes and families to go to.

JOHNSON: It is far better, sir, to live rich, than die rich.

[Children start lining up to receive JOHNSON's pennies. Soon, parents are bringing their children out of everywhere to take advantage of the bounty. BOSWELL and JOSEPH notice that a few of the adults, without kids of their own, are "borrowing" them.

When one clever little SCAMP *turns up for the third time in line –*
JOHNSON's *eyesight is bad, but not that bad...]*

JOHNSON: Haven't I seen you before, boy?

[Caught, the boy squirms. BOSWELL *watches closely. Then...]*

JOHNSON *[howling with delight]*: Well, sir! Since it seems we're meeting on
such a regular basis, it's time we introduced ourselves. I'm Samuel. Like
the Old Testament patriarch. And you are?
SCAMP: Angus MacDonald. Of clan MacDonald.
JOHNSON: And what will you do with your pennies, Angus MacDonald of
the MacDonald MacDonalds?
SCAMP: Buy bread for my sisters, sir.

[After a beat, JOHNSON *hands him the entire purse. The boy is stunned.
The others cluster around him.* BOSWELL *watches as* JOHNSON *walks
off, averting his face, wiping a tear from his eye.]*

INT. A TAVERN – NIGHT

[Music and dancing. A country Lass is teaching JOSEPH *how to dance.
The fiddler wails, a drummer thumps, the fifes trill, hornpipes and
tabors fill the air.
When* BOSWELL *feels* JOHNSON's *eyes on him...]*

BOSWELL: Music moves me to either pathetic dejection or daring reso-
lution. It either reduces me to tears or propels me, pell-mell, into the
thickest pitch of battle!
JOHNSON: If music made such a fool of me, I would avoid it all all costs.

*[The Fiddler, claiming thirst, sets aside his fiddle, much to the
disappointment of the partiers.* BOSWELL *downs his whisky, then
heads for the stage. He takes the fiddle from the player's hand. An
expectant hush. Then...
*BOSWELL *starts to play – first, a bit of Bach from which he segues
smoothly into a high-spirited Highland reel.*

The party kicks back into high gear. Even JOHNSON *is on his feet, stomping, trying to dance, and destroying furniture.*
BOSWELL *jams – the sudden darling of the ladies.]*

INT. A NEARBY BARN - LATER – NIGHT

[The party at the nearby tavern continues into the wee hours. JOHNSON *is in bed, massaging his aching feet in the dark. Then he hears…*
A young man and woman giggling and cooing in amorous play as they tiptoe into the barn, shushing each other's giggles – fondling, followed by smothered squeals. As they creep up to the hayloft, JOHNSON *sees that it's…*
BOSWELL *and the drummer Lass from the party. They disappear from sight. Sounds of love-making are sore reminders of old age. Agitated, he slips out into the night.]*

EXT. THE BARN - CONTINUOUS - NIGHT

*[*JOHNSON *stumbles in the dark, catching himself against the wall. He scans the area, then looks up to discover a heaven constellated with stars. It's awesome. Then, materializing out of nowhere…* JOSEPH. *In silence, they share the spectacle of the heavens.]*

JOSEPH: This modern celestial machinery may satisfy the reason, but in my heart, I prefer to see the ancient Gods and mythical beasts in these constellations. I miss the mystery, the majesty, the divine.

JOHNSON: Our theologians have turned God into a reflection of man.

JOSEPH: Performing a disservice to both.

JOHNSON: Well put, sir. Very well put.

JOSEPH: For such a strenuous Christian, I hear you rarely attend their services.

JOHNSON: Leading a cow into church instead of the cowshed does not make him a Christian.

[A hint of a grin from JOSEPH. *Then* JOHNSON *adds…]*

JOHNSON *[CONT'D]*: Besides, I hate the hymns.

[As they turn back to the barn, they see the Lass slipping away.]

JOHNSON: I sometimes think there are greater hymns in a young girl's heart than in all the cathedrals of Europe.

[Off their view of the Lass skipping off into the night...]

[DISSOLVE TO] TWO SHEEP – grazing on a grassy slope. Pulling back WIDER on a CROFTER'S HUT, built into a hillside with stone walls, its ROOF OF SOD so naturally extended from the grassy hill that it seems normal that sheep would graze on its roof. CHICKENS rush around the open front door. PULLING BACK FURTHER reveals...

EXT. THE LOWER HIGHLANDS - DAY

[The cart with JOHNSON, BOSWELL, *and* JOSEPH *rounds a bend in the narrow track, and rolls slowly up to the Sod Hut.*

THEIR POV – a WOMAN, barefoot, wrapped in a blanket cinched at the waist by a rope, much younger than she looks, materializes in the doorway, chickens at her feet. She eyes them warily.]

JOHNSON: Let's buy some fresh eggs.
BOSWELL *[attempting Erse]*: Madam, could we buy some eggs?

[She stares at BOSWELL *– bewildered. She doesn't understand.]*

JOSEPH *[smugly]*: Allow me.

*[*JOSEPH *climbs down off the cart and approaches the Woman.]*

JOSEPH *[in Erse]*: Madam, are your eggs fresh?

[She clutches the blanket tighter around her. JOSEPH, *stepping closer, and now a bit more aggressively...]*

JOSEPH *[in Erse]*: If your eggs are fresh, we'd like to buy them.

[She SLAPS JOSEPH *soundly. Turns heel and slams the door.*]

JOHNSON: Good God, man! What the deuce did you say to her?!
JOSEPH: I asked if her eggs were fresh.

[As JOSEPH *climbs into the cart, and they start off again, behind them… The hut's door opens. The Woman, now accompanied by her irate and equally filthy* HUSBAND, *come outside and start picking up stones. ANGLE on the cart. The first salvo of stones clatters all around, narrowly missing the trio.* JOSEPH *urgently snaps the reins.*]

EXT. CREST OF A HILL - THE HIGHLANDS – DAY

[THREE HIGHLAND WARRIORS *in full regalia. They are the* BROTHERS MACRAE. EUAN *(30s)*, MALCOLM *(late 20s), and their boy-faced baby brother* HUGH *(20). All three are a little red in the face from imbibing "The Water of Life."*
HUGH *is thrashing various thistles and flowers with his claymore (Remember that long steel monster that flew through the frames of the "Braveheart" trailer? That's a claymore!)*]

MALCOLM [*crossly*]: Aw for pity's sake, Hughie! Willya stop wavin' that damn thing around!
HUGH: I'm tellin' ya, it does'nay feel right! That smithie in Drumleck cheated me! [*slashing a bush*] It is'nay balanced properly!!

[EUAN *begins scratching furiously.*]

EUAN: I swear this damned wool's laden with fleas! Next time I think to don my tartans, remind me to…

[EUAN *tears at his chest and thighs.* MALCOLM *smiles.*]

MALCOLM: You wanted to impress cousin Kate. And so she was. I especially enjoyed her hoping the English'd lock us up for wearing the plaid.

[*While thrusting at and slashing an innocent thistle…*]

HUGH: Katie was upset because Malcolm called her an "auld bucket."

MALCOLM: She understood me perfectly. And I did'nay call her a "bucket."

HUGH: Aye, ye did, brother. Ye did.

MALCOLM: Can I help it if I'm nay perfect in the Old Tongue?!

EUAN: And if ye spent less time sluicing in Glasgow and more time at home ye'd be better practised.

[They march on. Homeward. MALCOLM *in a huff.* EUAN *scratching.* HUGH *battling the local flora.]*

MALCOLM: Hughie! I'll nay tell ye again!

[Hugh temporarily desists. Grumbling…]

HUGH: Mam should ha' let us take the –

MALCOLM: And stop with the damn horses! Da' said he'd bring 'em round.

HUGH: Just because Unkey Donald couldnay hold his whisky –

EUAN: We have to walk because that drunken idiot couldnay sit on his pony and broke his damn neck!

HUGH *[grumbling & slashing]*: Mam said –

ALL THREE: If ye'll drink then ye'll nay ride.

*[*HUGH *beheads a bush.* MALCOLM *glares.* EUAN *rakes his neck. Then, from below and just over the hill, they hear the clatter of cart wheels on rough ground. They freeze.]*

MALCOLM *[groaning]*: Ach, noooo. Father's brought the damned cart not the ponies!!

EXT. A ROUGH HIGHLAND TRACK – CONTINUOUS

[The cart. BOSWELL *and* JOSEPH *up front,* JOHNSON *in back. Then, out of the blue, to* JOSEPH…]*

BOSWELL: I know what you did! You didn't ask her if her eggs were fresh, you asked if she was fertile!!

*[*BOSWELL *and* JOHNSON *laugh.* JOSEPH *bristles.]*

JOHNSON: You've let us down, sir. And almost got us molested!!!

*[*BOSWELL *and* JOHNSON *yuck it up.* JOSEPH *seethes. The cart jars and bounces. But when they round the bend to discover that...*
The Three MACRAE BROTHERS *are blocking the road ahead – exactly what* BOSWELL *and* JOHNSON *imagined Highland bandits to look like. Their impression deepens with each mad and violent slash of* HUGH MACRAE's *claymore.*
BOSWELL *looks to* JOSEPH; JOSEPH *looks to* BOSWELL. *Uh-oh.*
Behind them, JOHNSON *is digging into his bag. He pulls out his pistol, powder, and shot. Neither* BOSWELL *nor* JOSEPH *notice.*
The gap between the parties closes.]

BOSWELL: We mustn't show fear. If we don't seem afraid, they won't harm us.

[But not even BOSWELL *believes that. The gap closes tighter.* BOSWELL *tenses when...*
HUGH's *claymore – its blade flashing ominously in the midday sun – swipes a roadside sapling off at the base. One moment it's there; the next, it's gone. Gulp.*
JOHNSON *tries to pour powder down the barrel, not easy in a bouncing cart and shifting wind.*
JOSEPH *hails the* MACRAES *in formal, articulated Erse...]*

JOSEPH: Greetings, gentlemen! Is this road the most direct route to Glenelg?

[REACTION – the MACRAES, *startled to hear the "Old Tongue" being spoken so well, and far better than they themselves can. Even* HUGH *stops his slashing. He and* MALCOLM *look to* EUAN.*]*

EUAN *[stumbling over the Erse] (in English subtitle)*: Uh, welcome, Tree-Dwellers! This is indeed the river to Glenelg!

[With JOHNSON *still loading his pistol behind him...]*

BOSWELL: What did he say? What's he want?

JOSEPH: I was under the impression that you didn't trust my translations.

BOSWELL: For God's sakes, man, this is no time to turn peevish! Do they want our money? Our horse? What?!

EUAN: Have you been traveling long?

[We see EUAN's *"Erse" line in English subtitle.* JOSEPH, *with a wicked gleam in his eye, whispers to* BOSWELL...]

JOSEPH: Looks bad, sir. They want it all. Including our clothes.

BOSWELL: Oh God. What do we do?

JOSEPH: Fight or run. What a sad end. You've been a kind master, master.

*[*BOSWELL *is just about to flee across the hills when he notices that* JOHNSON *has finished preparing his pistol.]*

JOHNSON *[to* BOSWELL*]*: Victory goes to those who come prepared!!

*[*BOSWELL *shields* JOHNSON, *and whispers over his shoulder...]*

BOSWELL: Just make the first shot count.

*[*JOSEPH *notices what* JOHNSON *is up to just as* EUAN MACRAE *steps up and grabs their pony's reins.* JOSEPH's *jest is quickly getting out of hand. He tries to block* EUAN's *view of the gunman, hissing to* JOHNSON...]*

JOSEPH: Put that away!

[Then quickly in Erse (subtitled in English)...]

JOSEPH: We'd offer a ride but...

EUAN *[in Erse, subtitled]*: I can see you're full up.

[Suddenly, BOSWELL *leaps from the cart, clearing* JOHNSON's *line of fire. When* EUAN *sees the pistol...]*

EUAN: Now that's a fine looking pistol!

[He steps closer – curious, friendly, and unsuspecting. JOHNSON *rises, aims (badly)…]*

JOSEPH: NO!

[He lunges as JOHNSON *pulls the trigger. The hammer snaps. Nothing. The BALL rolls harmlessly out of the down-tilted barrel, plops to the ground at* EUAN's *feet. All look at it.]*

EUAN: You did'nay prime it properly.
BOSWELL *[surprised]*: You speak English?
EUAN *[with an edge]*: And so do you. Are you Englishmen?
BOSWELL *[babbling]*: I'm Scots, he's Bohemian, and –

[When EUAN *takes the pistol from* JOHNSON, BOSWELL *blanches.* JOHNSON *grabs his huge walking stick.* EUAN *and* MALCOLM *examine the pistol closely.]*

EUAN: I once had a pistol like this, lowland made it was. Never shot worth a damn. D'ye mind?

[With which EUAN *tears off a patch of cloth from what was once* JOHNSON's *spare shirt, dusts off the ball, repacks it, then rams it home with the ramrod.* BOSWELL's *eye never strays far from…* HUGH, *who, still obsessed with his claymore, has resumed his crazed clearing of brush.]*

EUAN: For God's sakes, Hughie, stop it!

*[*HUGH *ignores him and continues attacking the vegetation.* EUAN *wheels. FIRES! A blast. The ball strikes the blade of* HUGH's *claymore inches above the handle. The blade snaps.* HUGH *is dumbfounded. Then…]*

HUGH: Look what ye've done! You ha' ruined it! Completely ruined it!

*[*MALCOLM *bursts out laughing.* JOSEPH, *relieved, grins.]*

HUGH: It's not funny! I paid good money for this and now it's ruined!

[BOSWELL *and* JOHNSON *look to one another. What is this? Suddenly, they hear the sound of POUNDING HOOVES, coming up from behind. They turn to find…*
MA *and* PA MACRAE *galloping up, leading a string of ponies.* MA MACRAE *barely hits five feet, but she's tough enough to fix her boys with a look. Her eye lands on the pistol in* EUAN'S *hand.]*

MA MACRAE: What the devil happened?

[*Belatedly,* EUAN *tries to hide the pistol behind his back.]*

EUAN: Nothing, Mam.

[HUGH *rushes up with his broken claymore.]*

HUGH: Look what Euan did to my sword!
MA MACRAE: It was nay good anyway.

[HUGH *sulks.* EUAN *squirms. And when he tries to scratch his itch discreetly…]*

MA MACRAE: Stop that, Euan!

[*He does. Instantly.]*

MA MACRAE: I caught yer Da tryin' ta slip away with the ponies. Did ye think I would not know what ye were up to?!

[*Suddenly, all four* MACRAE *men shuffle like scolded children. When she turns to* BOSWELL, *he turns as sheepish as the boys.]*

MALCOLM: They're goin' to Glenelg, Mam.
MA MACRAE: Where else might they be goin', ye great lummock?!

[*She gives* MALCOLM *a solid smack. Then smacks the cart.]*

MA MACRAE [to BOSWELL]: You'll never get there in this! Track's too narrow. [with a calculating eye] I'll rent ye' three ponies and a guide. Euan here. Ye got money?

[Since her accent is nearly incomprehensible…]

JOSEPH: She wants your money, sir.

[BOSWELL hands it over.]

MA MACRAE: Is he daft? All this, for ponies?!

[JOSEPH takes back the purse, explaining to BOSWELL…]

JOSEPH: They want to rent us three ponies for the road to Glenelg. The cart won't make it. Shall I negotiate?
BOSWELL [relieved]: Please do.

[BOSWELL watches as MA MACRAE gives the cart and pony another and closer look, and PA MACRAE examines HUGH's stunted claymore. MA MACRAE, satisfied with the condition of the cart and pony, spits, turns to JOSEPH, and grins.]

MA MACRAE: What say I make ye boys a trade?

[DISSOLVE TO] EXT. THE HIGHLANDS - LATER - THE GLOAMING

[Magnificence. Mountains, lochs, scudding clouds. Far below, people and ponies divides into two groups – one of FOUR MEN on the backs of ponies, one in plaid, moves on down the road to Glenelg; another group (the remaining MACRAES) with one pony (on which MA is riding) and a CART (taken in trade), head off across the hills. MA MACRAE fires JOHNSON's pistol. The shot echoes in the glens.]

EXT. THE HIGHLANDS – NIGHT

[Camping out. A flickering campfire. While EUAN and JOSEPH sleep,

BOSWELL *writes in his journal.* JOHNSON *watches.]*

JOHNSON: One could fill an entire volume explaining how you and I have come to this Scottish mountaintop.

*[*BOSWELL *sets aside his journal. Regards* JOHNSON *curiously.]*

JOHNSON: When I wrote my account of the Life of Richard Savage, I was trying to explain how a man of such learning, wit and literary talent could end up barefoot, broken and roaming the streets of London. He'd earn drinks in taverns by entertaining others with his conversation.
BOSWELL *[very carefully]*: Did you decide to write your biography of Savage before or after he died?
JOHNSON *[with equal care]*: Slightly before.

[There's something almost conspiratorial here – the smoking fire, the desolate Highland scapes, the hushed voices.]

JOHNSON: I entertained the notion that a man might make a name for himself as a biographer; Plutarch would have been forgotten had it not been for his *Lives of the Noble Romans and Greeks.*
BOSWELL: An account of your life would be far more engaging than Savage's.

*[*BOSWELL*'s implied offer to write* JJOHNSON*'s biography hangs there. Finally...]*

JOHNSON: If I were to entrust my life to another man's pen, it would be yours.
BOSWELL: A burden I would gladly but never lightly take up.

[After a long moment, JOHNSON *pulls up his cloak and lays down to sleep, watching* BOSWELL *muse on the embers.]*

JOHNSON: My English Plutarch.
BOSWELL: My Noble Brit.

[FADE OUT AND BACK UP ON TWO SHEEP – on a grassy slope. Pulling back wider to reveal...]

EXT. THE MAJESTIC, SWEEPING HIGHLANDS – DAY

[Mam Rattachan Mountain. The scenery is wild and spectacular.
ON A DANGEROUS WINDING TRAIL – JOHNSON's *bulk dwarfs*
his pony. He lacks an equestrian gene. EUAN MACRAE *rides alongside,*
guiding him along a narrow, rock-strewn trail as it hugs precipices and
deep defiles. Up ahead...
BOSWELL *and* JOSEPH *ride along easily and well. In this remote*
wilderness, employer-employee barriers begin to dissolve. We get the
sense that these two men are talking, man to man, in a way they
haven't in a long time.]

BOSWELL: But do you ever regret...
JOSEPH: Leaving Heidelberg? I had little choice. To stay would have meant...
BOSWELL: I hope my household has been better than a jail cell.

[Small smiles. Then...]

JOSEPH: I sometimes miss the life of a scholar. And I miss Mathilde.
BOSWELL: Life does take us down unexpected paths. Who would have
ever dreamed that you and I and Doctor Johnson would be here? In the
Highlands?

*[*BOSWELL *glances back to see* JOHNSON *and* MACRAE *in apparently*
deep conversation.]

BOSWELL: If only the Club could see him now! The lion of English letters
in deep conversation with a near savage!

*[*JOHNSON *and* EUAN MACRAE *ride side by side.[*

JOHNSON: It sometimes seems that all your countrymen are leaving for
the colonies.
EUAN: The English ha' helped us on our way, what with the confiscations
and enclosures.
JOHNSON: You must have been too young for the rebellion.
EUAN: Even a wee lad can fight. Bonny Prince Charlie still inspires and

I've heard it said that the glorious Flora MacDonald still abides in Skye.

JOHNSON: And thus the rebellion lives on.

EUAN: Aye. I also hear the Americans have got their own rebellion afoot.

JOHNSON: These colonials howl for freedom, yet why is it we hear the loudest yelps for liberty from the drivers of negroes?!

EUAN: If I go to America, I'll go a free man, not indentured like some lowland Scot bowing to his English master or enslaved like an African.

JOHNSON: Liberty, sir, is the just reward of loyalty to one's king, a privilege to be earned not demanded!

> [EUAN, *taking offense, gooses his pony and rides on ahead, leaving* JOHNSON *behind. Johnson grumbling, rides on at his own pace.*
> *JOHNSON'S POV –* First BOSWELL *and* JOSEPH *disappear around a bend in the trail ahead. Then* EUAN *disappears around the bend.*
> JOHNSON *suddenly finding himself very much alone in this wild and remote landscape, goads his pony sharply. No response. He kicks the pony hard, snapping the reins firmly. The pony suddenly rears.*
> JOHNSON *"steers." A very bad move.*
> *The pony loses its footing. Stumbles.* JOHNSON *struggles for control. He's making a bad situation worse, possibly fatal.*
> *Pony and rider perilously teeter on the edge. Loose rocks tumble over the side. Clatter into the abyss. Vertigo. At the last possible moment, the pony regains its footing and composure.*
> *The crisis has passed. But then, suddenly...*
> JOHNSON *gasps sharply. A look of shock and pain seizes his face. One hand clutches his chest. His breath turns ragged. He sways dangerously in the saddle. No one in sight. Terror. He opens his mouth to cry out. No sound emerges. With superhuman effort,* JOHNSON *draws in enough air to force out a strangled cry...]*

JOHNSON: Bozzy!

> [*No one comes. After another strained effort...*]

JOHNSON: Boswell!! Damn you! Come here!

> [*After a long moment,* BOSWELL *rounds the bend in the trail and*

gallops back. As he rides up to JOHNSON…]

BOSWELL: Sir? Are you all right?

[*Though the crisis has passed,* JOHNSON *is still obviously and deeply shaken. And still in pain. He covers with anger.*]

JOHNSON: How could you just ride off and leave me?! In this wilderness?! I must have been mad to leave London and come to this hellish desert in such hateful company!
BOSWELL: Maybe we should stop for a while.
JOHNSON: No.
BOSWELL: You need to rest. The pony needs to rest.

[*When* JOHNSON *spurs the pony on...*]

BOSWELL: I need to rest!

[JOSEPH *and* EUAN *are waiting for them at the bend in the trail. As* BOSWELL *and* JOHNSON *round the bend, they see…*
The sea-side town of Glenelg, far below.]

BOSWELL: I'll ride on ahead and make arrangements for the night. You need a meal, a bath, and a bed.
JOHNSON: No, sir! I am done with you! I shall return to my true friends as soon as I find a place in this miserable country where coaches run or ships sail! There is no excuse for such incivility! I would sooner pick your pocket than abandon you!! You, sir, lack character.

[JOHNSON *spurs his pony on.* BOSWELL *drops back. Humiliated. Hurt.* JOSEPH *and* EUAN *are embarrassed for him.*]

EXT. THE HARBOR AT GLENELG – DUSK

[BOSWELL *watches as* JOHNSON *makes inquiries among the ships' captains.* EUAN MACRAE *appears at his side, leading the three ponies.*]

EUAN: A good night's sleep and he'll have a change o' heart.

[BOSWELL *nods. He's crushed. He walks away as* JOSEPH *approaches* JOHNSON, *who's just been told by a Captain that his ship's heading for Ireland not south. A small horde of country people, their belongings bundled, pass, queuing at the gangway of a sea-going ship.*]

JOHNSON: Most of these ships are sailing for America. The rest are bound for the Hebrides or Ireland. It seems that every man, woman, and child in Scotland is trying to get out.

JOSEPH: Our rooms are ready, sir. You can make inquiries about the southbound coaches in the morning, if that is still your plan.

JOHNSON: Where's Boswell?

JOSEPH: Gone off. Your decision is sorely disappointing. Forgive my impudence, sir, but for his sake, you might reconsider.

JOHNSON: He might have thought of that this afternoon when he abandoned me in those damned mountains! The boy has been like a son to me.

JOSEPH: Sooner or later all sons disappoint their fathers.

JOHNSON: And do not fathers live in fear that one day the son will see his father as merely a man – flawed, diminished, unworthy of their former esteem?

EXT. END OF A WHARF – NIGHT

[BOSWELL *sits. Despondent. Watching waves, ships, the moon. He hears footsteps behind him. He turns. It's* JOHNSON. *Silence. Then...*]

BOSWELL: Perhaps this trip wasn't such a good idea.

JOHNSON: Rubbish.

BOSWELL: This afternoon...

JOHNSON: I was tired. And cross. Your Highlands proved more formidable than I'd anticipated. When you rode off...
[*off* BOSWELL's *look, with difficulty*] I became... frightened.

BOSWELL: Of...?

JOHNSON: Being left. Forgotten. Tumbling into nothingness.

[In the cover of darkness, JOHNSON *gives full vent to his soul searching.]*

JOHNSON: My life has been a preposterous failure.

BOSWELL: How can you possibly say such a thing?! You've written –

JOHNSON: A pile of trivialities, the works of a drudge who'd be too lazy to write a word if he didn't need the cash.

*[*JOHNSON *painfully lowers himself to sit at* BOSWELL'*s side.]*

JOHNSON *[CONT'D]*: I'm sixty-three years old, sixty-four on Wednesday. I'm half-blind, half-deaf, my limbs shake, my joints ache, and at any moment my heart could explode or I could lapse into… total insanity. *[off* BOSWELL'*s look]* I've already succumbed once. The only thing that's kept me on keel is my work. And now my best work's behind me. I'm washed up, Bozzy. My God, what will I do with what's left of my life?!

[His cry is almost plaintive – a full-bore mid-life crisis.]

BOSWELL: You are the acknowledged master of English letters. You have the universal admiration of men on two continents. I have the achievements of a child, a spoiled and foolish boy.

JOHNSON: You've been admitted to the Bar –

BOSWELL: And nearly flubbed my cases.

JOHNSON: You have a loving and understanding wife; the possibility of heirs. I have you.

BOSWELL: Margaret's pregnant. She doesn't think I know.

JOHNSON: And you've abandoned her? For this?!

BOSWELL: For the first time I'm ready to take my rightful place in the world. Here, in Scotland. As the laird of my family's estates. But to do that, I must first confront my father. Do not abandon me.

[Pause.]

JOHNSON: For better or worse, my boy, I am stuck here in the Hebrides. And apparently we are stuck with each other. … How goes the journal?

BOSWELL: It grows as it goes.

[Off the look between JOHNSON *and* BOSWELL...]

INT. THE INN – NIGHT

*[*BOSWELL *drinks and paces while watching* JOHNSON *read his journal. A nerve-wracking wait for the verdict,* BOSWELL *can't tell if* JOHNSON *is pleased or angry, whether he likes it or hates it. Will this seal their friendship or sever it forever?*
JOHNSON, *leaning heavily on his hand as he reads, seems to have fixated on a passage. He's been too still too long. What could this mean? What is he thinking? What have I done?* BOSWELL *finally screws up his courage and approaches.*
JOHNSON *snores. He's fallen asleep.* BOSWELL *tenderly removes the journal. Blows out the candle, and helps the still half-sleeping* JOHNSON *back to bed.]*

INT. THEIR ROOM AT THE INN – NIGHT

[As BOSWELL's *tucking him in...]*

JOHNSON: Boswell, you are a scoundrel!
BOSWELL: Sir?
JOHNSON: I could throttle the life out of you.
BOSWELL: If my sad attempt to –
JOHNSON: It's magnificent, you blockhead!

*[*BOSWELL's *dumbstruck.]*

JOHNSON: How dare you write so well? It's better than a novel! Your portrait has more life than its subject! That man Johnson you've created is far wittier than its original. And smarter. And better educated.

*[*BOSWELL *wilts with joy.]*

JOHNSON *[CONT'D]:* Now go to sleep. Tomorrow we brave the high seas and wend our way westward to the Outer Hebrides!

*[*JOHNSON *rolls over to go to sleep.* BOSWELL *returns to his bed. Each turns to the wall.* JOHNSON *is grinning. So is* BOSWELL. *So is* JOSEPH.]*

EXT. THE SOUND OF SLEAT - OFF THE ISLE OF SKYE – DAWN

[Beauty shot. Sunrise over the water. Reeling sea-birds.]

EXT. THE COAST OF SKYE – DAY

[Two CREWMEN row JOHNSON, BOSWELL, *and* JOSEPH *ashore. As the DINGHY rides the surf into the shallows, one Crewman tends the oars while the other leaps into the knee-deep water and offers his back as a conveyance.]*

JOHNSON *[to BOSWELL]*: You first.

*[*BOSWELL *climbs onto the Crewman's back.*
ON THE BEACH stands...
NORMAN MACLEOD *(30s) a vigorous, strapping man, in tartans.*
MACLEOD *marches out into the wave wash. Cruising right past*
BOSWELL...]*

MACLEOD: Welcome to Skye, Mister Boswell!
BOSWELL *[over his shoulder]*: Thank you for meeting us.

[AT THE DINGHY, MACLEOD *offers his back to* JOHNSON.]*

MACLEOD: Welcome, sir. I am Norman Macleod. Hop aboard. I'll take ye to land. Hate to see ye get yer feet soaked.
JOHNSON: I'm too big a package for you, sir.
MACLEOD: I've hauled bigger.
JOHNSON: Even so, I'll not have my host treated as a pack horse.
MACLEOD *[with a wink]*: Not to fear, sir. I've had me share of Scottish oats today.
JOHNSON: And I've had my fill of your Scottish ponies.

[With which, JOHNSON *jumps off the side into the water. Laughing*

heartily, MACLEOD *vigorously shakes* JOHNSON's *hand.* MACLEOD *glances back to find* JOSEPH *perched hesitantly on the gunwale.* JOSEPH *would be more than happy to take* MACLEOD *up on his offer, but it's not his place to ask.]*

MACLEOD: Come, sir. Since Doctor Johnson would rather be independent than dry, I'd like to think I haven't soaked me stockings for naught.

*[*JOSEPH *climbs onto* MACLEOD's *back. Johnson laughs loudly. BOSWELL'S POV –* JOHNSON *and* MACLEOD, *with the tall* JOSEPH *on his back, stride ashore, oblivious to the breaking sea. The Crewman who carried* BOSWELL *in, returns to the dinghy for the bags.]*

EXT. OPEN ROAD IN SKY – DAY

[The CARRIAGE, with MACLEOD *driving, clips along. Briskly.]*

BOSWELL: Doctor Johnson has always loved racing along in an open carriage.
MACLEOD *[with a twinkle]*: Do ye now?
JOHNSON: I like the speed, sir. For which I can offer no rational explanation.

[Grinning, MACLEOD *snaps the reins.* BOSWELL *nearly loses his wig. They almost lose* JOSEPH *over the tailgate.* JOHNSON *shouts with joy as they tear along.]*

EXT. DUNVEGAN - DAY

[The CARRIAGE approaches the sea-side castle – the oldest continuously inhabited castle in the Hebrides. JOHNSON *is obviously and deeply impressed with scenery and setting.]*

BOSWELL: What do you think of it so far?
JOHNSON: I think that we've come to the furthest reach of civilization!
MACLEOD *[waving seaward]*: There's still America out beyond.
JOHNSON: I said civilization, sir.

[… as they roll under the portcullis.]

INT. DUNVEGAN CASTLE – DAY

[MACLEOD ushers them into a large room, at the far end of which, a WOMAN feeds the roaring fire in the hearth.]

MACLEOD: We've not had as illustrious a guest since Bonnie Prince Charles passed this way with Miss Flora Macdonald at his side and English soldiers at his heels.

JOHNSON: I assure you, sir, we are neither fugitives nor pretenders to the throne.

[JOHNSON's shoes squish loudly as they approach the Woman. When she turns to them, BOSWELL is instantly reduced to a gawking teenager. The woman is none other than…
FLORA MACDONALD (50) a strikingly handsome woman with fearless, flashing eyes.]

MACLEOD: May I introduce…

BOSWELL: Flora Macdonald.

FLORA *[taking JOHNSON's hand]*: I trust your crossing wasn't too exciting.

JOHNSON: Being on a ship, madam, is like being in jail – with the chance of getting drowned.

[Laughter.]

FLORA: When Norman told me you were coming I invited myself as a guest.

JOHNSON: Had we known that you were waiting for us, we would have spurred our horses and found a faster ship.

[BOSWELL, effectively ignored, announces…]

BOSWELL: If you'll excuse me, I think I'll change to something dry.

JOHNSON: I think I'll steam.

MACLEOD: I think I'll join ye!

[The two men plop in front of the fire, stretching out their feet to the flames. As BOSWELL's *leaving…]*

MACLEOD *[to* JOHNSON*]*: A dram, sir, to remove the chill?
BOSWELL: Oh. Doctor Johnson doesn't drink.
FLORA: Not even a wee one?
JOHNSON: If truth be told, I can't just drink a little. What ferments the spirits also deranges the intellect, and mine needs no encouragement.

[Laughter. BOSWELL *exits, followed by* JOSEPH.*]*

JOHNSON: Abstinence is as easy to me as temperance would be difficult.
FLORA: You strike me as a man who can carry his liquor.
MACLEOD: And carry it well!
JOHNSON: No, sir, it carries me! But serve me a hogshead of tea and I'll drink it down!
MACLEOD: Then you shall have it. Annie!!

*[*ANNIE *(15),* MACLEOD's *pretty daughter, peeking in at the visitors from the doorway along with her* COUSINS, *steps in.]*

MACLEOD: Tell them in the kitchen to brew up a tub of tea for the Doctor; and a bottle for me from the cellar.
ANNIE: Yes, Father.

*[*ANNIE *curtsies, then exits with a glance back at* JOHNSON. *She rejoins her giggling companions then dashes off.]*

JOHNSON: Charming girl.

[Small smiles. JOHNSON *and* MACLEOD *watch the steam rise from their stockings.* FLORA *studies* JOHNSON *closely.]*

JOHNSON: Having seen this man brave the surf in his plaids with Boswell's giant on his back, I can now return to England and say I have truly met a Highland chief!
MACLEOD: And I a sober Englishman.

JOHNSON *[after a beat]*: Hah! Well said, sir! Well said!

INT. UPSTAIRS HALL - DUNVEGAN CASTLE - DAY

[THROUGH AN OPEN DOOR we see BOSWELL, *already in a fresh outfit, putting the finishing touches to a quick journal entry, then rushing out.*
IN THE HALLWAY Passing a mirror, BOSWELL *stops to check his appearance. Suddenly, he finds himself sharing his reflection with…* FLORA. BOSWELL *turns too quickly and blusters…]*

BOSWELL: Excuse me, madam, I…

*[*FLORA *grins.* BOSWELL *gawks.*
She presumes to straighten his wig for him.]

FLORA: There. Now you're presentable.

*[*FLORA *starts off toward the stairs.* BOSWELL *chases after.]*

BOSWELL: Madam, this is an honor.
FLORA: If it's an honor, then you haven't inherited your father's politics.
BOSWELL: Among other things.

[Bounding alongside, trying to keep up – she's clearly an energetic woman.]

BOSWELL: If I might be so bold, madam, the portraits I have seen of you do you little justice!
FLORA: Beauty, sir, is only skin deep.
BOSWELL: That may be. But I for one have never heard a man extol the beauties of a woman's liver.

*[*FLORA *laughs heartily and takes his arm.]*

[BACK TO] INT. DUNVEGAN - GREAT ROOM – CONTINUOUS

[LADY MACLEOD (30s), MACLEOD's wife and physical match, serves tea to JOHNSON and her husband. They hear FLORA's bright laughter from the hallway. They turn just as BOSWELL enters, arm-in-arm with a laughing FLORA MACDONALD.]

FLORA: Mister Boswell has just been telling me of their encounter with the Highland Macraes. *[to JOHNSON]* And here I thought you were one of the few Englishmen who've ever come into our country armed only with good intentions!

[JOHNSON glares at BOSWELL. A sheepish BOSWELL grins.]

INT. DINING HALL - DUNVEGAN - NIGHT

[The end of a sumptuous feast. Men, women, and children of all ages. All eyes are on JOHNSON, entertaining a wide-eyed LITTLE GIRL and BOY.]

LITTLE GIRL: You do not live in a house?
JOHNSON: Oh no! I live in a very big cave – and have done so ever since I got to be this size. When I was little like you, they kept me in a pantry!
LITTLE BOY: Why'd they let you out?
JOHNSON: They didn't. Mister Boswell there snuck me out in the middle of the night and dragged me off to Skye!

[The Guests laugh warmly. JOHNSON winks at FLORA. But then PRETTY ANNIE plants herself on JOHNSON's lap.]

JOHNSON: And what makes you so bold?!
PRETTY ANNIE: A wager.

[With a glance back at TWO GIRLS her own age, giggling.]

PRETTY ANNIE: They wagered that you would not allow yourself to be kissed.
JOHNSON: I hope that you wagered a bunch.

[With which he presents his cheek to her. She kisses him. The charmed Guests applaud. Before ANNIE *can run away…]*

JOHNSON: What?! Only one?! Kiss me again. And as many times as you wish. We shall see who will tire first!

[She kisses him twice more then stays there on his lap. FLORA *is much taken with* JOHNSON. *Their eyes meet. She smiles.]*

BOSWELL: It seems that Doctor Johnson has charmed all the ladies!

JOHNSON: And it seems Mister Boswell has done his best to deplete Mister Macleod's wine cellar!

BOSWELL: In vino veritas.

JOHNSON: That, sir, may well be an argument for drink, but only if you suppose all men to be liars.

[Chuckles.]

JOHNSON: I, for one, would not keep company with a fellow who lies when he is sober and whom you must make drunk to pry a word of truth out of him!

BOSWELL: The truth, sir, is that the ladies of Skye dote upon you. And not just those of Skye but of the Highlands as well. We came across this old woman in a crofter's hut –

JOHNSON *[overriding him]*: Who feared for her virtue when she spied Boswell!

BOSWELL: As I recall, it was I who had to protect the poor woman from you!

*[*BOSWELL *raises his glass to* JOHNSON, *then downs it.]*

JOHNSON: The woman's shift stank of her flock and smoke. If I were a pasha surrounded by a harem –

*[*BOSWELL's *eyes widen, a strange grin forming.]*

JOHNSON *[CONT'D]*: I would insist that all my beauties wear nothing but fabrics woven from vegetable. Linens, cottons, and silks; which are both more sanitary and more pleasing to the touch.

[BOSWELL *bursts out laughing.* JOHNSON, *never one to tolerate being the object of laughter, glowers.* BOSWELL *laughs on.*]

JOHNSON: Sir?

BOSWELL: The image of you, of all people, as master of a seraglio…

JOHNSON: You find such an image laughable?

BOSWELL: Merely amusing, sir.

JOHNSON: In what way? *[when* BOSWELL *says nothing]* If I told you that I have idled away entire days entertaining such exotic notions, what would you do?

FLORA: I'm sure he would pester you for an invitation.

JOHNSON: And I would grant my young and libertine friend free run of my house. I would even make him part and parcel of my establishment!

MACLEOD: You'd trust Boswell among the women?! With his reputation?!

JOHNSON: Indeed I would, sir. But only as my palace eunuch!

[Laughter at BOSWELL's *expense.]*

PRETTY ANNIE: Mother, what is a eunuch?

[More laughter.]

PRETTY ANNIE: Is Mister Boswell one?

[Howls of laughter. BOSWELL *is mortified.]*

JOHNSON: No, not at present, my dear. But he would, I think, make a very fine one, don't you think?

[Even more laughter.]

BOSWELL: You go too far, sir.

JOHNSON: A jest, sir, breaks no bones. Be of good cheer. Have another glass.

BOSWELL: Ah, so now you argue for drinking?!

JOHNSON: Some might argue that drinking improves a man's conversation.

BOSWELL: Then even you might encourage him to drink.

JOHNSON: Indeed I would, sir, especially if he sat next to you!

[Snickers of delight. BOSWELL *rises, a bit unsteadily.]*

BOSWELL: Once more, sir, I am defeated. *[with a slight bow]* Lady Macleod, thank you for a magnificent meal. Missus Macdonald, gentlemen, I must now retire.

*[*BOSWELL *exits.* JOHNSON *is suddenly and noticeably distraught.]*

JOHNSON: I fear I went too hard with him.

FLORA *[as she refills his teacup]*: Mister Boswell sought to draw you into debate and then, having done so, lost badly. As any of us might have predicted. Your reputation as a disputant precedes you. Which is as extreme as the rumors.

JOHNSON: Rumors? What rumors?

FLORA: Such as… that you've come north to propagate the growth of potatoes.

JOHNSON: To what possible end?!

MACLEOD: To make us as submissive as the Irish.

LADY MACLEOD: They say that at every house you stay you've been forced to eat oat-cakes as punishment –

FLORA: For your definition of "oats."

JOHNSON: Not a day has passed since I crossed the Border that I have not regretted that sad attempt at wit.

FLORA: One newspaper claims that you've challenged Macpherson to either produce the original of Finegal or meet you on the field of honor.

JOHNSON: Me?! In a duel?!

MACLEOD: Another reports that you've caught the pox from a female mountaineer!

*[*JOHNSON *just blinks. The guests' twitters subside.*
Silence. Then JOHNSON *bursts out laughing.]*

INT. UPSTAIRS BEDROOM – NIGHT

*[*BOSWELL *by candlelight, fighting his "buzz," records the evening's events in his journal.* JOHNSON *enters. At first,* BOSWELL *says nothing, then…]*

BOSWELL: That nonsense... about my being a eunuch in your harem...
JOHNSON: Tush, sir. Do you not know that I love you?

[BOSWELL *is only partly mollified.*]

JOHNSON *[CONT'D]*: Don't think of yourself as a man without balls...
[*off* BOSWELL*'s reaction*] But as a gentleman who, like the palace eunuch, has been entrusted with the most intimate secrets of his master's heart.

[*Small consolation.* JOHNSON *gives* BOSWELL*'s shoulder an affection-ate bear-like cuff, then exits. Beat.* BOSWELL *begins revising what he's just written.*]

EXT. BEN STORR – DAY

[*A wild and rugged mountainside with prospects of the sea. From down below we hear VOICES. A PARTY of climbers rounds a bend into view – everyone from last night's banquet, including the children. Out in front, leading the pack...*
JOHNSON *and* BOSWELL *silently and grimly set the pace. Both men are panting, sweat popping from their foreheads. Neither considers asking the other to slow down. This is serious competition.* JOHNSON *leans heavily on his man-sized walking stick.* BOSWELL *fights a cramp. Right behind them...*
FLORA *and* MACLEOD *traipse along with surprising ease – just a stroll through the hills, a morning jaunt. Watching* JOHNSON *and* BOSWELL*...*]

MACLEOD: The old goat's besotted with ye.
FLORA: Go to.
MACLEOD: It's not for me he's up there frisking like a ram in a rut.

[*Up ahead,* JOHNSON *leaps from one boulder to boulder.*]

MACLEOD: Look at him, showing off for you like a lad of seventeen!
FLORA: You have a fevered imagination, Norman Macleod. What possible interest could a man like Johnson have in a mad Scotswoman like me?

MACLEOD: Any man who's gone a-roving is primed to fall in love. It's as certain as the laws of physics.

[*Up ahead,* JOHNSON *strains to gain a few paces on* BOSWELL. *When he glances back…*]

MACLEOD: You ha' better go show him you've noticed before he breaks a bone.

[*After a few more steps…*]

MACLEOD: Well, what are ye waiting for?! Go to him, girl! Go!

[*Finally,* FLORA *rushes forward.*]

FLORA: Doctor Johnson! Hold to!

[JOHNSON *hearing her call, at last has an excuse to stop.* JOHNSON *and* BOSWELL *gasp for air. They manage to recover their composure just as* FLORA *joins them.*]

FLORA: We're none as vigorous as you!

[JOHNSON *beams; his chest swells, he thumps his stick.*]

FLORA: You really should show a bit o' mercy to your companion.

[BOSWELL *is about to object, but doesn't.*]

FLORA: Look at him, half your age and already flushed, with half as much again to go before the top!

[FLORA *takes* JOHNSON'S *arm and resumes the climb, taking it slowly.* BOSWELL *drops back until he's joined by* MACLEOD. *BOSWELL'S POV -* JOHNSON *and* FLORA *ahead of them, arm-in-arm.*]

MACLEOD: Just how old is Johnson?
BOSWELL: Sixty-four. Today.

MACLEOD: Today?

BOSWELL: It's his birthday. Though he's asked me to keep it a secret.

MACLEOD: Did he now?

EXT. SUMMIT OF BEN STORR - DAY

[A Highland picnic of cold mutton, bread, cheese, brandy, punch, and, for JOHNSON, *cold tea. The natives are dressed in full regalia – tartan kilts and bonnets.*
A FIDDLER begins to play. Led by ANNIE, *the children begin to dance.*
BOSWELL *joins in.* JOHNSON *and* FLORA *sit together. The prospects from the summit are grand.]*

FLORA: The morning Bonny Prince Charles took his leave, we climbed to this very spot. This was the last look he had of his homeland, and the one he'll hold near his heart till his exile's over and he returns to us again.

JOHNSON: The Prince is in Rome, isn't he?

FLORA: Aye. Living in poverty and neglect. But for fifteen months, some thirty years ago, we shared a great dream. Oh, you English chased him hard. You put a price of thirty thousand on his head, but none betrayed him....He and I together crossed these glens and mountains, taking shelter where we could, slipping past the British soldiers and coast patrols.

[Wind in their hair, they watch the dancers. Then...]

FLORA *[CONT'D]*: Ah, we lost so many at Culloden. And those who survived, the Lords executed or exiled to the colonies.

JOHNSON: And you?

FLORA: Captured, questioned, and clapped into a prison ship off London. Your Parliament and King banned all Highland dress and forbade us to ever carry arms. My own clan cannot gather in more than four at a time.

*[*JOHNSON *surveys the rifles, tartans, numerous Highlanders. When he glances back at* FLORA, *he finds her grinning.]*

FLORA *[CONT'D]*: 'Twould be a foolish Englishman to enforce such laws up here.

JOHNSON: I am not that man, Lady.

[FLORA, *smiling, leaps up and takes* JOHNSON'*s hand.*]

FLORA: It's time you learned to reel!

[*She hauls him to his feet – a small woman, lifting a bear. She leads him to the circle of dancers and begins to teach him a Highland dance. He's clumsy but game; she's patient and enthusiastic. Soon, everyone gathers to watch the couple dance, keeping time by vigorous clapping.* BOSWELL *is almost moved to tears. When the tune ends…* FLORA *presents* JOHNSON *to the crowd. He bows. They applaud and cheer, then, at* MACLEOD'*s prompting, shout in unison…*]

ALL: Happy Birthday!!!

[PRETTY ANNIE *rushes up and plants another kiss on* JOHNSON'*s cheek.* FLORA *laughs.* JOHNSON *searches the crowd for* BOSWELL. *When he finds him, he shakes a fist his way. Off* BOSWELL'*s grinning shrug…*]

[DISSOLVE TO]
EXT. BEN STORR - BELOW THE SUMMIT - LATER – DAY

[*The party's over, the group begins its descent. The Fiddler continues playing as they go.* BOSWELL *carries a sleeping* CHILD *in his arms.* JOHNSON, FLORA, *and* MACLEOD *stroll together,* FLORA'*s arm in* JOHNSON'*s.*]

FLORA: Have you ever met Boswell's Da?
JOHNSON: I've never met the man, though I know of him by reputation.
FLORA: They say he's learned and stern with a nasty sense of humor. But I've only encountered him once.
MACLEOD: Treated you warmly, did he?
FLORA: Ha! To him a Jacobite's a cross between a cattle-thief and baby-killer. He seemed horrified the English had let me out o' prison.

[All three glance back at BOSWELL. JOHNSON *holds up, and waits for* BOSWELL *while* FLORA *and* MACLEOD *continue on.* JOHNSON *and* BOSWELL, *walking. Finally...]*

BOSWELL: Remarkable woman, isn't she?
JOHNSON: She's had a remarkable life.

[Then, after a pause, with the hint of a Highland burr...]

JOHNSON *[CONT'D]*: 'Tis a grand country, Jamie, that can produce such women as her.
BOSWELL: And ones like Lady MacIntyre. Or have you long-forgotten her?
JOHNSON: I have not.

*[*BOSWELL *grins.* JOHNSON *huffs a bit, then...]*

JOHNSON *[CONT'D]*: Unlike some, sir, once my heart's been touched, I make an effort to remember them beyond morning.

[PULLING UP AND AWAY TO WIDE ON] The flanks of Ben Storr mountain, the picnickers descending, the sun beginning to set, the light diffusing to golden.

EXT. ATOP THE DUNVEGAN WALLS - MAGIC HOUR (THE GLOAMING)

*[*JOHNSON *strolls the battlements of the castle. There's a sense that he's searching for something.* BOSWELL *slips out of a niche, scampers on tiptoe across the cobbled walkway, then ducks behind the barrel of a tower. He's "stalking" the Bear.*
JOHNSON *reaches a promontory at the limits of the castle wall. He surveys the sea below, and then the hills behind. Only then do we begin to hear...*
A HAUNTINGLY LOVELY VOICE singing "Over the Sea to Skye," a plaintive lyrical ballad about Bonnie Prince Charlie's escape, sung in the voice of FLORA MACDONALD. *The woman's heart-felt voice filters down from the hills, insinuating itself in the air.*

JOHNSON, *deeply moved, begins to search it out.* BOSWELL *follows at a safe distance, hugging the walls. He sees* JOHNSON *disappear down a staircase.]*

EXT. DUNVEGAN CASTLE - MOMENTS LATER

*[*JOHNSON *emerges from a doorway into the open. He scans the hills. The WOMAN'S VOICE is stronger.* JOHNSON *starts off in its direction, walking slowly.* BOSWELL *peeks out from the doorway, then follows* JOHNSON *as he makes his way into the nearby hills. He discovers a WOMAN alone on a hilltop overlooking the sea, singing.]*

EXT. HILLTOP - NEAR DUNVEGAN – CONTINUOUS

*[*FLORA MACDONALD *sings, seemingly transported by the melody.* JOHNSON, *below her, listens, spellbound. Then, like some ancient and Homeric sailor unleashed from his mast and drawn by the song of the Sirens, he drifts ever closer and closer. As* FLORA *finishes her song,* JOHNSON *is almost at her side.*
BOSWELL, *respecting their moment, keeps his distance; but consumed with curiosity, keeps his watch.* JOHNSON *and* FLORA *stand side by side, drinking in the time and place and moment. Then, from across a glen, we hear…*
THE SOUND OF BAGPIPES *riding the air. Magic.* JOHNSON *and* FLORA *turn to one another. He takes her hand. Kisses it. Holding hands, they listen to the pipes.*
BOSWELL *is filled with emotion. His eyes well with tears. He too listens for a long moment, watching* JOHNSON *and* FLORA. *As he withdraws into the shadows, behind him are* JOHNSON *and* FLORA, *silhouetted on their hilltop.]*

[FADE OUT AND BACK UP ON]
EXT. THE SEA - SOUTH OF SKY – DAY

[AN OPEN SINGLE-SAILED BOAT runs southward before a steady wind over open water. JOHNSON *in the bow, one foot raised, his stick held high like some great wild-eyed patriarch leading his people on to*

the promised land, suddenly thunders...]

JOHNSON: Now this!! Is adventure!!

[JOHNSON turns to the others – BOSWELL, JOSEPH, FLORA, and NORMAN MACLEOD at the tiller.]

JOHNSON: Weeks from now I shall tell my Club how I crossed the cruel Atlantic in an open boat! Reynolds and Garrick will shudder, Burke will call me a fool to have exposed myself to such danger! Goldsmith will declare that crossing the sea in an open boat is nothing compared to the time he crossed Hampstead Heath in a driving rain without an overcoat! They'll all turn to Bozzy and ask, did he? did he really? Boswell will smile that smug yet sagacious smile of his and vouch for every word of my tale. They shall be awestruck!
BOSWELL: Sir, it might be safer if you sat.
JOHNSON: Aye, sir, safer, but more dull. More sail, Macleod! On to Iona!!

[The boat pitches, spray flies up into JOHNSON's face. He growls with exhilaration. His mood is infectious. JOHNSON staggers back to the stern, almost tumbling into FLORA's lap, then plops heavily next to MACLEOD.
Off to port is a LOVELY SMALL ISLAND. Seals bark.]

MACLEOD: Yon is Isa Island. Been Macleod land since the 12th century.... Do ye want it?
FLORA: Take care, sir, before you accept. A laird's gift demands a quid pro quo. You'll be Macleod's tenant. And once admitted to clan Macleod then you're one of us for life!

[After a pause...]

JOHNSON: I accept!
BOSWELL: Really?!
JOHNSON *[riffing]*: I shall built an ancestral fortress upon the headland with battlements greater than Dunvegan's and fortify its seaward walls with cannon!! I shall instill my tenants with such visions of glory that

we shall sally forth like Myrmidons from Isa and take Coll and Mull and Muck and expand the suzerainty of Macleod as far as Auchinleck! And there... *[with a nod to* BOSWELL*]* We shall treat with the future laird of Auchinleck for alliance!

[As FLORA *pours glasses of punch for each, a tumbler of lemonade for* JOHNSON, *she explains...]*

FLORA: It is the custom to address a man by the names of his lands, so... *[raising her glass to* MACLEOD*]* To Ulinish, Talisker, Dunvegan! *[then to* JOHNSON*]* Island Isa, your health!!

[All drink. JOHNSON *rises, claps a hand on* BOSWELL's *shoulder, and points to a SEA-ROCK, hardly big enough to support vegetation.]*

JOHNSON: And that shall be Boswell's.

*[*JOHNSON *and the others lift their glasses to* BOSWELL...*]*

JOHNSON: Inch Boswell! Your future!!

[They laugh. Drink.]

EXT. THE SEA NEAR ICOLMKILL (IONA) – DAY

[As the OPEN BOAT tacks for its run to the island, everyone aboard grows silent and solemn. The island appears sparsely populated, but what draws their focus is the stone TOWER OF THE CATHEDRAL, looming above the houses and abbey ruins.]

EXT. ABOVE THE BEACH AT ICOLMKILL (IONA) – DAY

*[*BOSWELL *and* JOHNSON *walk slowly toward the ruins. There is something ethereally calm about the place. Behind them,* MACLEOD *and* JOSEPH *secure the boat while* FLORA *surveys sea and coast, drinking in the heady atmosphere.]*

EXT. AMONG THE RUINS - ICOLMKILL – DAY

[The party of five strolls past ruined cloisters, skirting the ruin of a Romanesque arch, flanking the walls of the stone cathedral. A mysterious soughing of the sea breeze.
They enter sacred ground, the burial place of kings. The graves are marked with simple flat stones, their carved inscriptions all but weathered away.
Above them looms a CELTIC CROSS on its stone pedestal, the open sea beyond, the sun, now lower on the horizon, bursting brilliantly through interstices of the cross's ring and arms. BOSWELL *seems transfixed. He gasps sharply and staggers back.*
JOHNSON *and* FLORA *linger over the graves.* JOHNSON *stoops to read the worn inscriptions as if by braille. Their reverie is shattered by* COLIN *(40s) a local, self-appointed guide.]*

COLIN: These monuments mark the graves of ancient kings of Scotland, Ireland, Denmark, and even a king of France!

*[*JOHNSON *is about to explode at the interference.]*

COLIN *[CONT'D]*: Over here is the grave of Macbeth himself, whom you may know from William Shakespeare's tragic play. And beside him, in a shared peace they did not know in life, lies –
JOHNSON: Duncan was an Irish interloper! You disgrace good king Macbeth in this!

*[*COLIN *gapes. Even* FLORA *is surprised.* JOHNSON *takes* FLORA's *arm and hustles her away.]*

JOHNSON: Quick, madam. Let's make our escape while we have our chance.
MACLEOD: That may be difficult, as Colin's the only innkeeper on Iona.
JOHNSON: I would rather sleep in a cowbarn than put up with his prattle!

[Judging from COLIN's *angry skulking...]*

JOSEPH: You may well get that chance, sir.

JOHNSON [*scanning the area*]: Now where has Boswell run off to?

[*They spot* BOSWELL *slipping into the cathedral.*]

INT. THE ABBEY CATHEDRAL OF IONA – DAY

[BOSWELL *roams, his eyes scanning rafters. He seems dizzy, almost intoxicated by the place. He suddenly drops to his knees before the altar. Behind him,* JOHNSON, FLORA, MACLEOD, *and* JOSEPH *enter at the rear of the church.* JOHNSON *approaches. The others linger at the back.* JOHNSON *steps quietly to* BOSWELL'*s side. When* JOHNSON *notices* BOSWELL *daubing a misty eye,* JOHNSON *gently pats his shoulder. Leaning heavily on his stick,* JOHNSON *kneels beside* BOSWELL. *Off* BOSWELL'*s glance…*]

JOHNSON: We have drunk together in taverns, debated theories of government and poetry, made many a jest, yet you and I have never prayed together.

[JOHNSON *clasps* BOSWELL'*s hand, a grip of iron. They pray.*]

BOSWELL: From this day forth I shall reform. No more rambles or drunkenness. I shall become a man worthy of my father's respect, my wife's faith, and your good opinion.

JOHNSON: It's fitting, sir, that you should rediscover your faith, here where the gospel first came to Caledonia.

[*As* BOSWELL *rises, he seems to glow from within, a man suddenly freed from terrible burdens. He surveys the mote-sparkled BEAMS streaming through the windows, firing the CELTIC CROSS.* JOHNSON *rises beside him. Together, they walk out of the cathedral, passing the others, who note* BOSWELL'*s transformation.*]

INT. ICOLMKILL INN – NIGHT

[BOSWELL, *celebrating his moral conversion (by getting drunk) exults with all the fervor of a recently reformed sinner…*]

BOSWELL: I was such a rogue in my youth!

FLORA: You are but a lad of thirty!

BOSWELL: Thirty-three! The exact age of our Savior at his transformation!

[BOSWELL *remains blissfully oblivious to* JOHNSON's *scowl at this near-blasphemous analogy. He lubricates his tongue with another swallow then continues…*]

BOSWELL *[CONT'D]*: In my twenties, I was a rake! And when these fits of sensuality came upon me I sought out the foulest, darkest, most fornicatious corners of London to satisfy my lusts!

[BOSWELL's *frankness is becoming an embarrassment – to everyone but him. He takes another swig.* JOHNSON *rises.*]

JOHNSON: Enough, sir.

BOSWELL: I am a changed man. I have turned a corner! I shall clasp goodness to my bosom and banish all evil!

[In rising, BOSWELL *manages to knock a tankard of punch onto* JOHNSON's *trousers.*]

JOHNSON: And I leave you to your salvation.

BOSWELL: How could I be so clumsy?!!

[When BOSWELL *tries to clean up the mess…*]

JOHNSON: Enough! It was time I changed them.

BOSWELL: Sir, you are a good, kind, decent, brilliant, understanding –

JOHNSON: Goodnight, Boswell!

[JOHNSON *exits.* COLIN, *the innkeeper, slips up next to* BOSWELL *and in an almost seductive whisper…*]

COLIN: Another round, sir?

BOSWELL: None for me! I am a changed man!

[COLIN *signals the* BARMAID (19) *to keep the drinks coming.*]

FLORA: I'll see to Doctor Johnson.

[FLORA *exits, followed by* MACLEOD.]

BOSWELL [*woozily to* JOSEPH]: I am susceptible –

[*He has trouble getting his mouth around the word…*]

BOSWELL: Susceptible to influence.

[*The Barmaid plants a full glass in front of* BOSWELL *who instinctively picks it up, raises it…*]

BOSWELL: Henceforth, I shall cling only to those who inspire virtue!!

[BOSWELL *empties his glass, slams it onto the table, then bursts into… A HYMN!!*]

INT. ROOM AT THE INN - NIGHT

[FLORA *watches* JOHNSON *worry the wet splotch on his pants.*]

FLORA: If you'd been wearing a kilt, you'd only have had to wash your leg.
JOHNSON: If I'd been wearing a kilt, madam, I'd fear for my modesty!
FLORA: Aye. But you'd look grand.

[MACLEOD *enters with an armful of plaid clothing.*]

MACLEOD: I agree. Put these on. At least til your clothes dry.

[JOHNSON *balks.*]

FLORA: If Jamie Boswell can change his stripes, so can you!

[*Off* JOHNSON's *look…*]

EXT. A THATCHED COTTAGE - IONA - NIGHT

[Rocks tied in ropes, suspended from the cottage's eaves, secure the roof thatch. Stillness, then, BOSWELL *staggers up, having lost his way in the dark. He suddenly finds himself tangled in the ropes and attacked by the now swinging boulders. All efforts to extricate himself precipitate outrageously Chaplinesque prat-falls.]*

BOSWELL: Blasted stones!!!

*[*JOSEPH, *following at a discreet distance, is about to intervene when a* LASS *(20s) rushes out of the cottage, then bursts out laughing when she discovers* BOSWELL *flailing in the lines.* BOSWELL, *hearing her, turns, grinning sloppily. He's broadsided by a swinging rock the size of a watermelon.*
The LASS *tries to help. In trying to stop* BOSWELL's *manic pin-wheeling. She flings her arms around him and holds him. Finding a lovely young woman embracing him,* BOSWELL – *being* BOSWELL – *naturally assumes that her intent is amorous.]*

BOSWELL: Like some heaven-sent angel, you have delivered me from these snares! I am yours to command!

[He tries to bow. But in doing so, staggers; in staggering, he tries to catch himself by grabbing one of the ropes. He then swings off, tumbling on the return stroke, and finds himself sprawled at the LASS' *feet.* BOSWELL *grasps an ankle, then a calf, then lewdly tries to look up her dress. Just as he's lifting his head...*
HER BARE FOOT shoves his head to the dirt as a boulder grazes his skull. When the LASS *drags* BOSWELL *out from under the eaves...]*

BOSWELL: I am a new man!!
LASS *[in Erse]*: You're as wobbly as a seal!
BOSWELL: Never, my love, have I ever had such a divine invitation!

*[*JOSEPH *finally takes over from the* LASS.*]*

JOSEPH *[to the* LASS, *in Erse]*: If he were able, he'd apologize.
LASS *[in Erse, grinning]*: Oh I don't mind. He's very funny.

[But then BOSWELL *sees* JOHNSON *IN FULL HIGHLAND REGALIA – with* FLORA *and* MACLEOD.*]*

BOSWELL *[disbelief]*: Doctor Johnson?
JOHNSON: Unhand this maiden and come to bed.
BOSWELL: You're wearing – My God, look at you!!

*[*JOHNSON *and* JOSEPH *half-drag* BOSWELL *back to the Inn.]*

EXT. COAST OF IONA – DAY

[A rocky, rugged coast. Breakers roll in from the blue-green Atlantic and crash among the rocks, spewing foam. BOSWELL *brutally hung-over, sits on a rock overlooking the break, clutching his head, squinting against the vicious sun.*
JOHNSON *approaches. His shadow falls over* BOSWELL. BOSWELL *looks up at* JOHNSON *– the sun blocked by his body, daggers of light frame his silhouette. When* JOHNSON *takes a step to the side and the full force of the sun hits* BOSWELL's *eye.* BOSWELL *groans, clutching his temples.* JOHNSON *sits.]*

JOHNSON *[voice booming]*: Ah, Jamie, Jamie… Last night you set aside the playthings of your youth, then took up the past-times of an undergraduate!

[When that fails to raise a smile, JOHNSON *takes his arm.]*

JOHNSON *[CONT'D]*: Come.

*[*BOSWELL *balks. Then launches into an apostrophe of self-loathing…]*

BOSWELL: I am an idiot and a child. I lack common sense and make up for it with a huge propensity for vice.
JOHNSON: Where there is shame, there may, in time, be virtue.

BOSWELL: I live on a begrudging father's allowance, supplemented by a pitiful income from an occupation I loathe. And I am a bad husband of a patient and forbearing wife.

JOHNSON: And you parrot your father. *[off* BOSWELL's *reaction]* Has he not used identically vicious language to beat you with?

[Pause.]

BOSWELL: Within days we'll be at Auchinleck. *[with difficulty]* When I was twenty-one, he agreed to grant me an allowance of two hundred pounds a year, sufficient for a gentleman.

JOHNSON: But not enough for you.

BOSWELL: So in return for an additional one hundred per year for life, I agreed to renounce my claim to the estate.

JOHNSON: What?!

BOSWELL: In a fever of rebellion, I exposed myself to being disinherited. My father is a capricious, mean-tempered, vengeful man. Margaret and I invited him to our wedding, months in advance. But he was... otherwise engaged.

JOHNSON: What could be more important than his own son's wedding?!

BOSWELL: His Honor, Lord Alexander Boswell, scheduled his wedding for the same day. On the other side of town.

[A look exchanged. JOHNSON's *jaw clenches.]*

JOHNSON: And the new Lady Auchinleck?

BOSWELL: Hateful woman.

JOHNSON: To marry twice represents the triumph of hope over experience.

[Which evokes only a troubled grin from BOSWELL. *Then...]*

BOSWELL: I need your help. Unfortunately, you are as outspoken as he. And you each have contrary opinions.

JOHNSON: So, you'd have me avoid politics, religion, and nationalism.

*[*BOSWELL *timidly nods his head, yes.]*

JOHNSON *[CONT'D]*: I shall avoid all controversy and be as deferential as a courtier.

> [BOSWELL's *skeptical. He steals a glance at* JOHNSON *who stares seaward. Behind them,* FLORA *and* MACLEOD *are looking down on them.]*

MACLEOD: I met Auchinleck but once myself. As defendant in his court. And I'd rather face the Almighty with all my sins than go back before the Honorable Alexander Boswell.

FLORA: If he's as stern a parent as he is a judge, I pity his offspring. Perhaps by the time they reach Auchinleck, Jamie will ha' decided whom to claim as his "father."

> [*They watch* JOHNSON *put a comforting arm around* BOSWELL's *shoulder.*]

EXT. THE JETTY AT IONA – DAY

> [JOSEPH *climbs down into the dinghy which will take the trio out to the small sailing KETCH riding at anchor just off shore.* BOSWELL *lingers at the top of the rope ladder watching* JOHNSON *and* FLORA, *on the jetty, holding hands.* BOSWELL *leaves them, disappearing below the jetty wall.*
> CLOSE on JOHNSON *and* FLORA. *Silence. Finally…]*

JOHNSON: I've never been good with farewells.

FLORA: Nor I.

> [*They say nothing, losing themselves in one another's eyes.*]

INT. AUCHINLECK MANOR - AUCHINLECK'S OFFICE – DAY

> [*At a table near a window* LORD AUCHINLECK (64) *and his FACTOR (40s) pore over estate books, pens scratching, coats tossed over their chair-backs. When A POST-CHAISE rolls up outside,* AUCHINLECK *barely glances up.*]

AUCHINLECK: Let 'em wait.

EXT. AUCHINLECK MANOR - DAY

[While JOSEPH *helps unload their luggage from the coach,* BOSWELL *and* JOHNSON *survey THE MANOR HOUSE – an impressive pile of 18th century stone in the Adam style, surrounded by well-tended grounds.]*

BOSWELL *[babbling nervously]*: He prefers Greek to Roman authors and he's also prickly about...
JOHNSON: Religion, Whiggism and Scotland. Yes yes, you've already told me.
BOSWELL: Actually, he's prickly about just about everything.

[After a look at his overwrought friend...]

JOHNSON: A drink? Before we go in?
BOSWELL: If he smells liquor on me he'll – Do I look presentable?
JOHNSON: Like a laird in waiting.

INT. AUCHINLECK MANOR - MAIN HALL - DAY

*[*MARY *(50s) a longtime servant, admits* BOSWELL *and* JOHNSON*.]*

MARY: Ah, Jamie... Look at ye!
BOSWELL: Hello, Mary. Is my father...
MARY: He's in with his Factor doing the accounts. I told him of your coming but he asked not to be disturbed.
BOSWELL *[hurt but covering]*: I see. Well, then...

[But he's already lost JOHNSON*. Searching, he finds* JOHNSON *in a gallery of PORTRAITS of* BOSWELL *ancestors.* BOSWELL *identifies the faces...]*

BOSWELL: Thomas Boswell, originally of Fife. The first Lord Auchinleck.

TOGETHER - UNDER A PORTRAIT of Thomas Boswell.

BOSWELL *[CONT'D]*: King James the Fourth presented him with the title and castle. In 1504.

[BOSWELL moves them along to a PORTRAIT of David Boswell].

BOSWELL *[CONT'D]*: And this is David, the fifth laird. A supporter of Charles I who paid a fine rather than support Cromwell.

JOHNSON: Good for him! Sorry. Not another Tory peep shall cross my lips.

[JOHNSON moves them on to a PORTRAIT of James Boswell.]

BOSWELL: My grandfather and namesake, James.

[As BOSWELL waxes enthusiastic on his royal blood-lines, AUCHINLECK, still without his coat, enters behind them.]

BOSWELL *[CONT'D]*: It's through him I'm linked to both Prince Charles and George III.

AUCHINLECK: Boy!

[BOSWELL wheels too quickly. With a nervous flutter, he starts toward his father, then stops. Standing firm…]

BOSWELL: Father, may I introduce my friend, the eminent Doctor Samuel Johnson.

[AUCHINLECK making a quick comparison of JOHNSON's ill-fitted apparel and JOSEPH's more elegant attire, steps up to JOSEPH and extends his hand. JOSEPH covers well.]

AUCHINLECK: At long last, sir.

BOSWELL: That's Joseph, my servant. This is Doctor Johnson.

[JOHNSON and AUCHINLECK shake hands. Two bone-crunching grips. Eyes locked.]

AUCHINLECK: I expected you yesterday, Mister Johnson.

JOHNSON: Scottish roads delayed us, Mister Boswell.

[REACTION - BOSWELL who winces at this parrying over titles.]

AUCHINLECK: I just assumed that my son had, once again, been distracted by our Scottish beauties.

JOHNSON: Indeed he was, sir. As was I.

[BOSWELL *blanches, as* JOHNSON *continues...*]

JOHNSON *[CONT'D]*: There's such female strength in those fingers of sea and necks of land, it's no wonder you grill the testicles of your sheep.

[JOHNSON *winks at* BOSWELL, *who finally breathes.* AUCHINLECK *finally releases* JOHNSON'*s hand – intrigued but suspicious.*]

JOHNSON: It seems we've interrupted your work. Carry on. I'm happy to be left in your son's capable hands.

[*His hospitality challenged,* AUCHINLECK *ushers them DOWN THE HALLWAY.* AUCHINLECK *and* JOHNSON *walk side by side;* BOSWELL *trails behind; and bringing up the rear,* MARY, JOSEPH, *and staff.*]

AUCHINLECK: And having seen our country, sir, what is your impression – granny fries excepted?

JOHNSON: Rocks and water. *[off his look]* While there is some thin covering of soil, it is a bit like rags on a poor man's knee and elbow – the naked flesh always popping through.

AUCHINLECK: It's always reminded me of an old man's pate, his bald spots showing.

JOHNSON: It seems you are as instinctive a poet as you are a jurist, sir.

AUCHINLECK *[pleased but grumping]*: I leave poetry to those with time to indulge. I prefer to hone my wit on more sturdy whetstones.

JOHNSON: The Greeks?

[*They enter...*]

INT. AUCHINLECK'S LIBRARY – CONTINUOUS

[*A scholar's paradise.* AUCHINLECK *allows himself the pleasure of watching* JOHNSON'*s reaction to the abundance of volumes.*]

AUCHINLECK: I take it you prefer the Romans.

JOHNSON: I am more comfortable with Latin.

AUCHINLECK: You never graduated university, did you, Johnson?

BOSWELL: Oxford honored him with a Doctorate of Law. For his contributions to –

JOHNSON: In answer to your question, sir, I did not matriculate. I was too poor a scholar to stay at university.

AUCHINLECK: I cannot accept that you were ever a poor scholar, even as a youth.

JOHNSON: I could not afford the tuition.

AUCHINLECK: Ah. *[pause]* Did you like the Highlands?

JOHNSON: Who can like the Highlands? … I liked its people well enough.

AUCHINLECK: Do not trifle with me, sir. I know you hate the Scots. Please do me the honor of speaking your mind without prevarication, like a man.

[AUCHINLECK *baits the bear, but the bear steadfastly refuses to rise to the bait.* BOSWELL *suffers.*]

JOHNSON: Scotland, sir, has many fine views.

AUCHINLECK: And your favorite?

JOHNSON: The same that's most beloved by so many of your countrymen… The high road south to London.

[AUCHINLECK *freezes.* BOSWELL *gasps. Then,* AUCHINLECK *grins – though it's a bit sour and twisted.*]

INT. AUCHINLECK MANOR - DINING HALL – NIGHT

[BOSWELL *is seated at the vacant mid-point of the long table. His* STEP-MOTHER, AUCHINLECK'S *wife,* ELIZABETH *(50) sits at his father's left at one end of the table.* JOHNSON *sits at the other. It's been a tense meal, riddled with unnerving silences. Even the servants sense the tension in the air.*]

AUCHINLECK: Wealth, sir, is often a burden. And poverty, often a goad to industry.

[AUCHINLECK's eyes settle on his son. BOSWELL squirms. His STEP-MOTHER, gloating over BOSWELL's discomfort...]

STEP-MOTHER: Most young men with an allowance the size of his could live quite comfortably. But not our Jamie.

[JOHNSON looks from BOSWELL, whose eyes drop, to AUCHINLECK, who grimaces at his wife's remark before turning back to JOHNSON. Then, as if she'd never spoken...]

JOHNSON: I have always found that one must argue to convince others of the so-called "virtues" of being poor. But I have never known a man who had to convince anyone that it is possible to live happily on a fortune.

[JOHNSON eats – his table manners surprisingly meticulous.]

JOHNSON: We assume that wealth is good, but must convince that poverty has anything to recommend it.
STEP-MOTHER: Compassion is wasted on the poor. They have none for us or their own.
JOHNSON: Those who do not feel pain seldom think it is felt.
STEP-MOTHER: Poverty's no excuse for immorality!
JOHNSON: Nor is wealth, madam. If you were to go into the street and give one man a lecture on morality and another a shilling, which do you think will respect you more?
STEP-MOTHER: You are a cynic and a pessimist!
BOSWELL: And you are a blithering optimist!

[BOSWELL can't quite believe he just said what he did. With cheeks puffing and coloring, she's suddenly as speechless as a carp. She looks to her husband for support only to find AUCHINLECK watching with the kind of cool-eyed curiosity with which one might witness a cock-fight between utterly mismatched birds. The STEP-MOTHER, hurt and angry, fusses with her napkin, then rises.]

STEP-MOTHER: Excuse me. I am indisposed.

[She exits, her discomfiture balm to BOSWELL*'s wounded pride.]*

AUCHINLECK *[rising]*: Shall we retire to the library?

INT. AUCHINLECK'S LIBRARY – NIGHT

[The Three Men enter. AUCHINLECK *goes to a cabinet.]*

AUCHINLECK: In your travels, did you acquire a taste for our single-malt whiskies?

[He pulls out a bottle of old Scotch and three glasses.]

BOSWELL: My friend doesn't drink spirits.

*[*AUCHINLECK *sets out ALL THREE GLASSES and fills them. He slides one across the table to his son, lifts his own, then turns to* JOHNSON*. After a long moment,* JOHNSON *picks up the third glass.]*

JOHNSON: I suppose it behooves me to try the preferred drink of Scots, though it runs against my better judgment – especially after seeing what it's done to the judgment of most Scots.

[With which, JOHNSON *downs his glass in one swallow.* AUCHINLECK *and* BOSWELL *drink, then await* JOHNSON*'s verdict. But* JOHNSON *reaches for the bottle and pours another round. After the second round…]*

AUCHINLECK: Well, sir?
JOHNSON: Against my better judgment…

*[*JOHNSON *pours yet another round. They drink.* AUCHINLECK *and* JOHNSON *shove grins at one another. This time,* AUCHINLECK *does the honors of pouring the next round.]*

AUCHINLECK: I'd always assumed my ne'er-do-well son might learn something from you, but it seems you've learned a thing from him as well. Your health, sir!

[AUCHINLECK *raises his glass to* JOHNSON. *They drink.*
BOSWELL *watches, stunned.*]

AUCHINLECK: Drink up, boy!

[*He does.* JOHNSON *pours yet another round. Is this a drinking duel?*
Indeed it is. As another round is being poured…
CLOSE on AUCHINLECK's *eyes, starting to glaze.*
A SERIES OF SHOTS of glasses being filled and lifted. Swallowing. A
sheen of sweat on a brow, on a lip. A fresh bottle being opened.
BOSWELL *leans against a PEDESTAL, nursing his drink, arm draped*
companionably round a faux-Greek BUST OF ANACREON, watches
his two "fathers" go at it.
JOHNSON *and* AUCHINLECK *fighting the liquor's effects, each try*
to match and raise the other's capacity for self-control. JOHNSON *is*
dominating this twisted competition.]

AUCHINLECK: The danger of such drink is that it fuzzes the memory of
men our age.

JOHNSON: There is a wicked inclination to suppose that older men are
grown dotty. If a man of middle-age mislays his hat, it is nothing. But
let an older man do the same, people shrug and say, "Poor dog, his
memory is going!"

AUCHINLECK *[clapping his back]*: You, sir, have such a prodigious memory,
you can afford to squander.

JOHNSON: Memory can be occasionally useful, but it can also be a curse. For
example, I am able to repeat, verbatim, an entire chapter of Horrebow's
"Natural History of Iceland," which I read in passing some twenty-six
years ago.

AUCHINLECK: Impossible.

JOHNSON: I quote…

AUCHINLECK: Sir, if you insist on reciting, I insist on fortifying myself.

[AUCHINLECK *pours another round.* JOHNSON *clears his throat.*]

JOHNSON: "Chapter 72. The Natural History of Iceland. … Concerning
snakes. …There are no snakes to be met with throughout the whole island."

[That's it. When it registers on AUCHINLECK, *he barks out a loud laugh.]*

AUCHINLECK *[toasting]*: To brevity and understatement!!
JOHNSON: Succinctness and precision!

[They drink.]

AUCHINLECK: Jamie! Fetch another bottle!

*[*BOSWELL *slides off the statuary and sways to the cabinet.]*

AUCHINLECK *[CONT'D]*: Did you, sir, in passing through Saint Andrews have occasion to cross swords with Mister Hume?

[He searches out and pulls down a copy of Hume's "Treatise."]

AUCHINLECK *[CONT'D]*: He is after all our most notorious philosopher!

*[*BOSWELL *struggles to open the bottle.]*

JOHNSON: David Hume, sir, is a blockhead. His scepticism, a fraud!
AUCHINLECK: Hear, hear!

*[*AUCHINLECK *flings the book in the direction of the hearth. He misses, but almost hits his son.* BOSWELL *is shocked to find his father and* JOHNSON *in total agreement. For that matter, so are* AUCHINLECK *and* JOHNSON. JOHNSON *pulls a book from the shelf.]*

JOHNSON *[sneering]*: As for Bishop Berkeley's theories of the non-existence of matter…
AUCHINLECK: Preposterous and silly! And yet! Logically impossible to refute!
JOHNSON: I refute it thus!!!

[With which, JOHNSON *soundly KICKS the MARBLE PEDESTAL. The Bust Of Anacreon topples.* BOSWELL *dives to catch it, saving it from shattering.*

JOHNSON *limps around – he's probably broken a toe.* AUCHINLECK *cracks up, howling with laughter. REACTION –* BOSWELL, *who's never seen his father laugh.*]

AUCHINLECK: For that, sir, we break out the fifty year malt!

[AUCHINLECK *staggers out, almost colliding with his wife. The* STEP-MOTHER, *entering, surveys the scene...* BOSWELL *on the floor hugging the marble bust of Anacreon and* JOHNSON *still hobbling around the room.* JOHNSON *and* STEP-MOTHER *face off. The fumes off* JOHNSON *nearly knock her down.*]

STEP-MOTHER: You, sir, are drunk!
JOHNSON: And you, madam, are ugly! *[beat]* The difference being that in the morning, I shall be sober!

[*She blusters. He shoves the copy of Berkeley into her hands. She shoots a vicious look at* BOSWELL, *then exits.* BOSWELL *and* JOHNSON *swap boozy bad-boy grins, which broaden when they hear LOUD VOICES off – the Auchinlecks in conference.*]

INT. THE KITCHEN – CONTINUOUS

[JOSEPH *and* MARY *– over a contrastingly civilized supper.*]

MARY: Jamie's Mum, rest her soul, was so sweet and gentle. But this one...

[LORD *and* LADY AUCHINLECK's *shouts seem to fill the house. She refills his glass. Adds another portion to his plate.*]

EXT. GROUNDS - THE AUCHINLECK ESTATE - DAY

[*The gardens feature well-swept walks and shrubs precisely pruned in the Italian manner.* JOHNSON *and* BOSWELL *stroll.* BOSWELL *takes a nip from a flask, then offers it to* JOHNSON. JOHNSON *takes a sip then hands it back.* BOSWELL *points to an open lawn.*]

BOSWELL: Once I am laird, I intend to raise a monument to you. Right there.

JOHNSON: I'm touched and honored, but aren't you getting a bit ahead of yourself. You need to talk with your father.

BOSWELL: He'll be in a foul mood, from his drinking.

JOHNSON: And he'll be the same tomorrow and the day after.

[BOSWELL balks. Looks back at the house. Fusses with the stopper on his flask. He's about to take another swig, but stops himself. He corks the flask firmly and hands it off to JOHNSON.]

JOHNSON: Shall we?

[A deep breath. They start across the lawn toward the manor – a doomed man and his "spiritual advisor" heading for the gallows.]

INT. AUCHINLECK'S OFFICE – DAY

[BOSWELL waits. The shades are drawn, leaving only a long narrow slat of sunlight. He gravitates to the window, the slat of light cutting his shoulder.]

MARY *[from the doorway]*: He's on his way.

[She goes to him. He clutches her hand. She gives him a reassuring hug.]

INT. AUCHINLECK'S LIBRARY – DAY

[AUCHINLECK – cheeks stubbled, a haggard sag at his eyes and mouth – enters to find JOHNSON examining A COIN COLLECTION.]

JOHNSON: Your son's in your office. He wants to talk.

AUCHINLECK *[gruffly]*: About what?

JOHNSON: His future.

AUCHINLECK: Judging by his past, I wouldn't put much stock in it.

JOHNSON: The boy made a mistake.

AUCHINLECK: He's made so many, which one are you referring to?

JOHNSON: His renunciation of title.

AUCHINLECK: I'd sooner sell it all than –

BOSWELL [from the doorway]: You can't!

AUCHINLECK: Oh, but I can. You've said I could. In writing!

BOSWELL: Not so. I've checked the laws and consulted with counsel to know my rights.

AUCHINLECK [almost lunging at him]: You've forfeited your rights, boy! I know, because the best lawyer in Scotland drew those papers! Me. And you are the only lawyer foolish enough to bring suit against a Lord of Session!

JOHNSON: He wants to make his peace with you.

AUCHINLECK: He wants me to die!

[AUCHINLECK "hides" by going to the coin display. He takes out a COIN wrapped in velvet, then, almost reverentially, unwraps it. As he hands it to JOHNSON...]

JOHNSON: Collecting money for its aesthetic value is, I'm afraid, a luxury I have never been able to afford.

[The COMMEMORATIVE COIN features the embossed face of...]

JOHNSON: Oliver Cromwell?

AUCHINLECK: Aye. It's quite rare. It honors –

JOHNSON: The murder of an English King.

AUCHINLECK: The establishment of an Independent Scottish Presbyterian Church.

[Having hit the very hot-button issue that JOHNSON swore he'd avoid, JOHNSON struggles to restrain himself. LORD AUCHINLECK is under no comparable obligation.]

AUCHINLECK: Cromwell was –

JOHNSON: A regicide and vile usurper of a crown to which he had no right!

BOSWELL: Enough! Both of you.

[BOSWELL angrily yanks open the drapes, flooding the room with sunlight. AUCHINLECK winces, shunning the brightness.

BOSWELL'S POV – *his father's face, though fixed in a grim frightening scowl seems also poignantly fragile.]*

AUCHINLECK: We have nothing to discuss.

BOSWELL: Yes, Father, we do.

AUCHINLECK: This is not London, boy. We do not spend our days idling in taverns inventing topics for conversation. I am not one of your idiotic chums!

BOSWELL: My Club, sir, includes statesmen, actors, writers, and the finest gentlemen of our age!

AUCHINLECK: Then what possible reason could they have for letting you in?!

JOHNSON: I sponsored him. Your son, sir, besides providing excellent company, is a talented author. Men of substance value his friendship, even if you do not!

AUCHINLECK: I have known you, sir, for a day; I have known this pup all his life.

BOSWELL: You know nothing of me! And little of anything outside this backwater!

AUCHINLECK: Worldliness, boy, is no substitute for wisdom.

BOSWELL: You live in a fishpond and think it the ocean! You think of yourself as brilliant, but you are a pinprick in the darkness!

JOHNSON: Mind, sir. This man is your father!

BOSWELL: Whom I will acknowledge as such the moment he acknowledges me as his sole and rightful heir.

AUCHINLECK: There! Do you see the kind of dog I have raised?!

JOHNSON: While it is not my place to advise a man how to treat with his son…

AUCHINLECK: No, sir, it is not. Especially when you have never felt the pangs and disappointments of being a father.

BOSWELL: Or the anguish of being your son.

JOHNSON: Mind your tone, boy.

AUCHINLECK: You come here, dragging your Doctor Johnson like some war-trophy, as if that will impress me. *[turning away]* I might have been impressed had you bothered to come 'round some time during those long years after your mother died. But you chose not to.
[unable to meet his son's eyes] You had better things to do while I was here, alone, doing my duty!

[AUCHINLECK *paces – a caged, cornered and wounded lion.*]

AUCHINLECK *[CONT'D]*: Carousing with your actor friends and petty journalists, squandering your capital on whores and wine! And now you expect my generosity?!

BOSWELL: I expect neither generosity nor affection. I expect only to speak to the Laird of Auchinleck in order to settle the question of my succession.

AUCHINLECK *[taking his case to* JOHNSON*]*: He knows nothing of running an estate!

BOSWELL: I'll learn.

AUCHINLECK: Ha!

JOHNSON: You'll teach him.

AUCHINLECK: When?! In the few hours I have between sitting on the Courts and calculating how much the tenants owe and how little I'll collect?! I, for one, cannot afford to waste three months gadding about the country.

[*He ends at the window, facing out.* JOHNSON *approaches him.*]

JOHNSON: Among your son's reasons for this trip was to re-acquaint himself with his country. Which he'd put off ten years, in part, because of me.

AUCHINLECK: And for twenty I have toured it as a judge! If he wanted so badly to see his homeland –
[*to* BOSWELL*]* You could have come with me! With your own Da'!

[BOSWELL *steps up to him. Face to face, eye to eye.*]

BOSWELL: I cannot take back the past, sir. But whatever proofs you need, I shall provide. Whatever oaths you require, I shall take. Willingly.

[CLOSE *on* AUCHINLECK, *whose eyes bore into his son's soul.*
BOSWELL *meets his stare. Unflinching. A new and surprising strength.*
Finally, and with no change in expression... AUCHINLECK *nods his head in agreement.* BOSWELL *nods his head in assent.*

Without another word, AUCHINLECK *exits past* JOHNSON.
BOSWELL *stands taller and prouder than we've ever seen him.*
JOHNSON *flips the Cromwell coin to him.* BOSWELL *snatches it.]*

[MATCH DISSOLVE TO] BOSWELL'S FACE – glowing in flickering torchlight, his jaw firmly set, his eyes steady.

[CLOSE on BOSWELL'S HAND knocking THREE TIMES on an oak door. From beyond the door we hear, in ringing formal Erse…]

AUCHINLECK *[OS]*: Erinai slange currai?

INT. AUCHINLECK CHAPEL – NIGHT

[Almost dawn. The ancient stone chapel is lit by candles. Every pew and aisle is filled with the people of AUCHINLECK, *from well-dressed factors and stewards to simple crofters.* JOHNSON *and* JOSEPH *sit in the front pew.* JOSEPH *translates for* JOHNSON *(and us) – and, we soon realize, for the natives around them.]*

JOSEPH: "Who would enter?"

[Note: In the following "investiture" ceremony, the speeches of those speaking Erse will be JOSEPH's *translations.] ***

[AT THE ALTAR, AUCHINLECK, *in full regalia, flanked by his wife and VICAR, faces the rear door of the chapel.]*

BOSWELL *[OS]*: Lama, Sera Auchinleck, MacToi!

[As JOHNSON, JOSEPH, *and everyone in the chapel turns…]*

JOSEPH *[to* JOHNSON*]*: "Your true son, Auchinleck!"

[Everyone within earshot leans in closer to JOSEPH *to catch his translations since they don't know the language either.]*

AUCHINLECK * : "Enter, son of Auchinleck!"

[*The chapel doors open. Silent expectation.* BOSWELL *steps into the chapel. His polished breast-plate gleams in candlelight over the rich plaids of his clan regalia. The jeweled cap-badge on his Tam glitters. On his shoulder rests the long bare blade of a claymore.* BOSWELL *himself seems larger than life.*
REACTIONS - AUCHINLECK, *his wife, the Vicar,* MARY, *and various others.* JOHNSON'*s breath catches at the sight. And for the first time we see* JOSEPH'*s face break into a huge smile.*
A TRIO OF BAGPIPES inflate and swell into a solemn chord.
All rise instinctively as BOSWELL *marches solemnly forward.*]

BOSWELL * : "I have come to give and to take."

[*Overhearing* JOSEPH'*s translation for* JOHNSON...]

AUCHINLECK * : "To give what and take what?"
BOSWELL * : "To give my life and eternal pledge to my ancestors, the land, and the people of Auchinleck."
AUCHINLECK * : "And what do you take?"

[BOSWELL *kneels before his father, presenting his claymore – bare blade in his hands.*]

BOSWELL * : "Only that which is destined by blood to be rightfully mine."
JOHNSON [*aside to* JOSEPH]: These Scots are either more High Church than I'd imagined, or still living in the Tenth Century.
JOSEPH [*aside to* JOHNSON]: Fifteenth Century.

[AUCHINLECK *takes the sword and abruptly SNAPS the blade over a knee. KLAANG!* JOHNSON *and* JOSEPH *both jump.*
AUCHINLECK *turns and takes a huge claymore borne on a cushion by a YOUNG BOY. He holds the sword in front of* BOSWELL *who takes its pommel and blade in his bare hands. Each holding the weapon, they look into each other's eyes.*]

AUCHINLECK * : "Now say what must be said."

BOSWELL * : "Listen all! My words are those cut into stone and can never be washed away. I, who am the son of the sons of Auchinleck, take to me the rocks and grass and every living thing of our lands. They are my bones, my skin, my muscle. Each man and woman my blood. I am Auchinleck, you are Auchinleck!

[AUCHINLECK *steps back.* BOSWELL *rises, lifting the sword high above his head and turns to the congregation. All kneel. When* BOSWELL *lowers the sword...*
The entire clan leaps to its feet and erupts in cheers!
JOHNSON *and* JOSEPH *each discover that the other is in tears. They laugh. Then embrace. Then turn to* BOSWELL *who looks down at them, beaming. As* BOSWELL *heads for the door, the rays of a DAWNING SUN burst through the open door.]*

EXT. AUCHINLECK CHAPEL – DAY

[*The exhuberant crowd pours out behind* BOSWELL. *A pack of TORCHBEARERS is waiting for them.* JOHNSON *and* JOSEPH *step to the side to watch the procession move off around the chapel – torches dancing, air filled with song and cheers.]*

JOHNSON: Just what are the duties of the man-servant to a Scottish laird?

JOSEPH: As of this morning I am no longer in Master Boswell's service.

JOHNSON: What?! Have you been discharged?!

JOSEPH: I've decided to return to Bohemia. Then on to Heidelberg to resume my studies. Expect me at the Turk's Head Tavern in about three years.

[JOSEPH *takes* JOHNSON*'s hand. Shakes it warmly.]*

JOHNSON: Crescit eundo, Laddie!

[*The procession, having looped around the chapel, passes.*
BOSWELL *waves as he's carried off on the shoulders of the crowd toward the village.]*

INT. THE BOSWELL HOUSE - EDINBURGH – DAY

[MARGARET BOSWELL races down the hall toward the front door. She flings open the door to reveal JOHNSON and BOSWELL climbing out of a COACH.]

MARGARET: Welcome home!!!

[As BOSWELL rushes toward his wife we see the profoundly puzzled expressions on his and JOHNSON's faces – they fully expected to see MARGARET big with child. She isn't.]

BOSWELL *[as he embraces her]*: Are you… all right?

MARGARET *[brightly]*: I have never felt better in my life!
    [to JOHNSON] Please, come in. You must be parched from your journey. I've made lemonade, especially for you!

[JOHNSON is unable to take his eyes off her flat midriff.]

JOHNSON *[disconcerted]*: Umm… Capital idea. Thank you.

[They all go into…]

INT. THE BOSWELL HOUSE – CONTINUOUS

[MARGARET races off to the kitchen, leaving BOSWELL and JOHNSON to wait in the drawing room.]

JOHNSON *["loud" whisper]*: I thought you said she was with child?
BOSWELL: By my calculations she should be at least in her seventh month.

[A horrible conclusion strikes them both at the same moment. JOHNSON rests a comforting hand on BOSWELL's arm.]

JOHNSON: My dear fellow, I'm so sorry.

[BOSWELL's mounting distress is cut off by MARGARET's return with a pitcher of lemonade and glasses, smiling brightly. BOSWELL struggles to cover his emotions.]

MARGARET: I gather from your letter that things went well with your father.

BOSWELL: He was... accomodating. Thanks to Doctor Johnson.

JOHNSON: Your husband acquitted himself magnificently.

MARGARET: I'm sorry I couldn't attend the ceremony, but I just wasn't well enough to travel.

JOHNSON *[gravely]*: Understandable. Under the circumstances. As it were.

[BOSWELL "meaningfully" takes MARGARET's hand.]

BOSWELL: Oh, Margaret...

[LADY MACINTYRE enters carrying a small BUNDLE in the crook of her arm.]

MARGARET: I meant to tell you that we have a special house guest.

[BOSWELL turns, unable to take his eyes off the bundle, from which we now hear a very small CRY.]

BOSWELL: Alison, I...

JOHNSON: Madam! ... A baby!!

LADY MACINTYRE *[beaming]*: A lovely little girl. Ready to meet her father.

[When LADY MACINTYRE takes a step toward them, JOHNSON looks in horror at BOSWELL. BOSWELL, thinking that LADY MACINTYRE is moving toward JOHNSON with the baby, looks astounded. MARGARET starts to laugh.]

MARGARET: Our daughter was born on the very day of your investiture.

[LADY MACINTYRE places the infant in BOSWELL's arms.]

BOSWELL: Why didn't you write?

[MARGARET *joins him. While looking at the baby's face...*]

MARGARET: She was early. So tiny and weak... we really weren't sure. Alison thought it best to wait.
LADY MACINTYRE: But she's a fine strapping baby now.

[BOSWELL *beams. The baby lets loose a lusty WAIL. All four gather around.*]

MARGARET: I thought we might call her Elizabeth.
BOSWELL: Betsy is a fine name, but I did wonder if we mightn't call her... [*with a look toward* JOHNSON] Samantha.
JOHNSON [*thundering*]: You'll do no such thing, young man! Elizabeth it is!

[*At which the INFANT starts to wail.* BOSWELL *tries to coo and quiet her. To no apparent effect.* JOHNSON *takes the BABY in his big arms, rocks her, then begins to sing his own LULLABY version of "Over the Sea to Skye." But at the sound of* JOHNSON's *voice, BABY BOSWELL begins to howl in earnest.*
WIDER *on* JOHNSON *and the Baby:* JOHNSON *singing, the baby crying.*
The OTHERS gather around them. JOHNSON's *voice builds as the Baby's cries intensify. The SONG CONTINUES as we PULL BACK and...*]

[DISSOLVE TO]
EXT. THE AUCHINLECK ESTATE GROUND - YEARS LATER - DAY

[*A LOVELY ELEVEN YEAR OLD GIRL –* BETSY BOSWELL *in a white dress, sits on the green grass, reading a book.*
The sound of JOHNSON's *singing and the baby's cry insinuate themselves under the sounds of the park. A shadow falls across a page.*
BETSY *looks up from her book.*]

BETSY: Daddy, what's this mean?

[She points to a phrase. BOSWELL, *now a much stouter 44 year old laird, squats next to his daughter and grins as he explains…]*

BOSWELL: "Crescit eundo" is Latin. It means, It grows as it goes.
BETSY: What does that mean?
BOSWELL: Well… It means different things to different people.

[When he takes the book from her, we see that it's a copy of his recently published "Life of Doctor Samuel Johnson."
WIDER as BOSWELL *rises, drawing* BETSY *up with him. Right beside them we see a STATUE OF DR. SAMUEL JOHNSON. Looking up at the statue…]*

BOSWELL: You know, I was never altogether sure what it meant to him.

*[*BOSWELL *chuckles. Then, after a moment, they stroll off together, hand in hand toward the Auchinleck Manor House. As we PULL UP AND AWAY…* JOHNSON's *statue seems to be watching them go.]*

THE END

www.ingramcontent.com/pod-product-compliance
Lightning Source LLC
Chambersburg PA
CBHW052029090426
42739CB00010B/1836